The South Carolina Review
Locating African American Literature

Volume 46, Number 2   Spring 2014

Published by Clemson University Press, Clemson, SC

ISBN 978-1-942954-91-0

©2014 Clemson University.

EDITOR: Wayne Chapman.

FICTION EDITOR: Keith Morris.

BOOK REVIEW EDITOR: Cameron Bushnell

CONTRIBUTING EDITORS:
Sterling Eisminger, Martin Jacobi, Catherine Paul, Rhondda Thomas, and Jillian Weise.

ADVISORY BOARD:
Susanna Ashton, Ray Barfield, Cameron Bushnell, Jonathan Field, G. William Koon, Michael LeMahieu, Kimberly Manganelli, Dominic Mastroianni, Brian McGrath, John Morgenstern, Lee Morrissey, Angela Naimou, Angela Oberdan, John Pursley, and Aga Skrodzka-Bates.

BUSINESS MANAGER: Emily C. Clarke.

ACCOUNTING FISCAL ANALYST: Beverly Pressley.

EDITORIAL ASSISTANTS:
Charis Chapman, Chelsea Green, Dustin Mosley, and Tiffany Verkaik.

COVER: *Cane Women*, 1997, Oil on Canvas, 48" x 36" © Jonathan Green.

C O N T E N T S

LOCATING AFRICAN AMERICAN LITERATURE

Edited by Angela Naimou and Rhondda Robinson Thomas

ESSAYS

REGIONAL VOICES

CREATIVE WORKS

REVIEW ESSAY

REVIEWS

INTRODUCTION

LOCATING AFRICAN AMERICAN LITERATURE

by Angela Naimou

In Southern landscapes populated by plantation houses and monuments to the Confederacy, memorials explicitly naming the slave system that gave rise to both are rare.[1] Where memorials to the triumphs of the civil rights movement now stand, markers recognizing the turbulent century of history between the Civil War and the civil rights movement are virtually unknown. Unmarked in public space, these histories seem to fall out of public memory not only in the South, the nation, and the circum-Atlantic world but also at particular sites of everyday life—a campus, a building, a street, a house, or an open field.

Memorials locate history: their purpose is to affix historical meaning to places and produce spaces of public memory amid competing claims of the past on those places. They offer the appearance that space is neutral, there to be marked by a merely informative plaque, statue, or obelisk. As geographer Doreen Massey writes, however, space depends "on the notion of articulation" (Massey 1994, 8, quoted in Brady 2002, 7). May Pat Brady notes the potential for theories of space and spatiality to inform literary studies when she highlights "the sociality of space and the spatiality of language" (7). "Viewing space as produced, productive, and producing," Brady argues, "means viewing it as interanimating and dependent in part on narrative for its productive effects" (7). Space is never merely there, and it is never merely metaphorical. Locating places and affixing meaning to them in language is never a neutral act or a final one.

The Clemson University campus illustrates how memorials invent places as sites of memory and forgetting, what philosopher Paul Ricoeur calls "the unsettling spectacle offered by an excess of memory here, and an excess of forgetting elsewhere, to say nothing of the influence of commemorations and abuses of memory—and of forgetting" (2004, xv). At the center of campus sits the Fort Hill mansion, once home to the families of John C. Calhoun and Thomas Green Clemson, on land first settled by the Cherokee. A designated National Historic Landmark and listed on the National Register of Historic Places, the house was bequeathed by Clemson in his will to the State of South Carolina in 1888, along with his entire Fort Hill plantation, for the establishment of a scientific and agricultural college. Clemson willed that the Fort Hill house "shall never be torn down or altered, but shall be kept in repair" and "shall always be open for the inspection of visitors," making it the place wherein this public land-grant university locates its legacy and birthright ("The Will").[2]

On a small hilltop near Fort Hill and across from Tillman Hall stands a plaque that marks the start of another legacy, described as a legacy of inclusion.[3] Mounted in honor of Harvey Gantt, the first African American to be enrolled in what was then Clemson College, this two-sided plaque, along with other markers—a cement inscription of "Gantt Circle" in front of Tillman Hall, two cement block inscriptions within the Class of 1960 Memorial, and a center for student life named for Harvey and Lucinda Gantt—are Clemson's memorials to the history of forced racial integration on its campus following Gantt's successful lawsuit against the State of South Carolina.

Between the plantation and the civil rights memorials lie other histories of now-vanished places. About one-eighth of a mile from the Fort Hill plantation house stood the

Fort Hill slave quarters. The site is one of erasure, as the slave quarters were dismantled so that their granite stones could be used to construct the earliest campus buildings. Lee Hall, home to the School of Architecture and "one of the most elegant examples of mid-century modern architecture in the South" ("Facilities and Resources"), now occupies the land where the quarters once stood. The workers who hauled these stones from the slave quarters, made nearly one million bricks using local clay, and erected the original campus buildings were convict laborers, hundreds of mainly African American men and boys who labored and died to build the college under the brutal convict leasing system that transformed free African Americans into "slaves of the state," formally dead in law.[4] This history of forced convict labor may be found everywhere and nowhere at Clemson. The only remaining sign of these men's lives on the campus seems to be an unmarked potter's field at the edge of campus, where those who died while in captivity are buried. Their stories, like those of many African Americans who worked on this land, are part of a history that "appears to be not there" but, once acknowledged, asserts itself as a "seething presence, acting on and often meddling with taken-for-granted realities," much like Avery Gordon's account of the social functions of haunting (Gordon 2008, 8).

This special issue highlights the work of African American artists and intellectuals to locate sites of memory and to investigate the relationship between race, space, and place. Salamishah Tillet has argued that reconstructing "sites of slavery" in post-civil rights literature, art, and theory becomes a way for African Americans to "speak out against their racial plight" as full citizens who nonetheless remain estranged from the civic myths that give cultural meaning to legal citizenship. By imaginatively reconstructing the sites of slavery that have been forgotten or excised from narratives of national belonging, post-civil rights African American artists and intellectuals also speak out "on behalf of their enslaved ancestors (the dead)" while actively making space for memorializing the dead—for reconfiguring "these civic markers in order to accommodate the constitutive sites of American history that the national memory has forgotten" (Tillet 2012, 9). Novelist Octavia Butler points to the complex process of locating the sites of slavery, both spatially and in the literary imagination, in an interview on her visit to Mount Vernon, the estate of George Washington: "the tour guide did not refer to slaves but to 'servants' and there was all this very carefully orchestrated dancing around the fact that it had been a slave plantation." Maja Milatovic opens her essay in this special issue with Butler's account of her visit to Mount Vernon in order to examine the multiple forms of dislocations at work in Butler's fantasy novel *Kindred* (1979), in which an interracial couple shuttles between 1970s California and an antebellum Maryland plantation. Dana, an African American woman married to a white man, must ensure her own survival by protecting her white slaveholding ancestor long enough for him to rape her foremother and thus start Dana's family line. The trope of time-space travel juxtaposes antebellum and post-civil rights envelopes of time-spaces in ways that disrupt meanings of gender, sex, race, class, and family genealogies born out of the violence of the slave system. As Milatovic's essay demonstrates, Butler uses sites of slavery as spaces of dislocation to challenge both the civic myths of the post-civil rights era and the national myths of founding fathers.

Spatially locating the sites of slavery may also challenge the myth of its legal abolition. As H. Bruce Franklin notes, the Thirteenth Amendment wrote slavery into the Constitution when it proclaimed the end to slavery and involuntary servitude "except as a punishment for crime whereof the party shall have been duly convicted" (1998, 4). What emerges out of the failure of Reconstruction in the years after the Civil War is a harrowing legal regime that explicitly set out to recapture African Americans into a system of forced labor. This system at once provided for the massive industrial development of the post-Reconstruction South and the racial terror of white supremacy. An essay by Rhondda Robinson Thomas in this issue details the role of the convict lease system in the building of what was originally known as Clemson Agricultural College of South Carolina. She demonstrates how a college established decades after the Civil War is a site of slavery in a double sense, as both the legacy of antebellum fortunes produced by the enslaved and as the place built by convicts. By looking to a college established in 1889 and opened to students in 1893, Thomas extends recent scholarship by Craig Steven Wilder and others on how the antebellum slave system powered the growth of US universities. She draws extensively from little-known state archives and prison records to reconstruct the stories of the men and boys who lived, worked, and died as convict laborers on this land.

The construction in law of the convict, as a category of legal personhood that may be enslaved as punishment for a crime, is indebted to the centrality of race in legal thinking. Blackness has been figured as already criminal since the founding of the nation, and the criminalization of blackness continues in the current system of mass incarceration, what practicing lawyer and legal scholar Michelle Alexander has called "the New Jim Crow" (2010). As Jenifer L. Barclay incisively argues in her contribution to this special issue, the criminalization of blackness rested on antebellum legal reasoning that regarded enslaved blacks as inherently disabled. As blackness came to represent various forms of disability in US legal thought, court decisions used racial reasoning to inflict physically disabling punishments on the bodies of black subjects. Barclay analyzes state laws and court decisions that disabled African Americans as legal persons and physically as embodied humans. She then brings this legal history of disability to bear upon Frederick Douglass's *Narrative of the Life of Frederick Douglass* (1845) and especially the rhetoric of sympathy and slave capacity in white abolitionist literature, including Theodore Weld's *Slavery As It Is: Testimony of a Thousand Witnesses* (1839) and Harriet Beecher Stowe's *Uncle Tom's Cabin* (1852).

The essays in this special issue challenge US civic myths of citizenship and national belonging by redefining the interrelatedness of space, place, and the law for African Americans. Michael Ra-Shon Hall underscores the politics of location in the pre-Civil Rights era in his essay on Calvin A. Ramsey's *The Green Book: A Play in Two Acts* (2006) and Andrea Lee's musical, *The Golden Chariot* (2002). Hall shows how these works dramatize the experience of traveling through Southern spaces racially demarcated by Jim Crow laws. Hall also demonstrates how both works draw from the historical *Negro Motorist Green Book* (1949) by Victor H. Green, which served as a travel guide for African American motorists to help steer them away from spaces of racial exclusion and potential humiliation and violence. *The Green Book* listed the locations of those particular places (restaurants and motor lodges, gas stations, and public rest rooms) African Americans could enter in the course of their travels. The essay by Kenton Rambsy joins Hall's analysis of African American literary strategies for depicting location as a dynamic spatial process produced out of changing social relations.[5] Rambsy argues that Edward P. Jones' *New Yorker* short stories take up a process of "location-identification"—what Rambsy calls "literary geotagging"—of Washington, DC, in order to redefine the "racial-spatial dimensions" of our nation's capital.

Race, space, and place also have generated new literary forms and aesthetic strategies in African American literature written between the Civil War and the civil rights movement. In her essay, Kelly Clasen argues for a re-evaluation of Charles Chesnutt's multi-genre novel *Mandy Oxendine*, rejected by publishers in 1897 and first published a century later. Analyzing the shifting and contradictory depiction of the North Carolina piney woods in the novel, Clasen contends that the novel traces Chesnutt's emerging "environmental ethos," and that ecocriticism provides new insights into *Mandy Oxendine* as a text that examines the environment and society as part of a shared ecology. Shifting from the piney woods to the informally segregated streets of New York, the issue includes an essay by Ashley Bourgeois that uses spatial theories of liminality and mobility to contend that critics have largely neglected the spatial agency of Lutie Brown, the protagonist of Ann Petry's *The Street* (1946), in their readings of the novel. Bourgeois examines how Lutie actively rejects "black spaces" in favor of white spaces that ultimately leave her estranged and alienated from her family, her social circles, and her own labor. Literary critics have identified urban black life (and migration from the rural South to major Northern cities, including New York) as a primary theme of twentieth-century African American literature until the late 1960s, which marks a distinct aesthetic and thematic turn to the South. In her essay, Shaila Mehra astutely challenges literary scholarship on the southern turn in African American literature. Mehra demonstrates that the southern turn has been narrowly defined to reinforce critics' premise that it marks a literary evasion from considerations of modernity and postmodernity and toward the refuge of "nostalgic gestures" to a premodern, folksy rural South. Far from "freezing the South in a state of premodern plenitude at the precise moment when it is undergoing massive modernization," Alice Walker's *The Third Life of Grange Copeland* (1970) complicates dominant critiques of the southern turn by charting "the new South as a region in which folk tradition and political modernization exist in dynamic and productive tension."

Essays by Akel Ismail Kahera and David Borman reconfigure notions of the US North and the US South by expanding our parameters beyond the boundaries of the nation-state, underscoring circum-Atlantic crossings and identifying the African continent as an active site for forging circum-Atlantic affiliations among the black diaspora. Kahera's essay examines the slave narrative of Omar ibn Said, a Fulani Muslim tribesman from Futa Toro in what is now Senegal who received extensive education and religious training before his capture into the Atlantic slave system and his eventual sale in Charleston. Having fled one slaveholder, ibn Said was caught and imprisoned in a Fayetteville, North Carolina jail, where his Arabic writings on the jail walls gained local attention and led to his second sale—this time in North Carolina, where he lived the rest of his life. Kahera draws on recent scholarship that situates ibn Said within a broader context of enslaved African Muslims throughout the Americas. As Kahera demonstrates, ibn Said's Arabic literacy and religious training drive the complex narrative strategies at work in *The Life of Omar Ibn Said, Written by Himself* (1831) to challenge the distorted logics and cultures of US slavery. His essay also indirectly attests to the power of place for us as readers: after having been lost for decades, ibn Said's *Life* was rediscovered and found its way to the first auction of print and manuscript African Americana at Swann Galleries in New York City in 1996. It was there that Kahera held in his hands the only surviving American slave narrative written in Arabic. Such encounters reveal the enormous urgency of locating African

American literature and, in the process, broaden our understanding of its power to make places and to produce new spaces for intellectual and creative work between the African continent and the African diaspora.

Remapping the traditional narrative of the Middle Passage, which assumes a single crossing from the West African to the American coastline, Borman's essay reads Canadian novelist Lawrence Hill's *Someone Knows My Name* (2007) as "disorganizing the trajectory of black Atlantic diasporan theory," which has been criticized for its assumption of Africa as merely the provider of those raw materials that led to the complex improvisatory cultures of the Black Atlantic.[6] As Borman argues, Hill's novel is a "circum-Atlantic project of historical recovery" centered on a dynamic and expansive understanding of the African *djeli*, or village storyteller. The novel's narrator, Aminata Diallo, is captured from Bayo, Mali, and sold into slavery on an indigo plantation in colonial South Carolina: from there, her multiple cris-crossings between Africa, North America, and Europe lead not only to her authorship of *The Book of Negroes*, which lists the names of Black Loyalists, but also to her broadening of circum-Atlantic African collectivities through her work as *djeli*. Through deft close readings, Borman explores how Aminata's migrations and her work as book author and oral storyteller must be understood as actively shaped by the cultural meanings of literacy and storytelling in Aminata's village in Mali.

This themed issue also includes two pieces that explore what it means for individuals to grapple with, and to redefine, their particular locations within the US South. Meredith McCarroll's interview with poet Kelly Norman Ellis discusses the complex identifications of Affrilachia as a cultural, personal, and aesthetic location that seeks to upend official definitions of Appalachians as white. Susanna Ashton's biographical sketch of Jacob Stroyer examines his devastating experiences as an enslaved boy who was forced to labor for the Confederacy, first at Sullivan's Island in 1863 and then at Fort Sumter in 1864, when it was under Confederate control.

Sullivan's Island lies at the mouth of Charleston Harbor, on the way to North America's largest port of entry of enslaved Africans, where nearly half of all enslaved Africans entered the United States. Before disembarking at Charleston, slave ships for most of the eighteenth century brought unknown numbers of captured Africans to Sullivan's Island, where they were quarantined in "pest houses" before being transported to Charleston's international slave trade market. In 2008, crowds gathered at Fort Moultrie on Sullivan's island to inaugurate the Toni Morrison Society's "Bench by the Road" project—a memorial project inspired by Morrison's account of how her novel *Beloved* came into being: "There is no place you or I can go, to think about or not think about, to summon the presences of, or recollect the absences of slaves [...] There is no suitable memorial, or plaque, or wreath, or wall, or park, or skyscraper lobby. There's no 300-foot tower, there's no small bench by the road. [...] And because such a place doesn't exist [...] the book had to" (The World, 1989, quoted in "The Toni Morrison Society"). We are pleased to include the creative work of poets, short story writers, and visual artists that redirect Morrison's commentary to a wide range of subjects that involve remembering, forgetting, and place. Short stories by Tom Williams and Laura Good, poems by Lenard D. Moore and William Ramsey, and photography by Kaneesha Brownlee all invite us to think about the location of contemporary art in fresh ways. Also in this issue are reviews of current scholarship in African American studies that take seriously what Brady describes as the urgency of space, an urgency especially pressing for those who have long been under threat of forced labor and incarceration, racial segregation and the racially devastating effects of contemporary colorblind legislation, the extralegal violence of lynching and what theorists have described as "racial melancholia" in the post-civil rights era (Eng and Han 2000, 671, quoted in Tillet 2012, 9).

Finally, we are thrilled to reproduce the work of internationally acclaimed South Carolina low country artist Jonathan Green for the cover of this themed issue. Based in Daniel Island, just north of Charleston Harbor, Green's work explores the rich Gullah culture in which he was raised: it is his work that, perhaps even more than the steel bench memorial at Sullivan's Island, gives shape to the vibrant potential of locating African American literature and art.

Notes

As guest co-editors of this themed issue, Angela Naimou and Rhondda Robinson Thomas would like to thank the contributors as well as the staff of The South Carolina Review, *especially Dustin Mosley for typesetting, Tiffany Verkaik for cover design, Reviews Editor Cameron Bushnell for the reviews section, and* SCR *Editor Wayne Chapman for helping to bring this issue to completion. We also thank John Morgenstern for his copy edits, Dustin Pearson for his assistance, and the University Research Grant Committee (URGC) for funding through a 2013 Project Completion Grant.*

1. For a study of how slavery was excised from public memory of the Civil War as part of the narrative of reconciliation after the Civil War, see David Blight, *Race and Reunion: The Civil War in American Memory* (2002).
2. For a look at Clemson's efforts to incorporate the histories of African Americans at Fort Hill, see "African-Americans at Fort Hill: 1825-1888." Accessed December 1, 2013. http://www.clemson.edu/about/history/properties/fort-hill/forthill-aa.html.
3. Tillman Hall is the main building of the original campus, named after the avowed white supremacist Benjamin Tillman, who was then Governor of South Carolina and an original member of the Clemson Board of Trustees.
4. See *Ruffin v. The Commonwealth*. 1871. The Supreme Court of Virginia. November. 62 Va. 790; 1871 Va. LEXIS 89; 21 Gratt. 790. For an insightful reading of *Ruffin v. Commonwealth*, including its invocation of civil death, see Colin Dayan's genealogy of civil death in legal thought, *The Law is a White Dog: How Legal Rituals Make and Unmake Persons* (2013). There Dayan traces how *Ruffin v. Commonwealth* is one instance in which "the medieval fiction of civil death lives on in the present" (xii).
5. On critiques of unexamined uses of spatial metaphor and an insistence that using spatial metaphors be attentive to the metaphor and materiality as interconnected, see Neil Smith and Cindi Katz 1993.
6. Hill's novel was originally published in Canada and the United Kingdom as *The Book of Negroes*.

Works Cited

Brady, Mary Pat. 2002. *Extinct Lands, Temporal Geographies: Chicana Literature and the Urgency of Space*. Durham, NC: Duke University Press.

Dayan, Colin Dayan. 2013. *The Law is a White Dog: How Legal Rituals Make and Unmake Persons*. Princeton, NJ: Princeton University Press.

Eng, David L., and Shinhee Han. 2000. "A Dialogue on Racial Melancholia." *Psychoanalytic Dialogues* 10(4): 667–700.

Franklin, Howard Bruce. 1998. "Introduction." *Prison Writing in Twentieth Century America*. New York: Penguin.

Massey, Doreen. 1994. *Space, Place, and Gender*. Minneapolis: University of Minnesota Press.

Ricoeur, Paul. 2004. *Memory, History, Forgetting*, trans. Kathleen Blamey and David Pellauer. Chicago: University of Chicago Press.

Tillet, Salamishah. 2012. *Sites of Slavery: Citizenship and Racial Democracy in the Post–Civil Rights Imagination*. Durham, NC: Duke University Press.

Wilder, Craig Steven. 2013. *Ebony & Ivy: Race, Slavery, and the Troubled History of America's Universities*. New York: Bloomsbury Press.

"The Will." 1886. *Thomas Green Clemson*. Office of Web Services. Clemson University. Accessed December 10, 2013. http://www.clemson.edu/TGC200/the-will.htm.

"Facilities and Resources." Office of Web Services. Clemson University. Accessed December 10, 2013. http://www.clemson.edu/caah/architecture/facilities-and-resources/.

Smith, Neil, and Cindi Katz. 1993. "Grounding Metaphor: Towards a Spatialized Politics." *Place and the Politics of Identity*, edited by Michael Keith and Steve Pile. London: Routledge. 67–83.

Toni Morrison Society. Accessed December 5, 2013. http://www.tonimorrisonsociety.org/bench.html.

E S S A Y

"SLAVES OF THE STATE":
CONVICT LABOR AND CLEMSON UNIVERSITY LAND AND LEGACY

by Rhondda Robinson Thomas

November is an exciting "Month of Milestones" for Clemson University. We are indebted to the generosity and enthusiasm of those who have come before us, beginning with Thomas Green Clemson. Have you considered how many people have helped change the landscape of this University? Don't think about it? Let's take a moment to. Read and reflect on our November landmarks—each made possible by someone who cared enough.

—Legacy Month website, Clemson University (2013)

The convict labor heretofore furnished by the State has proved invaluable both in the construction of the buildings and the development of the farm. There still remains a large amount of work on the farm to fit it for experimental and other purposes, which can only be done economically by convict labor. We therefore ask that at least thirty-three convicts be furnished to the College next year upon the same terms as heretofore.

—R. W. Simpson, President of the Board of Trustees,
Annual Report to the South Carolina State Legislature (1894)

In October of 1891, 13-year-old African American Wade Foster, a convicted felon, reported for work at the South Carolina Experimental Farm, site of the new Clemson Agricultural College of South Carolina that would open in 1893. Foster, a laborer, had been found guilty of housebreaking, stealing six dollars worth of clothing in the daytime from Victoria Caldwell's home in Spartanburg, South Carolina. When Judge J. H. Hudson found that Foster, "having nothing to say only sentence should not be forced upon him," he sentenced the teenager to six months of hard labor at the state penitentiary (*The State v. Wade Foster* 1891). Soon thereafter, Foster found himself working among 50 other prisoners, hired by Clemson trustees through South Carolina's leased-convict system, to clear land, erect buildings, and plant and harvest crops at the site of the new public college in the Upstate made possible through a bequest in Thomas Green Clemson's will. Young Foster may have labored alongside 16-year-old African American Frank Taylor, a farmer who had been found guilty of housebreaking and compound larceny and sentenced to one year in the state penitentiary; 20-year-old African American Andrew Williams, a farmer who had been found guilty of assault with intent to kill and carrying a concealed weapon and sentenced to three years in the state penitentiary; 32-year-old African American Gabe Anderson, a blacksmith who had been convicted of assault and battery of a high and aggravated nature and sentenced to two months in the state penitentiary; and 53-year-old Jack Givins, a laborer who had been convicted of larceny of livestock and sentenced to two years in the state penitentiary—all listed in the prison register among the convicts assigned to Clemson College on August 1, 1891 (*Farm and Contract Registers* 1889-1892, 117).

The vast majority of the nearly 600 convicts whose names appear in the Farm and Contract Registers for Clemson College between 1890 and 1899 were African Americans. These men and boys comprised the third generation of people of African descent who toiled in conditions associated with slavery on the Fort Hill Plantation that became Clemson University. During the early to mid-nineteenth century, US Statesman John C. Calhoun and his family forced enslaved African Americans to work on a plantation they would never own, to care for the needs of a planter they dared not defy without risking detrimental consequences, and to take the name of a slaveholding statesman they would never know as family. After the Civil War, Calhoun's son-in-law and Clemson founder Thomas Green Clemson entered into agreements with freedmen and women who signed "X" on contracts that locked them into an exploitative sharecropper system that stripped them of their newly won rights as citizens, reverting them to a slave-like status. And when the Clemson College trustees searched for a means for a cash strapped, public education averse, white Democratic-controlled state to build a land-grant college on Fort Hill in the late nineteenth century, they leased convicts who were legally classified as "slaves of the State."[1] The majority of these convicts, African American men and boys, built a college that neither they nor their children or grandchildren could attend due to *de facto* racial segregation of South Carolina's public spaces and institutions, traditions that the State Assembly codified in Jim Crow laws during the 1895 state constitution convention convened at the urging of US Senator Benjamin R. "Pitchfork" Tillman, a Clemson College trustee.

Since Clemson University was founded after the Civil War, one might wonder what responsibility the institution has for acknowledging its connection to an antebellum plantation owned by a prominent white Southern American political family. Labor and criminal laws enacted by racist white politicians and supported by their constituents and the nation in the late nineteenth century created slavery by another name in the South: the convict-lease system that white legislators relied on to rebuild their states after the decimation of the Civil War. In South Carolina, the General Assembly empowered Clemson trustees to use the convict-lease system to expand its higher education system, beginning with Clemson College which enrolled white male students taught by white male faculty.[2] Uncovering the complex narrative of the Calhoun and Clemson families, the Fort Hill plantation, and America's peculiar institution is critical to understanding the relationship between the story and legacy of slavery in South Carolina and the history and mission of Clemson University.

The Politics of Public History: the Clemson Family, Land, and Legacy

Clemson University successfully markets itself as a top research university with a small college feel through the concept and experience of the Clemson family ("The Clemson Family" 2011). The University eases new administrators' and faculty's transition into campus life with assurances that they are now part of the Clemson family. The admissions staff introduces accepted students to the Clemson family through a website that features stories about student collaborations, faculty-mentored research projects, and locally made ice cream treats ("Clemson Family"). The University sponsors a Family Weekend each fall to welcome students' relatives into the Clemson family through participation in a football game and other social activities. Newly elected Clemson University President Jim Clements recently acknowledged the strength of the Clemson family in his first remarks to the University. According to Clements, "One of the things that excited us—me and (wife) Beth—so much about Clemson, is this is all about family. And there's something that's really special....So we are honored to be coming into a great university that has such a great history and I know it has a great future. So we're thrilled to be part of the Clemson family" ("New President" 2013). Clemson's eclipse of its $600 million goal in the Will to Lead capital campaign in the summer of 2013 reflects the loyalty and dedication of its family members—alumni, friends, corporations, and parents—whom the University confidently expects to help it reach the new $1 billion goal ("Clemson campaign"). Yet Clemson also counts among its family "Notable People" such as US Statesman and slavery proponent John C. Calhoun for whom the Calhoun Honors College is named, Confederate veterans such as Henry A. Strode who served as its first president and for whom Strode Tower is named, white supremacist and influential politician Benjamin Tillman who served as an original trustee and for whom Tillman Hall is named, and segregationist and influential politician Strom Thurmond for whom the Strom Thurmond Institute is named. Additionally, the University publicly lauds one African American family member, Harvey Gantt, who integrated Clemson with dignity in 1963, and has named the Center for Student Life, a scholarship, and a street in his honor. Yet no markers identify other important sites of significant nineteenth-century African American history, such as the slave quarters that once occupied the land where Lee Hall now stands, or the granite stones from those quarters that were recycled as the foundation for Hardin Hall and other campus buildings.

The circulation of revisionist history regarding Clemson University's complex connections to race, space, and place informs this careful construction of a cohesive Clemson family. In *Clemson: There's Something in These Hills* (2006), Clemson alumni Trent Allan and Kent Bray include an encomium for Bowman Field by then Clemson President James Barker that epitomizes the institution's efforts to construct a triumphant narrative about the Clemson family, land, and legacy. Bowman Field, named for Randolph T. V. Bowman, former Clemson instructor of forge and foundry and assistant football coach, stretches out like a green shag carpet in front of several of the oldest buildings on campus. The site is a popular gathering spot for celebrating First Friday festivals, building homecoming floats, and staging outdoor concerts. In "Sacred Soil of Bowman Field," Barker recounts the "drama of Clemson being acted out on this soil":

> This piece of earth, or nearby, marked the place where the first American died defending our country in the Revolutionary War, a Jewish soldier named Francis Salvador. This piece of earth was part of the farm of John C. Calhoun and Thomas Green Clemson. It produced crops of corn and cotton that supported the farm...
>
> Three Congressional Medal of Honor winners have marched on this field. When you walk on Bowman Field, you walk in their footsteps as well as the footsteps of Cherokees, the Jewish American hero, the African American farm workers, the athletic teams, the Clemson Cadet Corps and many ROTC unite across the generations. (182-83)

This multi-cultural yet uncritical revisionist history of Clemson family, land, and legacy obscures the harrowing narratives of forced removal and labor that engendered Bowman Field's existence, however. Many historians identify African American Crispus Attucks, rather than Francis Salvador, as the first casualty of the American Revolution. Although Calhoun and Thomas Green Clemson associated themselves with Upstate farmers, they were also slaveholders. European settlers and South Carolina colonists forced Cherokees from the land through wars and treaties, and then claimed it as their own. African American slaves, sharecroppers, and convicts, rather than African American farm workers, cultivated and harvested crops on the land that became Bowman Field. A statute of Thomas Green Clemson, an academic building named Tillman Hall, two nineteenth-century canons named "Tom and Jerry," and the Military Heritage Plaza stand as beacons of light on the edge of Bowman Field, guiding the footsteps of Clemson students, athletes, cadets, and ROTC units on a clear path to a legacy unmarked by memorials to Cherokees who settled the region and African Americans who lived, labored, and died on Clemson land prior to forced integration in 1964.

Indeed, the University bases its identity on the rich legacy created by founders Thomas Green and Anna Calhoun Clemson who generously provided educational opportunities to young white men in South Carolina through their gift of Fort Hill for the establishment of a "high seminary of learning…for the graduate of the common schools" ("The Will" 1886). The University commemorates their contribution through its annual fall Legacy Day. In October of 2013, Legacy Day was reintroduced as Legacy Month, however, and the University issued the following online invitation to the Clemson family and the public to participate in the celebration: "Legacy Day has quickly become a beloved fall tradition here at Clemson University, and this year we're stretching the celebrations to span the entire month of November. Honor our rich history, see the beautiful Fort Hill mansion, learn the importance of giving back and pay thanks to those who have given. Most importantly, consider what your legacy at Clemson will be" ("Legacy Month" 2013). The month-long celebration began with a "Will Signing Day" that included opportunities to view historic documents such as an early draft of Clemson's will. During the following week, guests celebrated the seventy-fifth anniversary of Thomas Green and Anna Calhoun Clemson's nuptials by eating wedding cupcakes. The next event was tailored for faculty and staff who toured the Fort Hill mansion and sampled nineteenth-century dishes. The celebration culminated in the annual Legacy Day event when hundreds of guests participated in scavenger hunt tours of Fort Hill; received a Legacy Day t-shirt and water bottle; enjoyed refreshments and listened to music on the Fort Hill lawn; viewed the final draft of Thomas Green Clemson's will; and signed the mat of a print that will be displayed in Cooper Library ("Legacy Month" 2013). The contributions of African Americans to the Fort Hill plantation and the Thomas Green Clemson family during the antebellum and post-bellum periods were not acknowledged, however.

The University has also commemorated its legacy through the publication of a biography of Thomas Green Clemson and a two-volume history of the university, which both briefly reference the labor of African Americans for Fort Hill and Clemson College. The biography, *Thomas Green Clemson* (2009) edited by Clemson English professor Alma Bennett, includes 15 chapters by a range of scholars who introduce readers to "…no ordinary man. He was, in fact, as unique as he was highly educated, skilled, pragmatic, visionary, and complex" ("Thomas Green Clemson" 2013). The text includes a chapter titled "Race, Reconstruction, and Post-bellum Education in Thomas Green Clemson's Life and World" by Clemson University history professor Abel Bartley. Bartley includes intriguing insights into Clemson's formative years in Philadelphia and his connections to slavery and Fort Hill through his marriage to Anna Calhoun, John C. Calhoun's daughter. Additionally, the chapter features mini-profiles and photographs of some of the enslaved African Americans who labored at Fort Hill, namely Susan Clemson Richardson, Nancy Legree, and Thomas and Frances Fuster, but does not include information about the freedmen and women who worked as tenant farmers for Thomas Green Clemson during Reconstruction ("Articles of Agreement," 1867, 1868, 1871, and 1875). In *The High Seminary: A History of Clemson University, 1889-1964,* Vol. 1 (2013), Clemson historian Jerome V. Reel adopts a similar historical strategy, opening his narrative with the chapter titled "The Land," which recounts the story of the Scots-Irish who eventually inhabited the Upstate South Carolina land that other Europeans had taken from the native population, Cherokee Indians (3-4). In Chapter 3, "Building the School, 1889-1893," he mentions convicts 24 times, limiting his examination of their contributions to Clemson to the trustees' requests to the State Assembly for convicts and the labor the convicts performed for the institution.

Overall, Clemson University's current public history narrative minimizes the institution's complex connections to slavery and its legacy in South Carolina. The most visible reminder that Clemson's current landscape filled with an array of stately buildings from historic structures to modern edifices is John C. Calhoun's Fort Hill Plantation is Calhoun's historic home that is located in the center of campus.[3] While historical markers exist for Fort Hill and other significant places, figures, and events, few resources mark the lives of the enslaved and free African-Americans who lived and labored on Clemson soil in the nineteenth century. Although scholars and historians have conducted some research to reconstruct the narrative that weaves the threads of race, place, and higher education in Upstate South Carolina, this multi-layered history is incomplete.

"There's Something in These Hills": from Cherokee Nation to Clemson Agricultural College

The story of the Clemson land is a five-part narrative that recounts its existence as a region in Cherokee Nation, establishment as the Frontier of one of the 13 colonies, transformation into the South Carolina Upstate, and operation as a plantation and farm before its development into a college. Historians have identified the Cherokee village of Essennaca as the settlement that was located closest to Clemson, about one mile from campus. During the American Revolution, Cherokees largely joined the British in attacks against the Scots-Irish colonists who established Fort Rutledge near University land to fortify themselves during battles (Rowan-Ricks 1992, 19-20). After the war ended, several different speculators purchased the land until Reverend James McElhenny, rector of the Old Stone Church in Pendleton, South Carolina, and a slaveholder, bought the property, built a parsonage named Clergy Hall, and eventually expanded the estate to 904 acres. Seventeen years later, Floride Bonneau Colhoun, John C. Calhoun's mother–in–law, purchased the property. Around 1825, John C. Calhoun and his wife Floride began renting Clergy Hall, which he renamed Fort Hill in honor of Fort Rutledge. After her mother's death in 1836, Floride Colhoun Calhoun inherited the property. Over the next fourteen years, the Calhouns enlarged their estate through inheritance and purchases of land and slaves. Following John C. Calhoun's death in 1850, Fort Hill changed hands within the family several times. In 1853, his wife sold the estate to their son, Andrew. When he defaulted on the property, his sister Anna Calhoun Clemson acquired Fort Hill. After she died in 1875, her husband Thomas G. Clemson became the last owner of the estate.

Thomas Green Clemson soon turned his attention to fulfilling his and his wife Anna's wish to establish an agricultural college in Upstate South Carolina. In the summer of 1886, he met with South Carolina politician Benjamin R. Tillman, businessman Daniel Keating Norris, and his attorney Richard Wright Simpson to discuss plans for the institution. By the fall of 1886, Clemson had drawn up his will, which included a bequest of the Fort Hill home and 814 acres of land for the establishment of a "high seminary of learning." After Thomas Green Clemson's death in 1888, the General Assembly began discussing the bequest. With three public colleges already operating in South Carolina, namely the College of Charleston (1770), the College of South Carolina (1801), and The Citadel (1842), state legislators were loathe to establish another institution of higher learning. In 1889, following a fractious, prolonged debate, the Assembly finally approved the establishment of the land-grant institution by a slim one-vote margin and South Carolina Governor John Richardson signed "An Act to Accept the Devise and Bequest of Thomas Green Clemson and to Establish an Agricultural College Connected Therewith" (*Acts and Joint Resolutions* 1890, 277-80). Legislators designated the college as a land grant institution, in accordance with the one-per-state stipulations of the 1862 Morrill Act, which also provided federal lands and funding for the establishment of higher education institutions that focused on agricultural and technical instruction and research, and military training to provide citizens with practical skills that would enrich their lives, communities, and nation. They also allocated state funds for its development and management. Clemson College trustees began operating the South Carolina Experimental Farm in 1890, authorized by the Hatch Act and Smith-Lever Act of 1887, which expanded the scope of the Morrill land-grant legislation, and proceeded with plans to open the college soon thereafter.

Tillman, one of the first of seven lifetime trustees that Thomas Clemson appointed, helped shape policies regarding curriculum and enrollment for Clemson College, as well as the Assembly's selection of six additional trustees to ensure white control of the new institution. In reflecting on his role in establishing Clemson College, Tillman declared in a speech titled "The Origin of Clemson College":

> Having in view the possible danger of the Negroes, who are so largely in the majority of our state, at some time getting control of the State Government, we suggested the scheme of seven trustees who would be self-perpetuating, and thus make it impossible for an averse Legislature to shipwreck the college, or make it a school to which negroes would be admitted…We were anxious to keep down the danger of negro domination of the school and at the same time to prevent the prostitution of the institution to ends not intended by its founder.

After the Civil War ended, Republicans, elected by majority African American populations in many Southern states including South Carolina, had controlled state and local governments until 1877 when Southern moderate Democrats brokered a deal with Republican Rutherford Hayes, promising not to block his election if he would withdraw federal troops from the South. That same year, white Democrats, under the leadership of Wade Hampton and the Red Shirts, a white paramilitary group that terrorized African American citizens particularly during elections, violently ousted South Carolina's last black majority Republican government.

Despite their dominance of South Carolina politics after Reconstruction ended, white Democrats feared a Republican comeback because African Americans still outnumbered white Americans in the state (Rogers and Taylor 1994). After being elected governor in 1890 and US Senator in 1894, Tillman initiated a series of legislative initiatives that stripped African American South Carolinians of the rights and privileges of citizenship. In his inaugural address for the governorship, he described his election as "a triumph of Democracy and white supremacy" and asserted that "[t]he whites have absolute control of the State Government, and we intend at any and all hazards to retain it" (1890, 3-4). During the next five years, Tillman secured whites' control of South Carolina through the enactment of Jim Crow laws, including the segregation of South Carolina's public education system, and the disenfranchisement of African American South Carolinians whom he regarded as unequal and unqualified to cast ballots (1890, 4).

The Failure of Reconstruction and the Criminalization of Black Life in Post-bellum South Carolina

Tillman and other white Democratic politicians utilized South Carolina's convict-lease system in attaining the goal of "keep[ing] down the danger of negro domination." In 1866, the South Carolina General Assembly had authorized the building of the state's first penitentiary, which would eventually include two cellblocks for 1,000 inmates and administrative offices. Legislators also amended state statues on criminal law that focused on substitution of punishments for crimes. If a sentence involved a fine that the convict could not pay immediately, the convict was detained and given another punishment. For offenses that did not involve "*crimen falsi*, or be infamous," the white prisoner would be imprisoned for a time equivalent to the fine at a rate of one dollar per day, but the person of color would be subjected to "enforced labor without unnecessary pain or restraint, for a time proportionate to the crime" at the rate of one dollar per day (*Acts and Joint Resolutions* 1866, 277). If the offense was "infamous," all prisoners would be sentenced to "hard labor, corporal punishment, solitary confinement, and confinement in tread-mill or stocks" at the discretion of the judge or magistrate who pronounced the sentence (277). Although some of these laws were modified during Reconstruction, legislators amended many of them to disadvantage the poor and minorities when white Democrats regained control of the state house.

When white Democrats took over the General Assembly in 1877, they enacted legislation to lease the state's majority black prison population to public and private individuals and businesses. During its first session in 1877, the General Assembly approved "An Act to Utilize the Convict Labor of this State" to generate revenue for South Carolina (*Acts and Joint Resolutions* 1877, 263). Leasing convicts involved contracting prisoners out to "businessmen, planters, and corporations in one of the harshest and most exploitative labor systems known in American history," according to Matthew J. Mancini (1996) in *One Dies Get Another: Convict Leasing in the American South, 1866-1928* (1-2). The roots of the system extend back into hiring-out practices developed during the antebellum period by slave owners who temporarily leased enslaved African Americans to another person or business to generate additional revenue, as well as the practice of individual states that purchased enslaved African Americans to complete specific projects, such as the South Carolina Railroad (Blackmon 2008).

Although Congress had abolished involuntary servitude in the Thirteenth Amendment, the law included a caveat: "except as a punishment for crime whereof the party shall have been duly convicted." Southern states quickly began to utilize this "exception" to "criminalize black life," according to Douglass A. Blackmon (2008) in *Slavery by Another Name: the Reenslavement of Black Americans from the Civil War to World War II*, and to severely limit convicts' rights (53). States were further empowered in their efforts to criminalize blackness through the Virginia State Supreme Court's 1871 decision in *Ruffin v. Commonwealth of Virginia*:

> For a time, during his service in the penitentiary, he is in a state of penal servitude to the State. He has, as a consequence of his crime, not only forfeited his liberty, but all his personal rights except those which the law in its humanity accords to him. He is for the time being *a slave of the State*. He is *civiliter mortus*; and his estate, if he has any, is administered like that of a dead man.

This view led to the establishment of the "hands-off doctrine," which protected state and penitentiary administrators from prisoners' lawsuits for ill treatment and their community's concerns about dire prison conditions (Champion 1994, 127). In "Exploitation in the Jim Crow South: the Market or the Law," economics professor Jennifer Roback (1984) explains the consequences of placing the well being of the convict in the hands of penitentiary officials: "In at least one respect, the lease system was worse than slavery. The slaveholder could expect to profit from a slave's future output for his entire working life and thus had an incentive to maintain the slave's health. But the lessee firm had no interest in keeping a convict alive past the end of his sentence or contract period, since the man had no 'scrap' or 'resale' value" (39). In effect, states were empowered to establish and enforce the rules, hire experts to operate their penitentiary systems, and faced no legal repercussions for ill treatment of prisoners. In America's nineteenth-century penal system, citizenship did not shield convicts from being treated as if they were dead, an experience that was worse than slavery for African American men and boys and their families.

Within a few years, overcrowding became a problem in the penitentiary, however, leading prison officials to increase their dependence on the lease-convict system and chain gangs to reduce the prison population and to increase state revenues. Beginning in 1878, the white Democratic controlled South Carolina General Assembly began amending its regulations regarding convict leasing to provide more opportunities for businesses and individuals to hire convicts. Legislators amended "An Act to Utilize the Convict Labor of this State," striking out the prohibition of hiring out convicts for agricultural labor, which paved the way for Clemson trustees to hire convicts to work the college farm (*Acts and Joint Resolutions* 1878, 721). They also passed "An Act to Regulate the Hiring of Convict Labor," enabling the penitentiary to employ convicts in the institution or hire them out to private companies (727). On December 24, 1879, legislators amended "An Act to Utilize the Convict Labor of this State," empowering the director of the Penitentiary to lease convicts to the "highest responsible bidder…to reject any and all bids…*Provided*, that no bid shall be received that does not include the board, clothing, and all other expenses connected with the transportation and safe keeping of said convicts by the bidder…" (*Acts and Joint Resolutions* 1880, 168). They also sought to insert a level of accountability into the state's convict-leasing program, mandating that "if any convict or convicts so hired shall be proved to the satisfaction of said Directors to have been ill-treated, or the contracts in relation to them to have been in any way violated, to return said convict or convicts to immediately to the Penitentiary upon the order of said Directors" (168). The convicts were returned the penitentiary but the contractors were not prosecuted for alleged abuse.

Thus, by the late 1870s, South Carolina was actively engaged in the convict-lease system to supply the massive labor pool the state needed to rebuild its infrastructure and increase revenues after the destruction of its infrastructure during the Civil War—just as incarceration rates for African American men and boys were escalating. Although the public and private sectors increased their profits through the leased-convict system, unskilled laborers were increasingly bereft of job opportunities because employers favored the more economical leased-convict option when filling working-class positions such as clearing land, planting and harvesting crops, repairing roads, building railroads, or erecting buildings. In states like South Carolina where African Americans outnumbered whites, unemployment rates skyrocketed for thousands of former slaves and their children whose occupational choices were often limited to farmer, domestic, or laborer. Although historians have cited vagrancy laws as one of the major means Southern states utilized to criminalize black manhood, in South Carolina, many poor African American men and teens became entrapped in the penal system due to varied forms of larceny, which also disqualified them from voting (*Acts and Joint Resolutions* 1891, 337).

African American Convicts and Ivory Towers in Post-bellum South Carolina

From 1878 through the end of the nineteenth century, convicts in South Carolina and throughout the South were leased for projects ranging from mining coal to building roads, but no state appears to have utilized convicts to expand its public higher education system as extensively as South Carolina.[4] Clemson trustees successfully petitioned the General Assembly at least three times to lease a minimum of 150 convicts to clear land, erect buildings, develop infrastructure, and establish the farm for the new public college in the Upstate. On December 23, 1889, the General Assembly approved the Clemson trustees' first request to lease convicts to initiate the work of building the new college. In "An Act to Provide for the Building and Maintenance of the Clemson Agricultural College of South Carolina," the Assembly authorized the State Penitentiary's Board of Directors to provide up to fifty "able-bodied convicts" for the employ of Clemson trustees to complete "work connection with the erection of the buildings of the said Clemson Agricultural College, or in the preparation of the ground and materials therefor" (*Acts and Joint Resolutions* 1890, 299-302). Trustees were required to provide transportation for the convicts from the penitentiary, medical care, food, and lodging. Here the State Penitentiary, Clemson

Trustees, and the State Legislature initiated a short-term business contract in the exploitative system of leasing convicts that mirrored the hiring out system utilized by slaveholders during the antebellum period. The "employer" was responsible for the slave/convict's sustenance in addition to paying the master/state for his services. Both systems enabled "masters" to enrich themselves while the slave's labor contributed to the local and national economies. Clemson trustees were so pleased with the work of the first 50 convicts that they petitioned the legislature for more convicts to expand and accelerate the work.

On December 23, 1890, state legislators approved the trustees' second request in "A Joint Resolution to Authorize and Require the Directors of the Penitentiary to Furnish the Trustees of Clemson Agricultural College One Hundred Additional Convicts" (*Acts and Joint Resolutions* 1891, 695). In the annual report to the State Assembly, the trustees had argued, "The fifty convicts heretofore furnished have saved to the board the expenditure of a large amount of money, but they are not sufficient to do all the work required, without the hire of much additional labor" (*Annual Report* 1890, 642). This request for additional labor included special instructions for the State Penitentiary's Board of Directors in choosing convicts to work at Clemson College: "In selecting such convicts care should be taken to send such as have most skill in brickmaking, carpentering, and blacksmithing" (*Acts and Join Resolutions* 1891, 695). The marginal note inserted besides the law underscored a major stipulation of the resolution: "To be skilled workmen," which suggests that trustees expected to find skilled laborers among the predominately African American prison population (695). By the end of 1892, hired carpenters and leased convicts had constructed a barn, stable, pasture fence, seven framed houses and three brick houses for professors, and a house for the Experimental Station, as well as restored and repaired the Calhoun plantation house. They had also erected a laboratory, dormitory, and kitchen; made over 900,000 bricks for various buildings; and nearly completed work on the infirmary, chapel, president's house, and main college building. Additionally, convicts cleared land for a garden and cut and stored hay (*Annual Report* 1891 and 1892, 6-7).

By July 1893, the convicts had completed enough buildings and infrastructure for trustees to open the Clemson Agricultural College of South Carolina for 446 white male students and 15 white male faculty members. The trustees continued to utilize convict labor to perform work on the college campus. On January 4, 1894, the General Assembly approved the trustees' third request for convict labor in "A Joint Resolution to Authorize and Require the Directors of the Penitentiary to Furnish the Trustees of Clemson Agricultural College, and to Furnish the Regents of the Lunatic Asylum Fifty Convicts, and to Furnish the Trustees of the South Carolina Industrial and Winthrop Normal College One Hundred Convicts" (*Acts and Joint Resolutions* 1893, 510-11). The Assembly authorized Clemson trustees to lease "able-bodied convicts, not to exceed fifty at any one time…[to be] employed by said Trustees in dyking Seneca River, adjoining the College Farm, and in other such work as to them may seem useful, for twelve months from the date of the approval of this Joint Resolution" (511). By 1894, convicts had built public buildings and support buildings, completed the dyke, and dug holding pools for water supplies and wells, and installed subterranean clay tile pipes that were routed from the reservoirs to the emerging campus.

Between 1890 and 1899, the convict population averaged about forty-seven but swelled to 150 at the height of the building initiative. Because the convicts were rotated in and out of the labor pool based on the length of their sentences, however, nearly 600 may have labored at Clemson during this time, according to the prison registers. My initial research on the first 250 convicts who are listed in the register for Clemson College indicates that most were African American farmers and laborers, though a few were identified as African American carpenters, waiters, butchers, wagoners, and brick masons. They came from nearly every county jurisdiction in the state. Most were convicted of some form of burglary, from housebreaking to grand larceny, but their crimes also included manslaughter, arson, rape, rioting, and murder—convictions for black men and boys that could be secured simply upon accusation, according to white journalist, author, and reformer Frank B. Sanborn (1904) in "Negro Crime," a paper given at the Ninth Conference for the Study of the Negro Problems at Atlanta University. The convicts' sentences ranged from a few months to life. Several died, including 21-year-old Furman Jones on May 24, 1891, 35-year-old Terry Abraham on May 28, 1891, and 22-year-old John Dacus on June 20, 1891, while working at the Clemson site and are believed to be buried in unmarked graves in a Potter's Field on campus (*Central Register of Prisoners*).

Preliminary research of prison records in the State Archives indicates that convicts assigned to Clemson College ranged in age from 13 years old to 53 years old, with most being in their late teens and twenties. Regardless of their ages, all were tried and sentenced as adults.[5] Court records for trials of the men and juveniles in county courthouses include indictments and subpoenas, as well as confessions from defendants, many who signed "X" on the legal documents. For example, Wade Foster and John Givins, mentioned in the introduction to this essay, were both tried in the Court of General Sessions in Spartanburg County. The indictment for *The State v. Wader Foster* reveals that 13-year-old Foster was arrested for "Housebreaking in Daytime." It includes an arrest warrant, which indicates Foster was arrested and examined in September of 1891 and committed to jail without bail to await his trial; a signed confession; signed statements from witnesses; appearance recognizance for the defendant, plaintiff, and witnesses; and a search warrant. On October 18, 1891, Foster affixed an X on outside cover of the indictment, pleading guilty to the charges of breaking and entering Victoria Caldwell's home and committing larceny (stealing six dollars worth of clothing), and accepting the sentence of one year in the penitentiary. His sentence reflected the common practice of the "indiscriminate herding of juvenile and adult prisoners," according to W. E. B. Du Bois (1901) in "The Spawn of Slavery: the Convict-Lease System in the South" (745). Givins faced a similar process when he was indicted for larceny of livestock, a heifer calf valued at six dollars, in October of 1892 and sentenced to two years hard labor in the state penitentiary. Indictment records for *The State v. Jack Givins* include an arrest warrant, statement by the trial justice, and recognizance of witnesses. Givins was found guilty of stealing the livestock and reselling it for four dollars. Seven months into serving his sentence, Givins escaped and was never recaptured (*Central Register of Prisoners* 1892–1899).

Instead of risking recapture through escape, other convicts whom the state leased to Clemson trustees successfully sought pardons while laboring at the Fort Hill site. During the nineteenth century, pardoning power in the states rested primarily under the control of the governor, who issued pardons to ease overcrowding in penitentiaries, award political favors to supporters, reward prisoners' good behavior, and clear the records of persons found innocent of the crimes they had been convicted of committing

(Whitman 2003, 182). At least two convicts who worked at the Fort Hill site mailed handwritten petitions directly to Governor Benjamin Tillman.[6] In 1891, Charles Jackson, a 38-year-old African American laborer who had been convicted of arson in Hampton County and sentenced to life in prison, petitioned Tillman for a pardon after serving over 12 years in prison. On August 2, 1890, Jackson initiated his petition process by penning the following letter:

> To B. R. Tillman Governor
>   Your Excellency will you be so kind as to take my case in consideration as I was convicted at the May term of Court for Hampton County 1879 for arson and sentence by your Hon. Judge Hudson. I wish your Excellency to do something for me & recommend me to your Hon. Board of Directors of the South Carolina Penitentiary. I have no one to intercede for me as you told me your would look over my case. I have been in prison 12 years and 2 months.
> Your humble servant,
> Charley Jackson

During the next year, Jackson received support from officers, guards, and employees of South Carolina Penitentiary who signed a petition in his behalf, and W. J. Talbert, Superintendent of Penitentiary, who attested to Jackson's good conduct while working at Clemson College. Governor Tillman granted Jackson a pardon on February 9, 1892, and he was immediately released from the Clemson work site.

Other convicts leased by Clemson trustees also relied on influential white friends who gathered signatures on petitions from upstanding members of the community, solicited letters from prominent businessmen, and pressured Tillman to honor their support as loyal Democrats. Like Jackson, thirty-six-year-old African American John Moore, a farmer who had been convicted of arson. He was tried in Abbeville County, and he was sentenced to 10 years in the penitentiary beginning on September 26, 1885. Nearly five years into his sentence on February 9, 1890, J. B. Arnold wrote Governor Tillman on Moore's behalf, requesting that he pardon the "colored man" other white people supported. Nearly four years later, Frank A. Arnold, Jr., owner of the gin house that Moore had robbed and burned down, wrote a letter to the governor in which he characterized Moore as "the Shrewdest and Most infernal Cotton thief that was ever about Ninety Six." He informed Tillman that he had voted for him and expected the governor to be an "honest firm Square man" who would not pardon a convicted felon. Moore's friends undermined the veracity of Arnold's characterization of Moore with a petition that described him as an "honest, industrious, law-abiding man and we are informed that his conduct since he has been in the Penitentiary has been above reproach." In the early months of 1894, Clemson trustee John E. Bradley sent Governor Tillman two letters reminding him to investigate the case of John Moore who was in the Fort Hill prison. Soon thereafter Moore also wrote the governor a follow-up inquiry regarding the status of his pardon request:

> Honored Sir:
>   You told me when you were up here that you would send my Pardon as soon as you went back. And you told me if you did not for me to write and I

remind you of it and as it has not come yet I thought I would write.
     Your humble Servant,
     John Moore

Eight days later, Moore sent a second, more urgent letter, imploring Governor Tillman to keep his promise to grant him a pardon:

Your Excellency Mr. B. R. Tillman Gov.
Dear Sir:
     When you were here at C.A.C last, you told me that you would discharge me in a few days after you returned to Columbia; and that if you did not to be sure and write and call your attention to this matter.
     My petition has been before you for some time and I do pray your executive clemency, remember me in mercy.
     Trusting your excellency for my freedom. I am your most humble servant,
     John Moore

On April 12, 1894, two days after Moore mailed his second letter, Governor Tillman granted Moore a pardon, releasing him from the work detail at Clemson College and restoring his freedom. Tillman also granted pardons for convicts at the Clemson College worksite as a political favor to an African American Democrat; in response to a persuasive petition signed by numerous members of a community, including the father of the plaintiff; letters from remorseful jurors who served at a trial; and solely due to a convict's handwritten plea.

Rather than submit themselves to the arduous task of seeking a pardon, some convicts took advantage of the remote, wooded site and took the more risky route to freedom through escape. In the *High Seminary*, Reel (2013) recounts the story of a nameless convict who disappeared from the worksite around Christmas but returned to the stockade where the convicts lived shortly thereafter, reporting that he had simply slipped away to spend some time with his family over the holidays (80). The registers for the convicts (see Figure 1, at right) assigned to Clemson College include notations of numerous escapes from the worksite, however. Escapees included laborers who were recaptured the same day, such as 23-year-old African American Fred Delvin, who had been convicted of forgery and sentenced to five years in the penitentiary, and 21-year-old William Gladden, a white fireman who had been convicted of house breaking and larceny and sentenced to one year in the penitentiary. Gladden later escaped a second time with Dillon D. Duncan, a 22-year-old white engineer who had been convicted of grand larceny and received a two-year sentence. Duncan was recaptured 10 years later and forced to complete his sentence, but there is no record of Gladden, a Pickens County resident, ever being returned to the penitentiary. Several other convicts escaped and remained at large for several years, such as 34-year-old African American Wallace Williams, a carpenter who had been convicted of burglary and grand larceny and sentenced to five years and five months in the penitentiary. Williams remained on the run for nearly three and one-half years before being recaptured and returned to the penitentiary to complete his sentence (*Central Register of Prisoners* 1883–1892).

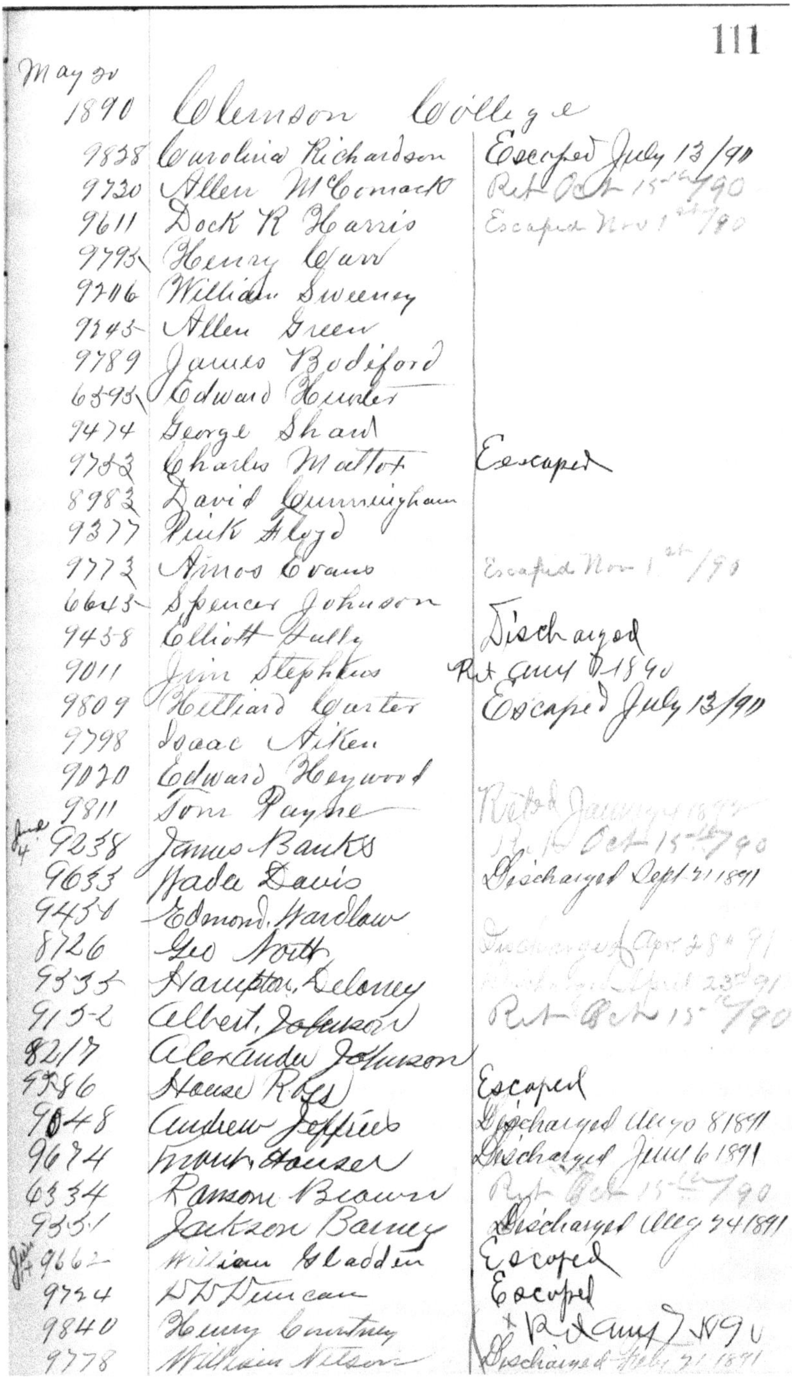

111

May 30 1890 Clemson College

9838	Carolina Richardson	Escaped July 13/90
9730	Allen McCormack	Ret Oct 15th 90
9611	Dock R Harris	Escaped Nov 1st 90
9795	Henry Carr	
9206	William Sweeney	
9343	Allen Green	
9789	James Bodiford	
6593	Edward Hunter	
9474	George Shaw	
9782	Charles Mattox	Escaped
8982	David Cunningham	
9377	Pink Floyd	
9772	Amos Evans	Escaped Nov 1st 90
6643	Spencer Johnson	
9438	Elliott Gully	Discharged
9011	Jim Stephens	Ret Aug 8 1890
9809	Hilliard Carter	Escaped July 13/90
9798	Isaac Aiken	
9020	Edward Heyward	
9811	Tom Payne	Retd January 1892
June 4 9238	James Banks	Ret Oct 15th 90
9633	Wade Davis	Discharged Sept 21 1891
9458	Edmond Wardlaw	
8726	Geo North	Discharged Apr 28th 91
9335	Hampton Deloney	Discharged April 23rd 91
9152	Albert Johnson	Ret Oct 15th 90
8217	Alexander Johnson	
9586	House Ross	Escaped
9048	Andrew Jeffries	Discharged Aug 20 1891
9674	Frank Houser	Discharged June 6 1891
6334	Ramson Brown	Ret Oct 15th 90
9351	Jackson Barney	Discharged Aug 24 1891
Jan 4 9662	William Gladden	Escaped
9724	D W Duncan	Escaped
9840	Henry Courtney	Ret Aug 7 1891
9778	William Wilson	Discharged Feb 21 1891

Figure 1. *Farm and Contract Register. 1889-1892. Department of Corrections.* South Carolina Department of Archives and History, Columbia, SC. Used with permission.

The convict-lease system worked so effectively at Clemson College that the General Assembly expanded its use to three other public colleges in the late nineteenth century. In 1895, Clemson trustee and US Senator Benjamin Tillman spearheaded the convening of a convention where the majority white Democratic delegation rewrote the state constitution to favor white citizens and relegate African American South Carolinians to second-class segregated citizenship. Legislators solidified the segregation of public higher education institutions through the establishment of an Agricultural, Mechanical and Industrial College for colored people (*Journal* 1895, 572). This land-grant institution for African Americans was made possible through provisions of the 1890 expansion of the Morrill Act, which stipulated that states refrain from using race as a criteria for admissions or establish a separate land-grant institution for minorities. South Carolina's General Assembly authorized the lease of convicts to erect this historically black college, as well as for building projects at Claflin College, the first higher education institution in South Carolina founded in 1869 for the training of African Americans, and Winthrop College, a public college founded in 1886 (*Acts and Joint Resolutions* 1893, 511; *Acts and Joint Resolutions* 1896, 382 and 386). Thus, the convicts, like antebellum slaves, returned to the auction block repeatedly and among the highest bidders were public college trustees. In effect, the white Democratic-controlled General Assembly relied on a slave system to carry out the expansion of the public higher education system that delegates to the Constitutional Convention convened in 1868 during Reconstruction had enacted.

Enslaved African Americans, exploited freedmen, and leased convicts are among the "many people [who] helped change the landscape of this University." Considerations of their presence and labor on Clemson land are essential components of conversations that need to be initiated about the legacy that members of the Clemson family—current, students, staff, faculty, and administrators—cultivate in this space. The history of the complicated, multilayered nexus of race, place, and space in Upstate South Carolina informs who we are and who we will become. It is only by deliberately choosing to locate and speak the unspeakable, the names, histories, and contributions of three generations of African Americans who lived and labored in various forms of slavery on Clemson land during the nineteenth century, that the Clemson family will be complete and its legacy fulfilled and sustained.

Notes

Special thanks to archivist Marion Chandler and the staff at the South Carolina Department of Archives and History who provided invaluable assistance in helping me to locate the historical court and prison records cited in this essay.

1. See *Ruffin v. The Commonwealth*. November 1871. The Supreme Court of Virginia. 62 Va. 790; 1871 Va. LEXIS 89; 21 Gratt. 790.
2. Although Thomas Green Clemson made no reference to the race of students eligible for enrollment in the "high seminary of learning" that would be established through the bequest in his will, African American students were not accepted at the college until Harvey Gantt successfully sued to gain admittance in 1963, nearly ten years after the US Supreme Court outlawed segregation in public schools in its 1954 *Brown v. Board of Education* decision. The college became a coeducational institution in 1955.
3. The campus is actually comprised of three plantations, Fort Hill; Hopewell owned by General Andrew Pickens' family; and Woodburn, owed by a series of wealthy low country slaveholders who retreated to Upstate South Carolina each summer to escape oppressive coastal heat.

4. In the Introduction to *Prison Writing in Twentieth Century America*, Howard Bruce Franklin (1998) asserts, "The infrastructure of many southern states was built and maintained by convicts. For example, aged African-American women overseen by armed guards dug the campus of Georgia State College" (5).
5. America's Juvenile Justice System was not established in the United States until the early 1900s. See William S. Boyd's (2004) *Juvenile Justice in the Making* for a history and analysis of this system of justice.
6. All of the letters cited in the paragraph on pardons are available in the convict's pardon file in the South Carolina Department of Archives and History. See Works Cited list for citations.

Works Cited

Acts of the General Assembly of the State of South Carolina, Passed at the Sessions of 1864-65. 1866. Columbia, SC: Julian A. Selby, Printer to the State. Google books.

Acts and Joint Resolutions of the General Assembly of the State of South Carolina, Passed at the Extra Session of 1877. 1877. Columbia, SC: Calvo & Patton, State Printers. Google books.

Acts and Joint Resolutions of the General Assembly of the State of South Carolina, Passed at the Regular Session of 1878. 1878. Columbia, SC: Calvo & Patton, State Printers. Google books.

Acts and Joint Resolutions of the General Assembly of the State of South Carolina, Passed at the Regular Session of 1879 and Extra Session of 1880. 1880. Columbia, SC: Calvo & Patton, State Printers. Google books.

Acts and Joint Resolutions of the General Assembly of the State of South Carolina, Passed at the Regular Session of 1889. 1890. Columbia, SC: James H. Woodrow, State Printer. Google books.

Acts and Joint Resolutions of the General Assembly of the State of South Carolina, Passed at the Regular Session of 1890. 1891. Columbia, SC: James H. Woodrow, State Printer. Google books.

Acts and Joint Resolutions of the General Assembly of the State of South Carolina, Passed at the Regular Session of 1893. 1893. Columbia, SC: Charles A. Calvo, Jr., State Printer. Google books.

Acts and Joint Resolutions of the General Assembly of the State of South Carolina, Passed at the Regular Session of 1896. 1896. Columbia, SC: Charles A. Calvo, Jr., State Printer. Google books.

Allen, Trent and Kevin Bray. 2006. *Clemson: There's Something in These Hills.* Anderson, SC: Fort Hill Press. 182-83.

Alexander, Michelle. 2012. *The New Jim Crow: Mass Incarceration in the Age of Colorblindness.* 2nd ed. New York, New Press, Kindle Edition.

Annual Report of the Board of Trustees of the Clemson College to the General Assembly of South Carolina. 1890-1901. Vol. 1. Special Collections. Clemson University Libraries, Clemson, SC.

"Articles of Agreement between Thomas G. Clemson and the Undersigned Freedmen and Women." Thomas Green Clemson Papers. Box 5, Files 4, 5, 7 and 10. Clemson University Libraries Special Collections, Clemson, SC.

Bartley, Abel. 2006. "Race, Reconstruction, and Post-bellum Education in Thomas Green Clemson's Life and World." *Thomas Green Clemson.* Clemson, SC: Clemson Digital Press. 159-86.

Bennett, Alma, ed. 2006. *Thomas Green Clemson.* Clemson, SC: Clemson Digital Press.

Blackmon, Douglas A. 2008. *Slavery by Another Name: The Reenslavement of Black Americans from the Civil War to World War II.* New York: Random.

Central Register of Prisoners, S. C. Department of Corrections. June 19, 1867 – May 28, 1872. Prisoners 49 – 1378. South Carolina Department of Archives and History, Columbia, SC.

Central Register of Prisoners, S. C. Department of Corrections. May 5, 1876 – June 1, 1883. Prisoners 2372 – 6145. South Carolina Department of Archives and History, Columbia, SC.

Central Register of Prisoners, S. C. Department of Corrections. June 7, 1883 – June 6, 1892. Prisoners 6146 – 10927. South Carolina Department of Archives and History, Columbia, SC.

Central Register of Prisoners, S. C. Department of Corrections,. June 16, 1892 – May 2, 1899. Prisoners 10928 – 14877. South Carolina Department of Archives and History, Columbia, SC.

Champion, Dean. 1994. *Measuring Offender Risk: A Criminal Justice Sourcebook.* Westport, CT: Greenwood.

"Clemson campaign achieves $608 million, now aiming for $1 billion." n.d. *The Newsstand.* Clemson University. Accessed December 15, 2013. http://newsstand.clemson.edu/mediarelations/campaign-news-releas/.

"Clemson Family." n.d. Accepted Students. Undergraduate Admissions. Clemson University. Accessed December 12, 2013. http://www.clemson.edu/accepted-students/stories/.

"The Clemson Family (Short Version)." 2011. Accessed December 12, 2013. https://www.youtube.com/watch?v=aVWIs_HXez0.

Cowan-Ricks, Carrel. 1992. "Cemetery Hill Archeological Project: In Search of John C. Calhoun's Pre-Emancipation African Americans." *South Carolina Antiquities* 24.1&2, 19-28.

Du Bois, W. E. B. "The Spawn of Slavery. The Convict-Lease System in the South." *Missionary View of the World* 24 October: 737-45.

Farm and Contract Registers, South Carolina Department of Corrections. 1889-1892. South Carolina Department of Archives and History. Columbia, SC.

Farm and Contract Registers, South Carolina Department of Corrections. 1893-1901. South Carolina Department of Archives and History. Columbia, SC. 28-40.

Index to General Sessions Judgments, Spartanburg County, Court of General Sessions, 1800-1908, (A-Z) C695. South Carolina Department of Archives and History. Columbia, SC. Microfilm.

Journal of the Constitutional Convention of the State of South Carolina. 1895. Columbia, SC: Charles A. Calvo, Jr., State Printer. Google books.

"New President introduced to Clemson Family." 2013. *Greenville News*, November 12. Accessed December 13, 2013. http://www.greenvilleonline.com/article/20131112/NEWS/311120013/.

"November is Legacy Month." 2013. Clemson University. Accessed December 12, 2013. http://www.clemson.edu//about/legacy-month/.

Petitions for Pardon of Charles Jackson, Hampton County. Gov. Benjamin R. Tillman's Papers. Petitions for Pardon. Florency-Horney Counties. Box 67, Folder 42. South Carolina Department of Archives and History. Columbia, SC.

Petitions for Pardon of John Moore, Hampton County. Gov. Benjamin R. Tillman's Papers. Petitions for Pardon. Florency-Horney Counties. Box 67, Folder 53. South Carolina Department of Archives and History. Columbia, SC.

Reel, Jerome V. 2013. *The High Seminary: A History of Clemson University, 1889-1964.* Vol. 1. Clemson, SC: Clemson Digital Press.

Roback, Jennifer. 1984. "Exploitation in the Jim Crow South: the Market or the Law." *Regulations* September/December: 37-43.

Rogers Jr., George C. and C. James Taylor. 1994. *A South Carolina Chronology 1497–1992.* University of South Carolina Press.

Ruffin v. The Commonwealth. 1871. The Supreme Court of Virginia. November. 62 Va. 790; 1871 Va. LEXIS 89; 21 Gratt. 790.

Sanborn, Frank B. 1904. "Negro Crime." *Some Notes on Negro Crime Particularly in Georgia.* Ed. W. E. B. Du Bois. Atlanta: Atlanta University Press. Accessed December 16, 2013. http://www.library.umass.edu/spcoll/digital/dubois/dubois9.pdf.

The State vs. Jack Givens. The State of South Carolina, County of Spartanburg Court of General Sessions. October Term 1892. Indictment for Larceny of live stock. Record No. 6. South Carolina Department of Archives and History. Columbia, SC.

The State vs. Wade Foster. The State of South Carolina. County of Spartanburg Court of General Sessions. October Term, 1891. Indictment for Housebreaking in daytime. Record No. 20. South Carolina Department of Archives and History. Columbia, SC.

Thirteenth Amendment to the US Constitution. National Archives. The US National Archives and Records Administration. Accessed December 15, 2013. http://www.archives.gov/exhibits/charters/charters_of_freedom_zoom_pages/charters_of_freedom_zoom_11.1.1.html.

"Thomas Green Clemson." 2013. Clemson Digital Press. April 26. Accessed December 15, 2013. http://www.clemson.edu/cedp/cudp/pubs/tclemson/index.html.

Tillman, Benjamin. 1890. "Inagural Address of Governor Benjamin R. Tillman, 4 December 1890." *Teaching American History in South Carolina.* 2006. Accessed December 15, 2013. http://www.teachinghistory.org/documents/InauguralAddress.htm.

——. "The Origin of Clemson College." Clemson University Libraries Special Collections, Clemson, S.C.

Whitman, James Q. 2003. *Harsh Justice: Criminal Punishment and the Widening Divide Between America and Europe.* New York: Oxford University Press.

"The Will." 1886. *Thomas Green Clemson.* Office of Web Services. Clemson University. 2006. Accessed December 15, 2013. http://www.clemson.edu/TGC200/the-will.htm.

E S S A Y

"THE GREATEST DEGREE OF PERFECTION": DISABILITY AND THE CONSTRUCTION OF RACE IN AMERICAN SLAVE LAW[1]

by Jenifer L. Barclay

In 1858, one of the South's preeminent legal thinkers, Thomas R. R. Cobb, championed the institution of racial slavery as the only way that blacks could "arriv[e] at the greatest degree of perfection of which [their] nature is capable" (1858, 51). His remarks capture the depth with which he internalized a sense of white superiority. From his perspective, even at their best, enslaved blacks were inherently defective, deviant, depraved—in a word, *imperfect*. Slavery, according to Cobb's logic, was an opportunity for benevolent whites to "improve" blacks and the only way through which they could ever presumably hope to reach some limited degree of "perfection." Cobb's baseline against which he judged the enslaved was, of course, elite white men like himself—men whose whiteness was an unmarked marker that assumed normativity and encompassed a range of beliefs, behaviors, and appearances that extended to the body and mind. For men like Cobb, whiteness claimed whole, able bodies and rational, sound minds as its ontological terrain, the embodiment of not only "normal" but also "perfect." In contrast, blackness represented various forms of defectiveness and abnormality—one might say *disability* —whether these characteristics were real or imagined, visible or invisible, physical or psychological. The fact that Cobb, a lawyer, wrote the southern states' only legal defense of slavery in 1858—*An Inquiry into the Law of Negro Slavery in the United States of America*— suggests that the law played a fundamental role in producing what was, by that time, a deeply entrenched and seemingly natural nexus of associations between blackness, defectiveness, and disability.

From their earliest iterations in the colonial years, the laws of slavery were overwhelmingly concerned with the state of enslaved people's bodies, which became a key index in shaping ideas of race from that point forward. Various subsets of slave law emerged, many with the goal of determining the answers to specific questions about slave bodies: Were they damaged or broken? Were they criminal? Were they worthy of manumission? As a labor system, slavery dictated that a person's perceived abilities and capacity to work determined their value. Slaveholders and traders even devised classifications like the "hand system" to evaluate their worth. "Full" hands were those deemed the most able and valuable, "three-quarter" hands slightly less so in comparison, "half" hands even less, and so on until the scale bottomed out with those considered "chargeable," meaning that the cost of their care was a liability to owners. In light of this reality, slave laws—designed to arbitrate property disputes, mete out punishments, and determine eligibility for manumission among other official tasks—were centered on black bodies and minds, particularly those considered damaged and defective. Regardless of whether they reflected or generated wider social beliefs, and despite variances between them over time and space, these laws constructed a legal narrative of blackness that persistently embedded a range of qualities often associated with disabilities within the meta-language of race (Higginbotham 1995, 5).

In the past two decades, scholars of disability have demonstrated that, despite embodied aspects, *ideas* about various disabilities are socially constructed, change over time, and are *always already* a constituent part of American life and history (Longmore and Umansky 2001). Much like race, class, or gender, disability can serve as a useful category of historical analysis—a *concept*—that illuminates how dominant groups justified patterns of injustice and inequality by attributing qualities associated with disability to specific groups of people (Baynton 2001, 32). Reading the laws of slavery in states of the upper and lower South through this lens highlights the conceptual relationship between race and disability and the myriad ways in which the bodies and minds of enslaved people were literally and metaphorically deformed and stigmatized by legal narratives of race. The institutionalization of these perceived links between race and disability in the legal realm were, by the mid-nineteenth century, so naturalized that they appeared to have always existed, though they had, in fact, been forged through statute and case law that reached back to the colonial era.

C3

The development of racial slavery in the New World arguably stemmed more from attitudes, customs, and labor needs than from formal laws, but there is little doubt that even in this era legal matters concerning enslaved people grew ever more important as slavery overtook indentured servitude as the preferred labor system (Bush 1997). Colonial laws in mainland North America, especially those of the southern regions of Virginia and South Carolina, sought to define a distinct "racial and status boundary" between whites and blacks to alleviate anxieties about the similar status of indentured servants and slaves (Bush 1997, 393). Virginia's 1705 slave codes unequivocally equated slavery with Africans and defined all "non-Christians" entering the colony as lifelong slaves, then quickly dispensed with the possibility that baptism could secure freedom (Hening v. III 1821, 447–62).

As the first slave codes took shape, they absorbed negative beliefs about African peoples and went on to influence emergent slave law in regions of North America that eventually became part of the United States. The first cohesive bodies of slave law were enacted in the 1680s in Virginia, by the early 1700s in South Carolina (which also borrowed heavily from Barbadian slave laws), and nearer to the middle of the century in Georgia, where slavery was initially banned (A. Higginbotham 1978, 38 and 167). Colonial whites generally viewed enslaved Africans as possessing "weak," "shallow" minds and, since lawmakers sought to mark them as visibly different from indentured whites in as many ways as possible, it is little surprise that these early laws began the process of linking blackness to other forms of perceived differences like disabilities (Bruce 1910, 9). These early slave codes served as models for other southern states that became part of the nation after the American Revolution, a process that further expanded and solidified this metaphorical relationship between blackness and disability (Flanigan 1973, 10–13). From their earliest, flexible incarnations, ideas about disabilities mediated and were embedded in the laws of slavery, which at once reflected and institutionalized then-nebulous social views of blackness as somehow deviant and defective, providing a legal basis for the emergence of increasingly crystalized racial beliefs.

Criminal laws represent one key facet of slave law that involved disabilities in obvious and disturbing ways. During the colonial era, violent punishments for criminal acts literally inscribed disability onto the bodies of enslaved blacks. This practice, which almost exclusively targeted slaves, helped maintain a legal distinction between enslaved blacks and indentured whites, which mirrored elites' desires for social separation between these similarly positioned groups—an especially important endeavor after Bacon's Rebellion of 1676 in Virginia when an interracial alliance threatened the white ruling class. Penal laws established and codified a number of double standards for trying, convicting, and punishing bondpeople for their alleged transgressions—they considered more crimes capital offenses for blacks than whites, targeted only enslaved people for insurrection, deliberately rushed the trials of enslaved people, and rejected slave testimony except in cases involving other slaves (Hening v. III 1821, 269–70). As part of these discriminatory procedures, colonial courts sentenced enslaved people to punishments that inflicted disabling injuries onto their bodies.

The actual function of disability in this practice is rarely if ever questioned because it is overshadowed by the courts' discriminatory tendency to mete out these violent punishments on an almost exclusively racial basis. The intentional disablement of enslaved blacks for their crimes far exceeded punishments that condemned whites faced for similar and even greater offenses (A. Higginbotham 1978 and Schwartz 1998). The courts clearly viewed the infliction of a permanent disability as the ultimate injury and insult to be levied against an individual and reserved this humiliating and stigmatizing punishment for enslaved (and sometimes free) blacks alone. In this way, they persistently linked enslaved blacks in particular and blackness in general to disabilities, yet the long-term implications of this practice in terms of social and legal constructions of race—that blackness and disability were collapsed into the same intellectual and legal space—remains almost invisible.

Because of the so-called "double character" of enslaved people in the eyes of the law, courts viewed them mostly as property and only as people for the purpose of holding them accountable for their crimes. As a result, physical injury became the only significant and viable means of punishing them. Fining enslaved criminals was contradictory since they could not legally own property, while imprisoning them burdened their owners by depriving them of access to their laborers. Since this quandary persisted until the antebellum years, the pro-slavery legal thinker Thomas R. R. Cobb's later remarks on it are useful. He explained, "The condition of the slave renders it impossible to inflict upon him the ordinary punishments by pecuniary fine, by imprisonment, or by banishment…he can be reached only through his body" (1858, 266). In the colonial years, courts established this precedent and began the practice of sentencing enslaved blacks with disabling punishments for many offenses—theft, running away, attempted rape, or sexual assault. As a result, they literally and brutally wrote disability onto the bodies of enslaved blacks, forever marking them with a visible stigma closely associated at that time with deviance, sin, God's displeasure, and—in the labor system of slavery—worthlessness.

Alleged thieves and runaways across the upper and lower South were one class of "criminals" targeted with these types of disabling and disfiguring punishments. A 1705 Virginia act found that it was inconvenient to consider theft committed by a slave a capital crime punishable by death. Instead, it called for thirty-nine lashes to the back for the first offense, but, for the second, the convicted slave "shall stand two hours in the pillory and have both his ears nailed thereto and at the expiration of the said two hours have the ears cut loose" (Hening v. III 1821, 179). Cropping enslaved people's ears was a practice that continued well into the antebellum years as a way both to punish and mark visibly slaves' bodies to render them more easily identifiable as criminally deviant.

In South Carolina, one 1712 act stands out as especially cruel for its increasingly severe punishment of those who repeatedly attempted to flee bondage, culminating with the deliberate "crippling" of enslaved people. There, authorities deemed that captured fugitives were to be whipped for their first escape attempt, branded with the letter *R* on the cheek for the second, have an ear cut off for the third, face castration for the fourth and then "in case any negro or slave shall run away the fifth time…the cord of one of the slave's legs [may] be cut off above the heel" (McCord v. VII 1840, 360). Habitual running away in South Carolina, then, led to increasingly disabling and disfiguring punishments, the most severe of which caused permanent physical disability by deliberately severing the achilles tendon. This practice also existed in Virginia, where runaway slaves faced the amputation of one of their legs throughout the colonial decades (Hening v. VIII 1821, 358). On a pragmatic level, deliberate disablement prevented further attempts at absconding; dramatically changed the everyday lives of those who experienced these punishments; and weaved together associations between blackness, deviance, and disability in the law and the wider society.

Enslaved men convicted of sexual assault and attempted rape of white women in colonial America also faced disabling and disfiguring punishments of a particularly gendered and intimate nature, namely castration, as was the case in Virginia (Hening v. VIII 1821, 358). While castration symbolized utter emasculation, it also inflicted a permanent physical disability intended to humiliate the condemned individual, cause intimate physical loss and sterility, and repulse those aware of it. Moreover, castration can lead to skeletal deformities resulting from severe osteoporosis as well as gynecomastia, the development of large and pendulous breasts (Wilson and Roehrborn 1999). Altogether, these physical changes marked enslaved men's bodies as deviant in colonial America, especially since individuals were expected to perform gender through their body, clothing, and behavior to preserve the very order of society itself (Brown 1996).

Even bondpeople who faced execution had their bodies brutally maimed and disabled prior to death and then further desecrated and displayed afterward as a warning to others. In 1729, Maryland determined that slaves convicted of murder or arson would "have their right hands cut off before they were hanged…[then] be beheaded, quartered, and their bodies left exposed" (Flanigan 1973, 12). Abolitionist Sarah Grimké recalled in 1830 that during her youth in South Carolina, when traveling along a public highway, she once witnessed such a gruesome spectacle. She saw "a human head stuck up on a high pole" that belonged to an "outlawed" slave, a violent display meant "as a terror to deter slaves from running away" (Weld 1839, 24).

In the decades following the American Revolution, a spirit of reform driven by a number of interlocking factors swept the nation and addressed these types of maiming and torturous punishments. The close of the Atlantic slave trade in 1808 largely shut off importations of enslaved Africans, bringing about an immediate need to preserve the health and able-bodied-ness of American slaves and safeguard slaveholders' existing property (Schwartz 1998, 24). The religious revivalism of the Great Awakening also provoked a greater sense of paternalism among slaveholders, which eventually evolved into the belief that slavery was a "positive good," all of which coincided with changing ideas about disabilities in American society. Throughout the years of the early Republic and, certainly, by the antebellum years with the advent of industrialization and growing professionalization of medicine, various disabilities were recast as anomalies or "errors" meant to be corrected by science as well as conditions sentimentalized as piteous spectacles worthy of benevolent Christian care. These views contrasted with former beliefs about disabilities as visible marks of God's wrath for sinful deviance or wondrous "freaks of nature" (Striker 2000 and Garland Thompson 1996).

Southern slave codes reflected these changing ideals and gradually established limits on the extent of physical injury allowed to be exacted on the bodies of enslaved people. By 1848, for instance, Georgia's slave codes declared that "the punishment of [a] slave for striking a white person" was whatever the justice "thought fit" with the exception that it could not "exten[d] to life or limb" (Hotchkiss 1848, 838). Inflicting disabilities as a punishment for criminal acts faded into the presumably more humane, less destructive, and certainly more familiar policy of whipping by the end of the eighteenth and beginning of the nineteenth century. Cobb lamented the quandary of this development from a legal standpoint, remarking:

> The extremes [of] death and whipping being the only available punishments, it becomes necessary in forming a slave code to throw all offences under the one or the other. Hence many offences are from public policy necessarily made capital, which when committed by a white person are not. (1858, 266–67)

By the antebellum years, the act of whipping—and all of the horrors related to slavery that it evokes—was a proxy for what had previously been a spectrum of physically disabling punishments for those deemed criminal. These colonial laws and their immediate aftermath demonstrate one of the primary means through which the courts embedded disability into slave law and drew a violent, direct parallel between a particular racial group and actual physical disabilities.

Commonplace ideas about disability also mediated colonial laws related to the manumission of enslaved people. Very early on, lawmakers expressed concerns that freed slaves would become social burdens or charges to the state. The issue of providing care for disabled or ill-indentured servants and lifelong slaves surfaced in the colonial era and clearly influenced slave manumission laws in later decades. In 1705 Virginia mandated:

> That if such servant be so sick and lame, or otherwise rendered so uncapable [sic] that he or she cannot be sold for such a value…the said court shall then order the church-wardens…to take care of and provide for the said servant…[T]he said court, from time to time, shall order the charges of keeping the said servant to be levied upon the goods and chattels of the master or owner of the said servant. (Hening v. III 1821, 449)

Anxieties about providing care for disabled, dependent bondpeople are clear, though the statute's uncertain language suggests lawmakers' reluctance to force masters to bear this burden alone. The courts eventually resolved this tension through more strict and pre-cise laws, which placed greater financial responsibility on slaveholders who emancipated their bondpeople. White fears of slave rebellion and the unchecked growth of "danger-ous" free black communities certainly guided manumission laws—a factor that scholars have long stressed—but concerns about the cost of caring for disabled men, women, and children were also at their core.

By the Revolutionary era, manumission laws grew far more specific. Slaveholders could only free bondpeople by legislative acts if they met a series of stringent physical qualifications and owners posted bonds to pay for their care in the event that they became disabled and unable to care for themselves (Klebaner 1955). Manumission laws varied widely from state to state, but such caveats were a staple of virtually all of them. A Virginia law from 1782, for example, required that emancipated bondpeople must be "of sound mind and body," not above the age of forty-five or under the age of twenty-one, and "sup-ported and maintained by the person so liberating them, or by his or her estate" (Hening v. XI 1821, 39). Over the course of the next half century, these directives further expanded and sometimes called for freed slaves to leave the state within a certain period of time or risk re-enslavement. This was the case in Florida, Louisiana, Mississippi, North Carolina, and Tennessee beginning in about the 1830s (Klebaner 1955, 446).

For states that did not require removal, stipulations that focused on emancipated people's able-bodied-ness and potential to remain independent were, by the antebellum years, a given precondition for manumission. Yet another Virginia law, from 1848, made clear that if a slaveholder emancipated a slave who was "likely to become chargeable to the county," the "overseers of the poor" would charge the owner or their estate an annual sum to provide for the freedperson (State of Virginia 1849, 459). By this point, rules determining how to provide care for manumitted people who were or became disabled, ill, or otherwise dependent on the state were clearly articulated and rivaled anxieties about limiting the size of a large, potentially insurrectionary free black population.

The vexing national issue of pauperism in the antebellum years likely contributed to these more aggressive manumission laws. Immigration, industrialization, and urbaniza-tion all contributed to a substantial increase in the number of people throughout the United States who sought social welfare, many of whom were disabled. The national pau-perism rate—"the total number receiving poor relief from public funds during the year, per thousand persons"—skyrocketed from 5.8 in 1850 to 10.2 in 1860, doubling in just a single decade (Kiesling and Margo 1997, 405). In the slaveholding states, however, south-erners argued that the institution of slavery mitigated local and state governments' need to establish significant social welfare systems for the indigent and disabled.

While slaveholders were legally responsible for the care of disabled and dependent slaves, social pressures also encouraged them to be honorable, "good" masters. Also, be-cause slavery was largely an agrarian institution, consumption and production occurred within the same place, which, in theory, should have alleviated outright pauperism among enslaved people. Occasionally, however, some bondpeople qualified for and received pub-lic assistance. This was the case if their owner was also indigent, disabled, and unable to provide for them or if they abandoned their "worthless" slaves in spite of laws that crimi-nalized this behavior. Louisiana, for example, mandated in an 1806 law that slaveholders care for "slaves disabled through old age, sickness, or any other cause" or be fined twenty-five dollars (Bullard and Curry 1842, 48–49).

Despite the presence of such laws, the personal narratives of formerly enslaved people often assert that especially cruel slaveholders had little qualms with abandoning slaves they deemed useless and worthless because of age or disability. Frederick Douglass, for example, described how his own elderly grandmother was "turned out to die" despite her many years of faithful service. He also detailed the less remarked-on experience of Henny, "a lame young woman" who "burned herself horribly" as a child and lost the use of her hands, to the point that she "could do very little but bear heavy burdens." According to Douglass:

> She was to master a bill of expense…[and] a constant offense…. He seemed desirous of getting the poor girl out of existence [and]…gave her away once to his sister; but, being a poor gift, she was not disposed to keep her. Finally, my benevolent master, to use his own words, "set her adrift to take care of herself." (1845, 381–82)

In this case, Henny's physical disabilities clearly devalued her in the eyes of her owner so, despite laws and social customs that frowned on such behavior, he simply manumitted her.

Some free blacks, perhaps in similar situations as Henny, received "outrelief"—aid that came by way of cash assistance, food provisions, and/or medical care that did not involve residency at a poorhouse—which further associated dependency and disability with blackness and "slaves without masters" (Ely 1985, 867–68 and Berlin 1974, 25–35). Indeed, lawmakers often attributed free blacks' financial need to a supposedly innate character defect—laziness—as opposed to a consequence of their lack of social, legal, political, and economic protections in southern society (Ely 1985, 867). For free blacks living with disabilities, these circumstances undoubtedly made life even more difficult. Pauperism among free blacks was clearly a significant concern and one that lawmakers understood as a racialized phenomenon that reflected a "natural" state of dysfunctionalism, which they sought to limit through manumission laws. These were not, however, the only category of slave law that dealt specifically with disabled slaves.

The egregious property laws of slavery also revolved in obvious ways around the state of enslaved people's bodies, further stitching together ideas about blackness and disability. While scholars recognize the inhumanity of equating people with property, their emphasis on race elides and tacitly excuses the simultaneous—and perhaps more familiar and acceptable—devaluation and objectification of people on the basis of visible and invisible disabilities, defects, and deformities. Civil disputes involving contested warranties about the soundness of enslaved people's bodies and minds were common by the antebellum years, as were those in which slaveholders sought compensation for "damage" done to their property. This subset of slave law involved debatable notions of what constituted "unsoundness"—socially constructed markers of disability and defectiveness, affixed with a corresponding value of diminished monetary worth (Gross 2000, 126–27). Even more, they categorically dismissed enslaved people's lived realities and experiences of disablement.

Laws that secured slaveholders' property rights and safeguarded their ability to seek compensation for disabilities sustained by their enslaved "property" through careless accidents and acts of cruelty by other liable parties reached back to the colonial era. South Carolina, for example, maintained in one 1740 act that:

[I]f any negro or other slave who shall be employed in the lawful business or service of his master, owner, overseer…[is] beaten, bruised, maimed, or disabled by any person or persons not having sufficient cause or lawful authority for so doing…[that person] shall for every such offence forfeit and pay the sum of forty shillings current money.… (McCord v. VII 1840, 399)

For slaves who were hired out when they were "maimed or disabled," the responsible party had to pay fifteen shilling for every day of lost time as well as medical expenses (McCord v. VII 1840, 399). Similar laws existed throughout the slaveholding states and remained in force until the antebellum era. In states like Kentucky and Louisiana, courts handed down even greater penalties to those responsible for disabling enslaved people (Stroud 1968, 40–41). Louisiana, for instance, required that the person responsible "pay the value of said slave" to his or her owner *and* forever "maintain and feed said slave" (Bullard and Curry 1842, 54). These laws provided no protections for enslaved people—only their owners—and denied them the right even to "own" the disabilities they sustained as a result of another's carelessness or cruelty. In fact, related laws forbid slaves from bringing any type of civil suit against whites "no matter how atrocious may have been the injury" received (Stroud 1968, 38).

Property laws vis-à-vis enslaved people determined the cost of physical and psycho- logical disabilities so that liable parties could pay compensation to slaveholders. Many cases dealing with compensation for slaveholders involved the outright death of enslaved people, but the remainder dealt with permanent or temporary disabilities caused by in- juries from violent beatings, accidents, or negligence. One case in particular captures the devastating effects that the property laws of slavery wrought for persons with disabilities and the doubly oppressive intersection of race and disability in their lives. In 1818 the Louisiana State Supreme Court issued a ruling on an appealed case, *Jourdan v. Patton*, which altered a lower court's decision regarding compensation due to a slaveholder for her injured bondman. Ms. Jourdan's property, a man who had long been blind in one eye, sus- tained an injury from the actions of one of the defendant's slaves that made him "wholly useless" because his "only [sighted] eye…[was] put out" (Wheeler 1837, 249). The lower parish court ruled that Jourdan should receive twelve hundred dollars for the value of her slave, twenty-five dollars a month "from the time he was deprived of his sight," the cost of the physician's bill, and two hundred dollars "for the sustenance of the slave during his life" (Wheeler 1837, 249). The initial decision, then, held that this now completely blind man would remain with his mistress, Jourdan.

Louisiana's Supreme Court, however, overturned this ruling because it supposedly compensated Jourdan far more than the estimated value of the slave and neglected to trans- fer ownership of the slave to the defendant. Viewing this enslaved man as property alone, the higher court ruled that since the defendant compensated Jourdan this constituted a "change of property" and he legally took ownership. The State Supreme Court argued:

The principle of humanity, which would lead us to suppose that the mistress, whom he had long served, would treat her miserable blind slave with more kind- ness than the defendant, to whom the judgment ought to transfer him, cannot be taken into consideration in deciding this case. (Wheeler 1837, 249)

In this instance, property rights trumped the potential humanity this "miserable blind slave" may have enjoyed with his "kind mistress," a determination that further affirmed the chattel principle of racial slavery and reduced enslaved blacks to a permanently inferior, disabled state. For the unnamed man—who was at once central but also inconsequential to the case—the historical record makes no mention of how his complete blindness or the judge's ruling affected his life. One might imagine his experience, though, as he lost the support of his family and community even as he grieved his total loss of sight, learned to navigate a disability that incapacitated him in a seeing world, and began the process of reconstituting his identity as "whole" in a society that viewed him as piteously incomplete.

The property laws of slavery also encompassed cases in which slaveholders disputed the physical and mental health of recently purchased slaves warranted as "sound," or free of defect and vice. These cases, as one scholar makes clear, were not simply about property law per se. They were also social enactments of southern honor in the courtroom in which white masters demonstrated their "proficiency" in interpreting enslaved people's bodies and character, a project that staked out white honor and black dishonor (Gross 2000). These civil disputes centered on thick descriptions of the condition of enslaved people's bodies and minds, particularly when a recently purchased slave died from or exhibited signs of terminal illness that were arguably present before sale. In other instances, recently purchased slaves exhibited vices—like being a habitual runaway or drunkard—that potentially revealed their innate defects of character, depending on how white slaveholding men interpreted them (Gross 2000, 79–80; 86–89). While these cases blurred the line between disease and disability, notions of disability suffused these debates about the worth of slaveholders' property, particularly those dealing with visible versus invisible afflictions—a theme that paralleled wider discussions of amorphous, ill-defined disabilities such as insanity, feeble-mindedness, and epilepsy in American society.

Enslaved people's invisible "defects"—presumably manifested in behaviors such as running away—served as ambiguous signs in the courtroom (Gross 2000, 130–32). Litigants alternately interpreted such behavior as either damning evidence of dishonorable slave character (the slave was a "perpetual runaway") or as markers of ineffectual masters whose incompetence encouraged recalcitrance. These interpretations reflected either dishonesty on the part of the seller for obscuring these qualities at the time of sale or ineptitude on the part of the purchaser for failing to manage slaves properly. Whichever party more convincingly argued their case determined the outcome of the contested warranty suit (Gross 2000, 79–86). These readings of slave behavior ultimately pivoted on a shared understanding of enslaved people's "innate" defects and abnormalities, again forging imagined links between blackness and disability that were intimately bound to constructions of enslaved people as dishonorable.

The objectifying processes of warranty disputes illuminates that, in the honorific society of the South, whites perceived slave dishonor as a characteristic with an "embodied nature," always either immediately visible or lurking beneath the surface (Gross 2000, 124). This was the backdrop against which they defined and debated their own sense of (white) honor and suggests the importance of ideas about ability/disability in this project. Honor, for white southerners, was a trait that reflected one's character as well as a ritualized code through which they negotiated their "superior" position in a deeply hierarchical society (Wyatt-Brown 2007). Those who were obviously disabled, disfigured, or unable to participate in routine activities and those whom white men perceived as dependent—such as women—were largely excluded from the realm of honor (Joyner 2004; Clinton 1991). Southern white men were indeed consumed with visible, superficial appearances that they linked to one's ability to enact and participate in the system of honor (Greenburg 1996). Signs of honor were manifested in displays of masculine independence like able-bodiedness (to physically defend oneself) and honest, rational, intellectual minds—all of which were the antithesis of qualities ascribed to enslaved blacks and supposedly evidenced by skin color. In the realm of property law—and specifically slave-warranty cases—litigants argued over and metaphorically ascribed the stigma of physical and psychological disability to enslaved people to uphold their notions of honor. This practice, however, permeated other facets of slave law, including those that codified "appropriate" slave behavior.

Restrictive slave codes governing behavior existed throughout the slaveholding states from the colonial era through the antebellum years, often supplemented by local municipal ordinances that further clarified them (Lucas 2002, 29–50). Many of these laws imposed metaphorical "handicaps" onto enslaved people, limiting them in ways similar to people living with various disabilities in a predominantly nondisabled world. Legal statutes restricted enslaved people's mobility, denied them the right to testify in court, and criminalized their access to literacy and education among many other things. In essence, they legally constructed enslaved blacks—in the coarse parlance of the day—as "cripples," "mutes," and "idiots."

Statutes such as the notorious pass laws, which required enslaved people to possess written permission to travel, emerged in the colonial era and began the process of metaphorically crippling enslaved people. Virginia's 1663 "Act prohibiting servants to go abroad without a lycence [sic]" is perhaps one of the earliest (Heming v. II 1821, 195). These laws remained in force in virtually all slaveholding states, but expanded in the 1830s in response to increased abolitionism and to Nat Turner's widely publicized 1831 rebellion in Virginia, both of which exacerbated fears of slave revolt. By this point, pass laws restricted enslaved people's mobility by denying them entry to toll roads and bridges and even limiting their use of watercraft and horses (McCord v. VI 1839, 314 and 552). Enslaved people often subverted these restrictions, sometimes by using the "rival geography" of their homes, local areas, and even the interior spaces of their own bodies and minds (Camp 2004). Local custom determined the degree to which pass laws were enforced, but their institutionalization in the law reflected slaveholders' desire to imagine and construct enslaved blacks as wholly dependent and limited cripples.

In addition to imposing mobility impairments, the courts denied enslaved people the right to testify against whites in court, keeping them officially, perpetually, and legally "mute" because of their imagined lack of intellectual "competency." Laws in Alabama, Kentucky, Maryland, Mississippi, Missouri, North Carolina, Tennessee, Virginia, and other states denied enslaved (and sometimes free) blacks a voice in the courtroom (Stroud 1968, 44). This drew a metaphorical parallel between enslaved blacks and, in particular, deaf individuals—the latter long perceived by Euro-Americans as suffering a "great calamity" and "peculiar misfortune" that forced them to "live in 'mental darkness'" (Joyner 2004, 9–20). By casting enslaved people as if they were virtually "deaf and dumb," these laws at once created and justified their exclusion from citizenship rights and legal personhood.

Lawmakers viewed the act of serving as a witness through the prism of "competency" and determined, on these grounds, that enslaved blacks could not testify against whites. In some cases free blacks could testify against whites and blacks, but many states, like South Carolina, entirely rejected even their testimony (Wheeler 1837, 194). Freedom sometimes served as "*prima facie* evidence…of competency," as in Louisiana, but most often the law viewed blackness as an indication of one's lack of the intellectual capacity necessary to bear witness, thereby effectively muting enslaved and many free blacks in the courts (Wheeler 1837, 195). This emphasis on competency also worked hand in glove with other socially disabling slave laws, particularly those involving education.

Laws forbidding literacy and writing helped legitimize views of black "incompetency" and metaphorically rendered enslaved people virtually "feeble-minded" as if they were perennially afflicted with intellectual deficiencies. The moral imperative of religious instruction in the colonial years initially suppressed white anxieties about slave literacy, but the infamous Stono Rebellion prompted South Carolina to the pass the first anti-literacy laws in 1740 and forbid whites from teaching enslaved people to write (McCord v. VII 1840, 397). This later expanded to include reading and other southern states followed suit, such as Georgia in 1755 (Monaghan 2004, 234). A spate of more rigorously enforced laws next emerged in the antebellum years in reaction to Turner's rebellion and the influx of abolitionist literature to the South, like David Walker's infamous 1829 *Appeal to the Coloured Citizens of the World.*

Enslaved people were well aware of the dire consequences of ignoring these laws. As one formerly enslaved man recalled, if a slave were caught writing "they would cut your finger off and if they caught you again they would cut your head off" (Oliphant 1941, 305). Another former slave, Henry Wright, also recalled that when his owner's son taught his father how to read and write, his owner warned him "to keep it to himself, because if the men of the community found out that he could write they would cut his fingers or his hand off" (Driskell 1941, 201). As each of these cases demonstrates, the metaphorical sometimes intersected with the real, and slaves' failure to acquiesce to social disabilities could be met with disabling punishments. The widespread belief that educated and literate slaves would grow disillusioned underpinned these laws, which sought to preempt this by imposing a state similar to "idiocy" onto enslaved people.

Of all the socially disabling aspects of slave law, denying literacy and education to enslaved people was one of the most well-known and deeply resented. Not only did it demand subservience and deference by denying slaves access to knowledge, but it also quite literally attempted to liken enslaved people to those with intellectual disabilities, commonly referred to then as "idiots," "imbeciles," or "the feebleminded." Frederick Douglass eloquently captured this when he explained, "I have found that, to make a contented slave, it is necessary to make a thoughtless one. It is necessary to darken his moral and mental vision, and, as far as possible, to annihilate the power of reason" (1845, 415). Indeed, from the post-Revolutionary years onward, many Americans viewed those labeled idiotic as able-bodied but ignorant with an innocent, almost childlike nature, though perhaps with the propensity to be criminal in their ignorance. They were often the brunt of mean-spirited jokes and were sometimes the objects of pity and charity. After the Panic of 1819, views of idiocy became more anxious and reconstructed it as a "failure of the will" by the mid-1850s (Trent 1995, 16). In many ways, these views of idiocy correspond to stereotypes of enslaved men, in particular, as "Sambos"—an imagined figure that was supposedly "docile but irresponsible, loyal but lazy, humble but chronically given to lying and stealing…full of infantile silliness…and childish exaggeration" (Elkins 1968, 82). The long history of laws forbidding literacy and education for enslaved people bespeak attempts to mark enslaved people as "feeble-minded" and to embed slaveholders' desire for all blacks to act in a Sambo-like fashion into the law itself.

While state laws encompassed a range of metaphorical handicaps that linked together ideas of race and disability, lawmakers also occasionally institutionalized such sentiments at the federal level. One of the most well-known of the few references to slavery present in the nation's Constitution, for example, is the "three-fifths clause." In an effort to protect disadvantaged southern states, this clause gave them greater representation in national politics and federal government by taking into consideration their large slave populations and enumerating slaves as three-fifths of a person to level the political playing field. Federal law, then, neither considered enslaved people citizens nor did it entirely dehumanize them. Rather, it constructed them as disabled and disadvantaged in comparison to elite, white, able-bodied male citizens whose worth in terms of political representation was whole and complete.

The series of literal and metaphorical links drawn between enslaved blacks and disabled people in southern slave law were not lost on antebellum abolitionists. They often targeted slave law to demonstrate not only the inhumanity of the institution but also its contradictory presence in a presumably free, democratic society. By the 1830s, as William Lloyd Garrison began amassing white support, abolitionists capitalized on changing views of physical, psychological, and intellectual disabilities in the larger society to advance their cause. Those "afflicted" with disabilities were increasingly sentimentalized as deserving objects of pity and benevolence (Klages 1999). Schools for the blind, "deaf and dumb," and "idiots" cropped up throughout northern states where kind-hearted—albeit paternalistic—whites sought to "fix" people and help them overcome their presumably unfortunate circumstances. Reformers, like Dorothea Dix, targeted hospitals, almshouses, and asylums to expose horrific, inhumane conditions and lobby for change. In this atmosphere, it is little surprise that one of the first major abolitionist tracts to garner considerable attention centered on the spectacle of disability to emphasize the inhumanity of legally sanctioned slavery.

In 1839 abolitionist Theodore Weld (along with Angelina Grimké Weld) and Sarah Grimké), illuminated the brutal nature of southern slave life and the laws that upheld it in *American Slavery As It Is: Testimony of a Thousand Witnesses*. As suggested in the subtitle, Weld's work takes on the characteristics of a legal treatise by presenting a series of ordered, logical arguments against slavery. Through amassing the "testimony" of eyewitnesses and "facts" inadvertently reported by southerners themselves, Weld presents empirical evidence about the brutality of the institution to readers whom he addresses as "jurors." The text, according to one scholar, is filled with such a litany of slave abuse that to read it "is to confront a savagery so nauseating that it can only be witnessed in glances"—in much the same way that disabled bodies are met with furtive peeks to avoid the social blunder of staring. Not only the violence itself, but also the freak show–like spectacle of "mutilations," "tortures," and "suicides" embodied in "limbs, teeth, and tongues" with "whippings, everywhere [in the text] whippings" make Weld's *Slavery* a disturbing read for contemporary audiences (Browne 1994, 277). Recalling the way that the whip came to stand in for the outright infliction of disabilities and that those abuses had likely not faded from living memory by this point, it seems that in the changing historical context of reformist-driven antebellum America Weld's *Slavery* resonated. It became the largest-selling antislavery tract up to that point, selling twenty-two thousand copies in its first four months in print and a hundred thousand by the end of its first year (Leonard 1995, 121). The emotive rhetoric of disability, precipitated by changing mid-nineteenth century views that sentimentalized disability, played a central role in the text's appeal to a wide readership and its ability to denounce laws sanctioning the brutality of slavery.

Slavery As It Is, however, also drew on older understandings of disability, which were only just then becoming *passé* to cast slaveholders, other agents of slavery, and even the institution itself as disabled in a way that conjured up evil, deformity, and depravity. For many long centuries Europeans, and later Euro-Americans, interpreted birth defects, blindness, deafness, epilepsy, conjoined twins, and other disabilities as marks of God's displeasure and punishment for sin, views that a new "medical model" of disability began to displace in the antebellum era (Garland-Thompson 1996). Contributors throughout *Slavery As It Is,* including Weld, deployed this older, more damning language of disability as "monstrous" to denounce slaveholders, traders, and overseers as well as the entire institution of slavery. Weld argues in the work's introduction, for instance, that "[Human nature] uttered her testimony against slavery with a shriek ever since the monster was begotten" (1839, 7). Weld's *Slavery*, then, was an abolitionist interpretation of the matrix of race, disability, and law that reframed enslaved people as "disabled" to elicit sympathy for their plight while casting slavery and slaveholders as monstrously disabled—quite the opposite of apologists, like Cobb, who envisioned slavery as a benevolent asylum for the enslaved and a virtual "cure" for blackness itself.

Abolitionist writers after Weld continued to deploy the rhetoric of disability, even in literary representations of slavery. Harriet Beecher Stowe's classic abolitionist portrayal of enslaved life, *Uncle Tom's Cabin* (1852), mirrors Weld's *Slavery As It Is* in many ways. Stowe reportedly slept with Weld's text under her pillow, drawing on it for background to capture the brutalities of slave life. Her depictions of hard-hearted traders, abusive overseers and owners, and scenes of slaves' physical and psychological torment often directly or obliquely reference disability. For example, after the coarse slave trader Mr. Haley purchases Uncle Tom from the indebted Arthur Shelby he buys additional slaves at a sale in Washington, D.C.—including fourteen-year-old Albert who was cruelly sold away from his aged and disabled mother, Aunt Hagar. According to Haley, Hagar is "not worth her salt…[because she was] half-blind, crooked with rheumatis and foolish to boot," a cold, calculated description of a tormented enslaved mother, which, for the reader, dramatizes how slavery deadened men's moral senses (Stowe 1852, 195). Other characters, like Cassy and Prue, experience varying degrees of disablement as a direct consequence of their enslavement. Cassy, the concubine of the exceptionally cruel Simon Legree, has a "half-crazed and wandering mind" because she is "stung to madness and despair" while Prue, who has one child after another sold away and daily experiences abuse, falls into depression and alcoholism (Stowe 1852, 560). In addition to using the spectacle of disability to convey the violence and injury heaped upon enslaved people, Stowe—like Weld—also deploys it in other ways.

Stowe repeatedly assails the legal system that upheld slavery in *Uncle Tom's Cabin,* drawing particular attention to bondpeople's legal disabilities and fundamental lack of legal personhood. Throughout the text, she draws attention to laws forbidding slave marriage and education, sanctioning the domestic trade, making it illegal to help or harbor fugitive slaves, and legitimizing slave catching with the passage of the Fugitive Slave Act in 1850. Stowe even addresses the issue of denying enslaved people a legal voice through the actions of Simon Legree, who ensured that no whites witnessed the daily barrage of violence he meted out to those he enslaved. When the young George Shelby threatens to bring charges against him for brutally beating Tom and causing his death, Legree sneers "Where you going to get witnesses?—how you going to prove it?—Come, now!" and "George saw, at once, the force of this defiance. There was not a white person on the place; and, in all southern courts, the testimony of colored blood is nothing" (Stowe 1852, 592). In another instance, fugitive slave George Harris crosses paths with Mr. Wilson, who had once employed George as a hired hand in his factory. Troubled by the fact that George was running away, Wilson attempts to sway him by pointing out that he was breaking the laws of his country. George responds:

> "What country have *I,* or any one like me, born of slave mothers? What laws are there for us? We don't make them,—we don't consent to them,—we have nothing to do with them; all they do for us is to crush us, and keep us down…Can't a fellow *think,* that hears such things? Can't he put this and that together, and see what it comes to? …Don't I sit before you, every way, just as much a man as you are? Look at my face,—look at my hands,—look at my body…why am I *not* a man, as much as anybody?" (Stowe 1852, 185)

In a few short sentences, this exchange highlights the disabling aspects of laws that "crush" slaves, asserts that enslaved people are not "competent," and illuminates the importance of the body itself in marking out George's ability and masculinity. Even beyond these examples of how Stowe, like Weld, engaged the intertwined issues of race, disability, slavery, and law, she also echoed Weld's methodology by closing *Uncle Tom's Cabin* with a chapter explaining that the characters she wrote about were based on real-life individuals. By evoking the testimony of first-person witnesses and her own personal experiences, Stowe establishes the legitimacy of her narrative by standing on facts and evidence.

Laws pertaining to enslaved people indeed consistently and repetitively linked ideas about blackness to those about disability. In some cases, they outright inflicted disabling injuries onto the bodies of enslaved people, expressed anxieties about providing care for disabled freedpeople, established compensation guidelines for slaveholders for their "damaged" property, or metaphorically handicapped enslaved blacks in society—sometimes even to the point of classifying their symbolic worth as a mere fraction of that of white men. Given Americans' widespread and long-held beliefs in the inferiority of people with disabilities that presumably justified their exclusion from the body politic, it is little wonder that white southern lawmakers from the colonial to the antebellum years imagined, legislated, and then exploited parallels between disabled people and enslaved people as a way to legitimize, justify, and excuse racial slavery.

Social death, legal disabilities, and arbitrary boundaries of legal personhood all factor into antebellum legal narratives of race, though scholars often overlook the centrality of disability to these constructs even as they draw on the language of disability to discuss them. In her poignant analysis of the creation of a legal personality for enslaved people, scholar Colin Dayan describes this process as "a birth as monstrous as that of Victor Frankenstein's creature" and notes that radical qualifications of slaves' legal identity were "shored up by fictions of disability which treat the figure of the slave as more or less human, not yet born and already dead" (2011, 54–55). Such language finds easy parallels in contemporary debates about issues like assisted suicide and euthanasia as disability rights activists proclaim that individuals with conditions deemed "severe" or with terminal illnesses are "not dead yet." In antebellum America, abolitionists sought to re-imagine associations between blackness and disability as a piteous spectacle in both fiction and nonfiction, while the laws of slavery sought to reinforce the belief that blackness was "real" and that it was inherently connected to the same contemptible, dependent state that presumably beleaguered people with disabilities. Thomas R. R. Cobb's statement—that only through slavery could blacks attain the "greatest degree of perfection" they could possibly achieve—bespeaks the way that slaveholders perceived blackness as always innately disabled in comparison to white men who staked out able-bodied-ness and sound-mindedness as their own racialized terrain.

Note

1. Jenifer L. Barclay would like to acknowledge the generous support of the Carter G. Woodson Institute at the University of Virginia that enabled her to conduct research and draft portions of this article as a pre-doctoral fellow. She benefitted tremendously from the insights of faculty members—particularly Deborah McDowell, Marlon Ross, Claudrena Harold, Risa Goluboff, and Charles McCurdy—as well as from other fellows who were part of the 2009–2011 and 2010–2012 cohorts. She also acknowledges the continued support she received as a Case Western Reserve University 2011-12 Postdoctoral Fellow in African American Studies, with many thanks to Rhonda Williams for her sage advice and constructive criticism. Nik Ribianszky and Tshepo Masango Chery also gave freely of their time to read and comment on this work.

Works Cited

Baynton, Douglas. 2001. "Disability and the Justification of Inequality in American History." In *The New Disability History: American Perspectives*, edited by Paul K. Longmore and Lauri Umanski. New York: New York University Press.

Berlin, Ira. 1974. *Slaves without Masters: The Free Negro in the Antebellum South*. New York: Pantheon Books.

Brown, Kathleen. 1996. *Good Wives, Nasty Wenches, and Anxious Patriarchs: Gender, Race and Power in Colonial Virginia*. Chapel Hill: University of North Carolina Press.

Browne, Stephen. 1994. "'Like Gory Spectres': Representing Evil in Theodore Weld's *American Slavery As It Is*." *Quarterly Journal of Speech*, 80: 277–92.

Bruce, Phillip Alexander. 1910. *Institutional History of Virginia in the Seventeenth Century: An Inquiry into the Religious, Moral and Educational, Legal, Military, and Political Condition of the* People, v. I. New York: The Knickerbocker Press.

Bullard, Henry A. and Thomas Curry, eds. 1842. *A New Digest of the Statute Laws of the State of Louisiana*. New Orleans: E. Johns & Company.

Bush, Jonathan A. 1997. "The British Constitution and the Creation of American Slavery." In *Slavery and the Law*, edited by Paul Finkleman. Madison, WI: Madison House Publishers.

Camp, Stephanie. 2004. *Closer to Freedom: Enslaved Women and Everyday Resistance in the Plantation South*. Chapel Hill: University of North Carolina Press.

Clinton, Catherine. 1991. "'Southern Dishonor': Flesh, Blood, Race, and Bondage." In *In Joy and In Sorrow: Women, Family, and Marriage in the Victorian South, 1830–1900*, edited by Carol Bleser. New York: Oxford University Press.

Cobb, Thomas R. R. 1858. *An Inquiry into the Law of Negro Slavery in the United States of America*. Philadelphia: T. and J. W. Johnson and Company.

Dayan, Collin. 2011. *The Law is a White Dog: How Legal Rituals Make and Unmake Persons*. Princeton: Princeton University Press.

Douglass, Frederick. 1845. *Narrative of Frederick Douglass: An American Slave*, edited by Henry Louis Gates, Jr. New York: Penguin, 2002.

Driskell, E. 1941. "Slavery as seen through the eyes of Henry Wright." *Slave Narratives: A Folk History of Slavery in the United States from Interviews with Former Slaves,* Georgia Narratives IV, Part 4. Washington, DC: Library of Congress.

Elkins, Stanley. 1968. *Slavery: A Problem in American Institutional and Intellectual Life*. Chicago: University of Chicago Press.

Ely, Jr., James W. 1985. "'There are Few Subjects in Political Economy of Greater Difficulty': The Poor Laws of the Antebellum South." *American Bar Foundation Research Journal* 10 (4): 849–79.

Flanigan, Daniel. 1973. "The Criminal Law of Slavery and Freedom, 1800–1868." Ph.D. Dissertation (Rice University).

Garland-Thompson, Rosemarie. 1996. "From Wonder to Error." In *Freakery: Cultural Spectacles of the Extraordinary Body*, edited by Rosemarie Garland Thompson. New York: New York University Press.

Greenburg, Kenneth S. 1996. *Honor and Slavery: Lies, Duels, Noses, Masks, Dressing as a Woman, Gifts, Strangers, Humanitarianism, Death, Slave Rebellions, the Proslavery Argument, Baseball, Hunting, and Gambling in the Old South*. Princeton: Princeton University Press.

Gross, Ariela. 2000. *Double Character: Slavery and Mastery in the Antebellum Southern Courtroom*. Athens, GA: The University of Georgia Press.

Hening, William Walter, ed. 1821 v. II, v. III, v. VIII, v. XI. *Statutes at Large of Virginia Being a Collection of All the Laws of Virginia, From the First Session of the Legislature in the Year 1619*. Richmond, VA: J & G Cochran.

Higginbotham, Jr., A. Leon. 1978. *In the Matter of Color: Race and the American Legal Process, The Colonial Period*. New York: Oxford University Press.

Higginbotham, Evelyn. 1995. "African American Women's History and the Metalanguage of Race." In *"We Specialize in the Wholly Impossible": A Reader in Black Women's History*, edited by Darlene Clark Hine, Wilma King, and Linda Reed. Brooklyn: Carlson Publishing Company.

Hotchkiss, William A., ed. 1848. *Codification of the Statute Law of Georgia*. Augusta: Charles E. Grenville.

Joyner, Hannah. 2004. *From Pity to Pride: Growing up Deaf in the Old South*. Washington, DC: Gallaudet University Press.

Kiesling, L. Lynne and Robert A. Margo. 1997. "Explaining the Rise in Antebellum Pauperism, 1800–1860: New Evidence." *The Quarterly Review of Economics and Finance* 37 (2): 405–17.

Klages, Mary. 1999. *Woeful Afflictions: Disability and Sentimentality in Victorian America*. Philadelphia: University of Pennsylvania Press.

Klebaner, Benjamin Joseph. 1955. "American Manumission Laws and the Responsibility for Supporting Slaves." *The Virginia Magazine of History and Biography* 62 (4): 443–53.

Leonard, Thomas C. 1995. "Anti-Slavery, Civil Rights, and Incendiary Material." *Media and Revolution: Comparative Perspectives*, edited by Jeremy D. Popkin. Louisville: University Press of Kentucky.

Longmore, Paul and Lauri Umansky, eds. 2001. *The New Disability History: American Perspectives*. New York: New York University Press.

Lucas, Marion B. 2002. *A History of Blacks in Kentucky: From Slavery to Segregation, 1760–1891*. Lexington: University Press of Kentucky.

McCord, David J., ed. 1839 v. VI. *The Statutes at Large of South Carolina*. Columbia, SC: A.S. Johnson.

——. 1840 v. VII. *The Statutes at Large of South Carolina*. Columbia, SC: A.S. Johnson.

Monaghan, E. Jennifer. 2004. *Learning to Read and Write in Colonial America*. Amherst: University of Massachusetts Press.

Oliphant, Louis. 1941. "Mistreatment of Slaves." *Slave Narratives: A Folk History of Slavery in the United States from Interviews with Former Slaves*, Georgia Narratives IV, Part 4. Washington, DC: Library of Congress.

Schwartz, Philip. 1998. *Twice Condemned: Slaves and the Criminal Laws of Virginia, 1705–1865*. Union, NJ: The Lawbook Exchange.

State of Virginia. 1849. *The Code of Virginia with the Declaration of Independence and Constitution of the United States and the Declaration of Rights and Constitution of Virginia*. Richmond, VA: William F. Richie.

Striker, Henri-Jacques. 2000. *A History of Disability*. Ann Arbor: University of Michigan Press.

Stowe, Harriet Beecher. 1986. *Uncle Tom's Cabin, Or, Life among the Lowly*. New York: Penguin Books.

Stroud, George. 1968. *A Sketch of the Laws of Slavery in the Several States of the United States of America*. New York: Negro Universities Press.

Trent, James W. 1994. *Inventing the Feeble Mind: A History of Mental Retardation in the United States*. Berkeley: University of California Press.

Weld, Theodore Dwight, ed. 1839. *American Slavery As It Is: Testimony of a Thousand Witnesses*. New York: American Anti-Slavery Society.

Wheeler, Jacob D., ed. 1837. *A Practical Treatise on the Law of Slavery: Being a Compilation of All the Decisions Made on that Subject, in the Several Courts of the United States, and the State Courts*. New York: Allan Pollock, Jr. and New Orleans: Benjamin Levy.

Wilson, Jean D. and Claus Roehrborn. 1999. "The Long Term Consequences of Castration in Men: Lessons from the Skoptzy and the Eunichs of the Chinese and Ottoman Courts." *The Journal of Clinical Endocrinology and Metabolism* 84 (12): 4324–31.

Wyatt-Brown, Bertram. 2007. *Southern Honor: Ethics and Behavior in the Old South*. New York: Oxford University Press.

E S S A Y

"WHAT HAPPENED IN BETWEEN":
LAWRENCE HILL AND *THE BOOK OF NEGROES*

by David Borman

In many ways, Lawrence Hill has always been concerned with representing the route from Canada to Africa in his fiction. His first novel, *Some Great Thing* (1992), includes the protagonist's brief press visit to Cameroon. *Any Known Blood* (1998), Hill's follow-up, has a pivotal moment when the narrator's research trip to Mali proves disastrous for his marriage in Canada. But with *Someone Knows My Name* (2007) (published in Canada and in the UK as *The Book of Negroes*), the links between Africa, North America, and Great Britain are the focus of the entire plot, as Hill presents the fictional autobiography of Aminata Diallo, an African woman who is enslaved, escapes, and returns to the continent with the founding of Freetown, Sierra Leone.

Winner of the Commonwealth Writers' Prize Best Book in 2008, *Someone Knows My Name* is possibly the best-known fictional account of the Black Loyalists.[1] These former slaves responded to a variety of British proclamations at the outset of the American Revolution, and Aminata's "autobiography" pivots around her experience as one of these emigrants. The historical narrative of this revolutionary moment generally frames the Black Loyalists in two distinct manners: as an ironic counter-narrative to the mythology surrounding the Founding Fathers or as a powerful example of the quest for freedom in an age of revolutionary ideals. *Someone Knows My Name,* however, uses the Black Loyalist migration as a suggestive moment for theorizing international affiliation with Africa. In Hill's novel, Aminata tells her narrative as a circum-Atlantic project of historical recovery that centers on the ever-changing nature of "the village" in her experience. As her sense of African-affiliated community expands throughout her narrative, Aminata also develops her capacity to give narrative shape to her community. Beginning with her earliest attempts at repeating the names of her slave ship captives, Aminata's life story is immersed in her attempts at understanding and defining her affiliations as they broaden.[2]

In its concern with multiple migrations around the Atlantic, Hill's novel articulates a space for Africa as a site of collective affiliation that is less rigorously associated with the original transportation of the slave trade. To be sure, Aminata's capture and sale into the Atlantic slave system is one of the defining features of her life, but her insistence on her various movements around the world, especially her return to Africa as a self-identified Black Loyalist, suggests that the African continent holds an active presence in her life as well as in the cultural connections seen throughout the novel. Much of her time is spent in contact with the established and hybridized slave cultures of the American colonies, yet the cultural affiliation Aminata develops is distinct from the traditions of the low-country slaves or black New Yorkers during the Revolution. In her ever-expanding village, Africa remains an enduring presence with the ability to enrich her collective affiliations. Such a vision of Africa interrogates some of the major assumptions of widely influential diasporan and hybridity theories, most notably articulated by Paul Gilroy (1993) and Stuart Hall (1990). Charles Piot (2001) critiques Gilroy in particular, noting that *The Black Atlantic,* "suggests, of course, that Africa has played little role in the development of Black Atlantic cultural production, other than as provider of raw materials—bodies and cultural templates/origins—that were then processed or elaborated upon by the improvisational cultures of the Americas" (156). Following Piot, it makes sense to see Hill's novel as disorganizing the trajectory of black Atlantic diasporan theory. By maintaining active ties to Africa as more than the provider of raw materials, especially in her return to the continent, Aminata's narrative carves out a space for African collective affiliation in specifically nonhybridized ways.

Aminata Diallo, the story's protagonist and narrator, is taken from her home in Bayo, Mali at the age of eleven. She is sold into slavery at Bance Island (Sierra Leone) and works in indigo production in South Carolina, where she learns to read and write in English. Eventually, Aminata is sold to the Jewish indigo inspector, Solomon Lindo, and works for him as an accountant. In an attempt to stabilize the indigo market through legislative channels, Aminata and Lindo travel to New York City just before the American Revolution, and Aminata escapes into Canvas Town, where many other escaped slaves have set up crude shelters and begun a community. While teaching reading and writing at a local church, Aminata is hired by the British government to record the names of Black Loyalists leaving New York for other points in the Commonwealth. In addition to having her write this fictional autobiography, Hill also situates Aminata as the anonymous author of the Book of Negroes.[3] When she departs from New York for Shelburne, Nova Scotia, Aminata experiences more of the same—she finds little work and less acceptance outside of the black community. After the African emigration movement is underway, Aminata's literacy is again put to use coordinating the sailing to Sierra Leone. She ends the novel in London, writing her autobiography, after leaving the Freetown settlement in a failed attempt to return once more to her hometown of Bayo.

In the novel's movement from Bayo to London, Aminata's chosen collective identity—along with her awareness of it—branches outward. While the ten families in the Bayo of her childhood are the only community she can imagine at the beginning of the novel, in her final days in London, she has embraced an imagined community of readers in her autobiography. Such expansion of her sense of connection is based upon the totality of her story and her insistence that her identity is predicated upon more than her former-slave status or her experience of the Middle Passage. She demands to be known by her name, and the gradual expansion of her audience as well as "her people" indicates that connection across the globe is based upon understanding the whole of her historical experience. It is based upon the circuitous nature of her travel, yet it still maintains powerful roots in Africa.

The desire to understand these connections is consistently tied to Aminata's attempts at articulating her community, either orally or in print. From her earliest days in Bayo, Aminata's foremost desire is to become a *djeli,* the village storyteller, usually referred to as *griot* in Anglophone contexts. A *djeli* traditionally tells stories that recount the collective history and genealogies of those living in a village, and Aminata remarks that this form of oral history-keeping is revered throughout her homeland: "It was said that when a *djeli* passed away, the knowledge of one hundred men died with him" (Hill 2007, 55). Fulfilling such a role is impossible for Aminata, for she is doubly handicapped: She is both a woman and enslaved. Her desire to see, record, and recount the history that unfolds before her, however, is one of the reasons Aminata is able to survive various traumas. The first instance in which she performs this role is during her Atlantic crossing, as she learns the names and hometowns of a majority of slaves being transported below decks: "When I was carried up the ladder and dropped like a sack of meal on the deck of the toubabu's ship, I sought comfort by imagining that I had been made a *djeli,* and was required to see and remember everything. My purpose would be to witness, and to prepare to testify" (55–56). To witness and testify are impulses that Christian Krampe (2009) identifies as "externaliz[ing] and spread[ing]" the traumatic memories of abduction, the Middle Passage, and plantation slavery (71). Krampe is right to locate Aminata's agency in her role as witness, as is his reminder that "the collective voice embodied by Aminata is an important aspect of stressing collective rather than personal memory" (2009, 71). But, whereas Krampe sees the book's influence as chiefly responding to the Canadian image of itself as a promised land, Aminata's own rhetoric pushes outward toward an African diaspora, fostering a sense of affiliation built upon the collective uses of these memories.

This expansive rhetoric begins with Aminata's narration of her Atlantic crossing, a moment in which she begins to expand the *djeli* role to include a more global audience. She recalls, "In telling my story, I remember all those who never made it through the musket balls and the sharks and the nightmares, all those who never found a group of listeners, and all those who never touched a quill and an inkpot" (Hill 2007, 56–57). While Aminata imagines the group that experienced similar atrocities, this passage also implies the greater collective of readers and listeners who might gain from her story. To perform the role of *djeli* is, in many respects, to catalog and recite a community's history so that it can be remembered and celebrated by that community—it is to bear witness to the past so that it may inform the present. In some respects, her narrative is meant for her fellow sufferers, yet Aminata's impulse also seems directed toward another community, that of the "men, women and children walking about the streets without the faintest idea of our nightmares" (56). Seen as an expansive gesture, such authorship fosters an imagined community within her reading audience while narrating the methods by which the transported slaves formed their own collective.

That the Middle Passage would be a moment of collective formation amongst the slaves is not surprising; indeed, this is one of the central tenets of African American literature and Black Atlantic literary theory. However, this Middle Passage is noteworthy in that it is only the beginning in a process for Aminata: it is on the slave ship that her notion of group identity begins to expand and where she first tries to articulate that community. Rather than see herself only as a child of Bayo, Aminata begins to understand herself in relation to the other captives. In fact, her exchange with Biton, a captured chief who eventually leads a slave rebellion onboard, causes Aminata to look outward. Although Fomba—a *woloso,* or second-generation slave, from her village—has lost his mind in captivity, Aminata still tries to get him privileges with the captains of the slave vessel. Biton, however, urges Aminata to use her influence with the white men in order to have other slaves useful to the rebellion put into positions of relative privilege. At this point, Aminata clings to traditional ties of kinship when she defends her position: "He is from my village." Biton, however, can only respond, "We are all from a village, child" (Hill 2007, 70).

This initially seems to be a moment in which the slave ship takes primacy over the African village for identity formation, as Biton certainly tells Aminata that Bayo ceases to enrich actively her daily life after capture. However, Biton's response hints at another possibility. Their exchange comes in the middle of Aminata's growing awareness of the particular community forming on the slave ship, for she recognizes that with each dead slave thrown overboard those remaining are brought together by the fact of their survival. With the most recent body thrown overboard, Aminata "wondered how many of *us* would end up in the sea" (Hill 2007, 70, emphasis added). Biton's assertion that "we are all from a village," spoken as the surviving slaves continue to band together, would seem to be a statement that asserts a new collective identity rather than erasing the African village past. Although Biton's remark is an understandably brutal severance from former ties, Aminata receives his sentiment differently. Rather than deny the importance of the village for an individual captive, Aminata uses Biton's words to rethink a more expansive notion of collectivity that makes the idea of the village more inclusive; indeed, the village is reconstructed on the slave ship's Atlantic crossing.

What Biton relates to Aminata is the beginning of a negotiation central to the progression of her narrative. In asserting the importance of the village for the slave ship, Biton's remarks speak to identity formation on both an individual and collective level. The captives will understandably identify with their places of origin in Africa, yet the experience of the Middle Passage is such that many disparate people and groups are inextricably bound together. The collective sense of identity will only expand throughout Aminata's account, and the process begins on the slave ship when the captives are made to dance for the white sailors. To make the experience less traumatic, Aminata begins to sing a song that weaves together the names and villages of each person on deck. As she sings out a name, the man or woman would "clap if I got it right, and the others would call it out, once. When I got a name wrong or didn't know it, the person would clap twice and dance a little with me and sing out his or her name and village" (Hill 2007, 80). Such clapping and dancing transforms the forced ritual into a community building exercise. Soon, the captives genuinely forge ties with one another: "Everybody took to this activity, and on other occasions when we were made to dance, homelanders took turns calling out the names and villages of the people around them" (80). The experience of dancing over the slavers' whip thus becomes a moment in which the captives both band together as one and assert their individual identities and places of origin. For Aminata, who "could call out the names of almost every person," this experience begins a lifetime of performing the role of a *djeli* and recognizing individual names and collective identities simultaneously (80).

Aminata barely survives her transport across the Atlantic and is so sickly that she is sold in Charleston, along with Fomba the *woloso,* as a refuse slave to Robinson Appleby, who intends for her to work his indigo plantation in the South Carolina Sea Islands. There, she learns to speak three languages—the vernacular English used by plantation slaves, the dialect used by the planters, and Gullah used by low-country slaves—as well as the customs of the South Carolina slave population. At the same time, under the tutelage of a slave overseer, Aminata secretly learns to read from planters' almanacs. These two influences leave Aminata struggling to understand the new community into which she has been thrown as well as the place from which she was taken and with which she still strongly identifies.

Upon arriving at Appleby's indigo plantation, Aminata is taken in by Georgia, an enslaved woman who works in the fields and as a midwife for the local slave population. She introduces Aminata to low-country customs and the Gullah language, and it is by traveling throughout the low-country with Georgia that Aminata gains a richer sense of the culture that exists all around her new home. From Georgia she learns practical medical advice, like how to cure particular ailments with herbs, but more importantly she begins to understand the network of information that travels between plantations all along the coast. They call it "the fishnet," as Georgia explains: "Niggers got mouths like rivers. Our words swim the rivers, all the way from Savannah to St. Helena to Charles Town and farther up.... Our words swim farther than a man can walk. When we find someone, up he comes in the fishnet" (Hill 2007, 141). The fishnet proves to be the defining feature of this low-country slave community, and it proves to be a powerful tool for interpersonal connections in Aminata's life. At the beginning of her enslavement to Appleby, Aminata immediately looks for a boy named Chekura, who had become something like a brother to her on their Atlantic crossing and who was sold to a different low-country planter. Nevertheless, it is Chekura who finds Aminata in the fishnet, as he is more intimately involved in the shadow economy of South Carolina slave culture: "During [the sick] season, Chekura said, dozens of Negroes could be found at night, roaming and boating, trading poultry for rice, vegetables for gourds, rabbits for rum, exchanging news of brothers and sisters and wives and children, sinking the fishnet and pulling it back up" (158). Constantly reaching for information creates a sense of community in the low-country that Aminata cannot help but become a part of, and when she and Chekura are eventually married on Appleby's plantation, it is a community event, complete with food, gifts, music, and a long night of celebration.

As her awareness of and involvement in the slave community grows, so does Aminata's personal sense of identity in relation to her home in Africa. Making sense of her social life in the colonies means "sinking the fishnet," but understanding her place of birth, and what it means to be African, requires the ability to read European and American accounts of her homeland. Although she is far removed from Bayo and the customs of her childhood, Aminata's developing literacy allows her to begin reading about where she comes from. She mostly searches for information about how to get back to Africa from the colonies, but none of the books at her disposal are very useful for this. However, reading almanacs, medicine guides, and the Bible does leave Aminata with a growing desire to understand and give an account of her place in the world.

Very early upon arriving in South Carolina, Aminata realizes that Bayo holds no meaning across the Atlantic—to slaves and owners alike—for she is *African*, a term she had never heard until this point. Reading books, however, allows her to get a better sense of herself, even as she reads exclusively about the planter class and their concerns:

> Books were all about the ways of the buckra, but soon I felt that I could not do without them. And I lived in hope that one day I would find a book that answered my questions. *Where was Africa, exactly, and how did you get there?* Sometimes I felt ashamed to have no answer. How could I come from a place but not know where it was? (Hill 2007, 165)

This individual quest for knowledge carries on throughout her life, and her search for information about her homeland always takes place parallel to her involvement in building, sustaining, and narrating a community. She most keenly feels the desire for information about Africa while in Charleston after being sold to Solomon Lindo, the indigo inspector.

Recognizing Aminata's intellectual abilities, Lindo purchases her to keep the ledgers of his indigo-inspecting and consulting business, teaching her writing and arithmetic in the process. After her morning lessons, Lindo rewards Aminata with books by Jonathan Swift, Voltaire, and William Falconer to read in the evenings. The reading continues to inspire questions about the ways in which the world is run, and Aminata cannot escape the feeling that her own personal identity is tied together with the workings of the global markets: "How much had been paid for me, I wondered, and who had arranged to have me brought to this land? How were the black men who stole me from Bayo tied to the Christians and Jews who traded in slaves in South Carolina? …Answers only led to more questions" (Hill 2007, 205). While her personal and cultural connections to Georgia, Chekura, and others strengthen in South Carolina, Aminata continues to find her individual identity through memories of Bayo. As on the slave ship, community life both contracts and expands—she still considers Bayo her home, yet her identity continues to be influenced by an expanding group consciousness that has little connection to that African village.

The course of her enslavement to Lindo coincides with the growing hostilities between the colonists and the British government, and Lindo eventually takes Aminata to New York City to help lobby for governmental policy that can stabilize the South Carolina indigo market. While the two are in the North, fighting breaks out in Lexington and Concord, and Aminata takes her opportunity to run away, eventually settling in the makeshift black neighborhood of Canvas Town. Her entry into a larger community in New York begins almost immediately upon fleeing Lindo and the slave system he represents, when Aminata walks through the city and into the burial ground for African Americans. A funeral for a child is taking place, and when she sees the mourning adults and listens to their songs, Aminata cannot help but join them in their grief:

> They took me into their dancing, and did not ask where I came from, for all they had to do was look at me and hear my own sobs in my maternal tongue and they knew that I was one of them. The dead infant was…every person who had been tossed into the unforgiving sea on the endless journey across the big river. (Hill 2007, 256)

Although the infant's burial is a powerful moment of communal gathering and collective identity, it is one that takes place without comment from any of the participants, and it ends almost as suddenly as it begins. Aminata speaks to one woman after the ceremony, but their encounter ends quite abruptly: "She raised her fingers in salutation, and turned away. The Africans kept walking south through the woods, and none looked back at me" (257). Thus, Aminata has no personal connections to foster from this exchange, yet she is left with an entire African-based collective to imagine and identify with in the abstract. Much like the fishnet in South Carolina, the network of blacks in New York City is extensive and has its own methods of connection. Yet, in contrast to the more direct exchange of information in the fishnet, the community Aminata finds in New York is largely imagined.

After gaining a stronger sense of ethnic identity and collectivity in New York, Aminata begins to foster personal connections in Canvas Town through acts of literacy. She teaches reading and writing to a handful of free blacks and runaways, and her lessons always begin with names: "In a private room lit with lamps and candles, they told me their names, huddled around me, put their hands on my shoulders and arms and back, and peered at the words taking shape under my hand" (Hill 2007, 259). In an echo of the song from the slave ship, and in anticipation of her employment writing the Book of Negroes, Aminata forges personal relationships through asking, repeating, and even writing the names of those she meets. This moment both continues and expands her role as a *djeli*, as she continues to attest to her community but does so by reading and writing in addition to oral recitation.

Her time teaching in New York spans the American Revolution, and when Loyalist New York finally needs to be evacuated, Aminata is known around the city as the member of the black community who knows everyone and can read and write. The British army then hires her to record the names and descriptions of each departing black in the Book of Negroes. It is notable that Aminata's public writing—which culminates with her auto-biography at the end of her life—begins in New York, where she eventually records names and descriptions of blacks evacuating with the British in the Book of Negroes. In this moment, Aminata seems to take on the role of the *djeli* yet again. Indeed, listening to the emigrants and recording their names thus combines the written and oral traditions with which she is so familiar. The path to authorship, however, is yet another manifestation of the process Aminata negotiates throughout her life, as she must imagine and identify with a community much larger than any she has ever known; yet the intimacy of the Book of Negroes requires knowing each individual's story and recording each one on its own.

As she listens to the stories of those wishing to emigrate for Nova Scotia, Aminata's sense of community and personal identity fuse together, and she develops an understanding of her own place within the world. While the questions of relation that lingered in Charleston are still unanswered, listening to the emigrants' accounts of "unexpected migrations" gives Aminata a sense of belonging: "I loved my new work. I felt that I was giving something special to the Negroes seeking asylum in Nova Scotia, and that they were giving something special to me. They were telling me that I was not alone" (Hill 2007, 291). At the same time, recording individual names of emigrants allows for Aminata to assert individual identity, and she is careful to give each former slave a moment of personal attention: "I showed them their tickets, read out their names and made sure they saw that their names had been recorded" (291).[4] The experience of hearing and recording so many stories leads to one of Aminata's refrains for the rest of the novel: "We are travelling peoples" (301). The "we" here is certainly inclusive of an African diasporic community, one in almost perpetual migration, but the formulation of "peoples" hints at the primacy of individuals to this collectivity—the "stout wenches" and "likely fellows" described in the Book of Negroes count, their histories matter in themselves and as part of the collective.

At this point in the novel, Aminata rapidly gains two further claims upon her identity: she self-identifies as a Black Loyalist and joins the emigration to Shelburne, Nova Scotia, then joins the movement to Sierra Leone. A relatively small narrative space is actually given to the experience in Nova Scotia, as most of the events seem directed toward the mass exodus to Sierra Leone ten disappointing years later. For Aminata, Nova Scotia brings the birth of her daughter and the child's subsequent kidnapping by the white family for whom Aminata works. While in Nova Scotia, she also learns the news of Chekura's death at sea during the British evacuation. Organizing the mass return to Africa yet again requires Aminata's literacy, as she records names and testimonies of potential emigrants for the Sierra Leone Company's evaluation. The experience also propels her toward her dream of returning to Bayo, resurrecting her lifelong process of negotiating her personal experiences with the claims of community upon her identity. After aiding John Clarkson in the organization of the Sierra Leone emigration, Aminata arrives in Freetown with only one desire: to make the trip inland

and settle in her childhood village. It takes many years and an unfavorable bargain with an African slaver before the opportunity to travel to Bayo arises. The Freetown settlement sees its share of problems in these years, and Hill includes the historically real controversies over land allotments and quitrents, bombardment by French warships in 1794, an armed-settler rebellion over land ownership in 1800, and the influx of hundreds of Jamaican maroons who subsequently put down that rebellion. But amidst these community efforts at meaningful freedom and settler solidarity is Aminata's own struggle with how to identify with her homeland after a lifetime of migrations around the Atlantic.

At the forefront of this struggle is Aminata's partial self-identification as a diasporan, alongside her strong desire to return to Bayo and live as she did before her capture four decades earlier. Returning to Africa provides Aminata with an undeniable lesson: although she may still consider herself undeniably connected to the region, the local Temne think of her as closer to white. Her notions of group belonging, which have expanded since her capture, must change again to encompass her African origins and her identification with the Black Loyalists and Nova Scotian returnees. In the beginning, the colony is built based on a community ethic of hard work and Christianity, and Aminata joins in the spirit of this, even if she does not completely identify with Nova Scotian culture: "In South Carolina, I had been an African. In Nova Scotia, I had become known as a Loyalist or a Negro, or both. And now, finally back in Africa, I was seen as a Nova Scotian, and in some respects thought of myself that way too" (Hill 2007, 385). Yet, despite her uncertainty about what place Africa holds in her life, Aminata's strongest desire is to connect with the local Africans in the market and eventually to return to Bayo, to be home again: "[W]hat part of me was still African? I would never feel truly at home again until I found my way back to Bayo" (386).

Her return inland, back to Bayo, fails. She cannot keep up with the slave-trading crew, and after about a month of walking, she overhears the leader's plans to sell her back into slavery at the next town. Near exhaustion, she runs away and is taken in at a small village and nursed back to health. The trip to Bayo fails on the most elementary level, as Aminata cannot complete the walk and will never see her hometown again. But the inability to return also removes the final barrier to Aminata's realization of a stable sense of belonging. From the moment she returns to Africa as part of the Sierra Leone settlement, she understands Freetown to be "nothing more than a stepping stone" (Hill 2007, 387). The lack of complete attachment to Nova Scotian and Freetown culture is only attributable to her insistence on returning to a home village. In a sense, the more circumscribed notions of village identity that occupied her childhood sense of self reappear in Freetown, and her obsession with returning "to the place where [her] life began" clouds any sense of collective identity she had developed in her life of migrations. Her month recuperating, however, puts Aminata into the position of *djeli* and reanimates the desire to understand her life and collective identity together.

The final movement in Aminata's progression involves her acceptance of the *djeli* role, both in an unnamed African village as well as in the abolitionist circle of London, where she sails at the request of the Sierra Leone company leaders after escaping the slavers. In immediate terms, Aminata's abandonment of her quest for return to Bayo, and her escape of a second enslavement, reinforces her commitment to an imagined community of listeners and readers, where her life's story has the power to bring people together under a common commitment. Reaching this audience begins during her recovery, as she offers to "tell stories of all the places I have been and all that I have seen in the toubabu's land" (Hill 2007, 446). As she stays for "one revolution of the moon," Aminata becomes the *djeli* that she had always wanted to be as a child and fulfills the role she imagined for herself on the slave ship and enacted as a recorder for the Book of Negroes decades earlier. Her story is a combination of the personal and the collective, a culmination of her individual journeys around the Atlantic. and of the collective black journeys to find meaningful freedom in the British world:

> I told the story of my youth, the story of my trek to Bance Island and how I had caught babies along the way. Always, with each story, I was asked for names....I told the story of the ship's passage, the revolt on the ocean, the conditions on board the ships, and of Sullivan's Island. I told of growing indigo, and harvesting it, and Negroes enslaved in America regardless of where they were born....I told of the wars between the white men in America and our betrayal in Nova Scotia, and, ultimately, of our passage to Sierra Leone and my futile search for my home. (446–47)

The shifting subjects of Aminata's stories, from her individual capture to the collective betrayal in Nova Scotia, indicate the degree to which she can finally integrate her personal sense of identity with a collective notion of belonging. She is at home with her African audience and equally comfortable identifying herself as an African-born woman, a former slave, and a betrayed colonist. Such a composite worldview in Africa makes her trip to London almost superfluous, as she has already embraced her role as *djeli*—she can already understand herself and her people as globally relevant, even when enslaved.

Her time in London deepens both of Aminata's narrative roles: She continues to be an African oral historian when lecturing to the public and to schoolchildren, and she expands her role as a published author through the completion of her memoir. As an author and testifier against the slave trade, she is able to reach an even wider imagined community of readers, and she is careful to teach this community about her entire life. Amidst the immediate political crusade against the slave trade, she once again asserts that her identity, and that of blacks worldwide, is not reducible to slavery or to the Middle Passage. When addressing a group of British schoolchildren every Friday, Aminata once again emphasizes that the importance of her story goes beyond her slave past, highlighting the totality of her lifelong journey: "I always began the same way. Unrolling a map of the world, I would put one finger on a dot I had drawn to represent my village of Bayo, put another finger on London and say: 'I was born there, and we are here now, and I'm going to tell you all about what happened in between'" (Hill 2007, 469).

Someone Knows My Name is perpetually concerned with the in-between, all of it. Aminata demands that her readers and listeners understand her story, and the story of the Black Loyalists, in its totality. And by asking such complete vision of her audience, she asserts the need for understanding a way of belonging for blacks that cannot rely only on notions of national citizenship. Hill addresses his own concerns about the problems of identity formation in Canada by looking to the Black Loyalist story as a whole, by understanding it as a circum-Atlantic narrative about more than slavery, more than racism, more than the Middle Passage. If Hill comments on how African-Canadians are to make sense of their cultural heritage, it is by affirming a place for Africa within that worldview.

The point is not that Canada lacks a place for blacks, but that Canada is not even the right place to look. Aminata is not Canadian, nor is she completely African either. Africa is her home, blacks around the globe are her people, and she is a *djeli* for anyone who will listen. *Someone Knows My Name* asks to be heard in its entirety.

Notes

1. Beginning with Lord Dunmore's in 1775, the British made various promises of freedom in exchange for military service, certainly as a military expedient rather than an act of humanitarianism. Thousands of slaves ran away to join their ranks. Many were asked to serve as foot soldiers against the revolutionaries, while others became cooks, servants, and even river guides through the swamps of Georgia and South Carolina. The Loyalist forces accepted all runaways, not just men capable of serving on the front lines, resulting in large groups of women, children, and the elderly making their ways from the southern work fields to the camps of the British army. In the immediate aftermath of the war, after British defeat, Commander Sir Guy Carleton kept the promise of freedom to any black who could prove to have been behind British lines for at least one year. Thousands of Loyalists, black and white, were transported to various parts of the British Atlantic world, including the West Indies, Nova Scotia, British Columbia, and England itself. A portion of those transported to Canada migrated to Sierra Leone in 1792 as part of the Sierra Leone Company's efforts to promote "legitimate commerce," trade in Africa that did not deal in humans. For the historical treatment of the Black Loyalists as a counter-narrative to the accepted story of the American Revolution, see Frey (1992), Nash (2005), Schama (2006), and Quarles (1973). On the other hand, Pybus (2006), Walker (1992), and Wilson (1976) narrate this story chiefly in terms of individual quests for liberty.

2. *Someone Knows My Name* (2007) is often commended as a work that asserts the presence and importance of African Canadians in the Canadian national story in more complicated ways than are typically seen. Hill's former slaves in Shelburne, Nova Scotia, struggle to survive amidst a society where slavery still thrives and heavy racial prejudice is a fact of life. Far from presenting Canada as an unproblematic haven for freed slaves—or, implicitly, as a happy, multicultural land in the present day—Hill gives a complex, often contradictory vision of black Canadian life. See Virgo (2011), Krampe (2009), and Yorke (2010). By contrast, the novel itself reaches beyond national borders throughout. More specifically, *Someone Knows My Name* is a work about identity formation intimately linked to narratives of national belonging yet also freed from the constraints of personal identification based solely on one's citizenship.

3. The Book of Negroes is the longest document about African Americans written before the nineteenth century. It lists around three thousand freed or escaped slaves who joined the ranks of the British Army and were evacuated at the end of the American Revolution. The book was compiled in 1783 as a record for Americans to calculate the value of former property that had been evacuated with the British. Authorship of the Book of Negroes is anonymous, although it was certainly compiled by a variety of British and American officers on board the departing ships. It can be found in its entirety in Hodges (1996), and a digitized copy is available online through the Nova Scotia Archives (Province of Nova Scotia 2006).

4. The dynamic interplay between individual and collective is played out again in the composition of the historical Book of Negroes. Although most descriptions are short and lack much actual description (e.g. "stout wench," "worn out," "fine boy"), the collective power of the names, descriptions, and brief histories of these individuals is almost overwhelming. Hill himself described seeing the document as "a very rich experience" and as a great teaching tool (Sagawa 2008, 315): "Looking at 'The Book of Negroes' and learning to decipher it and take meaning from it, I think, could be a rich exercise for any enterprising university or senior high school student" (Sagawa 2008, 321).

Works Cited

Frey, Sylvia R. 1992. *Water from the Rock: Black Resistance in a Revolutionary Age*. Princeton: Princeton University Press.

Gilroy, Paul. 1993. *The Black Atlantic: Modernity and Double-Consciousness*. Cambridge, MA: Harvard University Press.

Hall, Stuart. 1990. "Cultural Identity and Diaspora." In *Identity: Community, Culture, Difference*, edited by Jonathan Rutherford. London: Lawrence and Wishart.

Hill, Lawrence. 2002. *Black Berry, Sweet Juice: On Being Black and White in Canada*. Toronto: Harper Perennial.
———. *Someone Knows My Name*. 2007. New York: Norton.
———. 2008. *Any Known Blood*. Toronto: HarperCollins. First published 1998 by William Morrow.
———. *Some Great Thing*. 2009. Toronto: Harper Perennial. First published 1992 by Turnstone Press.
Hodges, Graham Russell. 1996. *The Black Loyalist Directory : African Americans in Exile After the American Revolution*. New York: Garland.
Krampe, Christian J. 2009. "Inserting Trauma into the Canadian Collective Memory: Lawrence Hill's *The Book of Negroes* and Selected African-Canadian Poetry." *Zeitschrift für Kanada-Studien* 29(1): 62–83.
Nash, Gary B. 2005. *The Unknown American Revolution: The Unruly Birth of Democracy and the Struggle to Create America*. New York: Viking.
Piot, Charles. 2001. "Atlantic Aporias: Africa and Gilroy's Black Atlantic." *The South Atlantic Quarterly* 100(1): 155–70.
Province of Nova Scotia. 2006. "African Nova Scotians: in the Age of Slavery and Abolition." Last modified January 3. http://www.gov.ns.ca/nsarm/virtual/africanns/BN.asp.
Pybus, Cassandra. 2006. *Epic Journeys of Freedom : Runaway Slaves of the American Revolution and Their Global Quest for Liberty*. Boston: Beacon.
Quarles, Benjamin. 1973. *The Negro in the American Revolution*. New York: Norton.
Sagawa, Jessie. 2008. "Projecting History Honestly: An Interview with Lawrence Hill." *Studies in Canadian Literature/Etudes en Littérature Canadienne* 33(1): 307–22.
Schama, Simon. 2006. *Rough Crossings : Britain, the Slaves, and the American Revolution*. New York: Ecco.
Virgo, Clement. 2011. "Where We Need 'The Book of Negroes.'" *Maclean's* 124(8): 77.
Walker, James W. St. G. 1992. *The Black Loyalists: The Search for a Promised Land in Nova Scotia and Sierra Leone, 1783–1870*. Toronto: University of Toronto Press.
Wilson, Ellen Gibson. 1976. *The Loyal Blacks*. New York: Putnam.
Yorke, Stephanie. 2010. "The Slave Narrative Tradition in Lawrence Hill's *The Book of Negroes*." *Studies in Canadian Literature/Etudes en Littérature Canadienne* 35(2): 129–44.

E S S A Y

THE GEOGRAPHY OF *MANDY OXENDINE* AND THE EMERGENCE OF CHESNUTT'S ENVIRONMENTAL ETHOS

by Kelly Clasen

Charles Chesnutt's earliest novel, *Mandy Oxendine,* rejected by Houghton Mifflin in 1897 and pushed aside for the remainder of his lifetime, focuses, as so much of Chesnutt's fiction does, on the mixed-race people who occupied a liminal space in a society divided along a color line.[1] Its frank attention to passing and miscegenation likely made it too scandalous for late nineteenth-century publishers, and Chesnutt moved on to other pursuits, including the publication of his most well-known work, *The Conjure Woman* (1899). When *Mandy Oxendine* was finally published a full century after its rejection, readers were met with a dichotomous text, its plot both prescriptive and pioneering. Chesnutt's critique of racial injustice and employment of regionalist characteristics compete with an abruptly introduced murder-mystery plot, which results in an innovative story line but compromises the cohesiveness of the work. Moreover, this unusual fusion of genres contributes to an erratic portrayal of a threatened piney woods that is both a resource to be protected and a realm of danger to be avoided by the disenfranchised racial minority—a portrayal that contradicts Chesnutt's solidly sympathetic rendering of the natural world presented in *The Conjure Woman.* That is, as *Mandy Oxendine* swerves between regionalism, race fiction, and mystery novel, Chesnutt's depiction of the natural world takes on a mutable nature as well, shifting to conform to the conventions of each particular genre. Despite *Mandy Oxendine's* resistance to genre conventions, Chesnutt imaginatively intertwines his disenfranchised mixed-race characters and the southern landscape they inhabit, condemning the exploitation of both and envisioning a more environmentally aware, egalitarian future for the region. Addressing the intersection of these motives invigorates Chesnutt studies by stretching the boundaries of his legacy as a regionalist who employed creative discursive strategies to critique racial injustice to acknowledge his historically forward-thinking environmental ethos.

At the beginning of *Mandy Oxendine,* Chesnutt celebrates the "tangled profusion" of the piney woods of his North Carolina setting, and even criticizes the inhabitants of this community for going "out into the woods to cut down the saplings for fire wood" (6). However, as the novel progresses, the forest takes on a decidedly more ominous personality, its shadows the cover for a series of sexually and racially motivated violent crimes. Chesnutt's forest ultimately exhibits rather anachronistic similarities to the woods of earlier American gothic literature, sites brimming with anxiety about the frontier wilderness—as often seen, for example, in works by Nathanial Hawthorne, for whom "wild country was still…a powerful symbol of man's dark and untamed heart" (Nash 2001, 39). As Chesnutt's mystery plot develops, his forest also grows increasingly symbolic, its shadows closely aligned with the ugliest human impulses. The violence unleashed by the novel's white characters in the forest against people they wish to dominate parallels the compulsion by American settlers to conquer, in the name of progress, a "wild country," which they perceived as "cursed and ungodly land" (Nash 2001, 44). This sort of anxiety conflicts with the rather progressive view of environmental stewardship presented early in the novel, however, and we can only conclude that as Chesnutt struggled to find his way in a white publishing world, he lost sight of this environmental ethos or saw it as significantly less important than his critique of the "one-drop rule" and its painful implications for his protagonists.

Mandy Oxendine is noteworthy not only as Chesnutt's first novel and a pioneering treatise on the performativity of race, but also as an introduction to understanding Chesnutt's environmental ethos, one that has previously been acknowledged only in relation to his conjure stories.[2] Part regionalism, part race fiction, and part mystery—with a strong undercurrent of social commentary that dissipates somewhat as the novel progresses—the book has been called "the most important of his novels that were not published during his lifetime" (Hackenberry 1997, xi). Nevertheless, only a few critics have written at length on the slim novel (some call it a novella), and the limited criticism that exists has primarily drawn attention to the book's incongruous fusion of genres.[3] In an attempt to categorize the book, Joanna Penn Cooper has argued that the "text's ideological and stylistic ambiguity marks it as an important contribution to the category of post-Reconstruction American fiction that we might call the racialized gothic," which she associates with authors such as Pauline Hopkins, Mark Twain, Kate Chopin, and Stephen Crane (2009, 119). Without focusing on the role of the forest specifically, Cooper calls attention to the "atmosphere of gloom and secrecy" that predominates in the latter half of the novel and that contributes its gothic qualities (131), an atmosphere which pivots on Chesnutt's increasing reliance upon the woods as a site of violence. Ultimately, just as Chesnutt struggles to settle on a genre for his story and to uphold a thematic structure centered on race, so does he seem to grapple with how to present the natural world—a problem that finds resolution in the supernatural elements of his conjure stories and that coalesces in a clear denunciation of practices like large-scale agriculture and timber production that both harm the natural world and uphold economic systems based on the subjugation of the African American population.

Certainly, it is not my goal to cast Chesnutt's novel as overtly environmentalist in its agenda or to attach such motives to his more well-known Uncle Julius tales. Although the novel's initial focus on race gets buried in plot twists, Chesnutt's primary purpose with *Mandy Oxendine* remains to expose his mostly white audience to the particular hardships of America's mixed-race population at the end of the nineteenth century, including the polarizing effects of prejudice. As William Andrews observes, the book's conclusion "urges understanding, tolerance, and sympathy toward mulattoes like Mandy, whether they seek happiness on the black or white side of the color line" (1980, 147). Despite its prominent focus on race relations, however, *Mandy Oxendine* warrants ecocritical analysis, as do the Uncle Julius tales, because "ecocriticism's attention to place reflects its recognition of the interconnectedness between human life/history and physical environments to which works of imagination (in all media, including literature) bear witness" (Buell, Heise, and Thornber 2011, 420). By examining the geography of Chesnutt's setting and his fluctuating depictions of nature, we begin to see him establish a connection between the piney woods and the people who populate them, at times and to varying degrees promoting greater consideration of both.

With origins in the study of setting (making regional writing, like Chesnutt's, ripe for analysis), ecocriticism has morphed well beyond its original focus on literary renditions of the natural world that suggest the value of place attachment and promote individual contact with nature (Buell, Heise, and Thornber 2011, 419). Although it is my goal to examine Chesnutt's regional novel within this setting-based tradition of ecocentric study, I seek also to advance ecocriticism's continued ideological expansion by embracing the movement's evolution beyond an initial focus on the Anglo-American imagination, and also by promoting ecofeminism's acknowledgement of the connection between the domination of nature and the subjugation of disenfranchised people. In this case, that includes the no-nonsense heroine Mandy, as well as the mixed-race population of North Carolina in which Chesnutt was so invested.[4] Although Chesnutt clearly calls attention to the social confines plaguing light-complexioned mulattoes in this work, a cautionary message about the state of the forest that is the center of economic opportunity in the region underlies what finally spirals into a tale of intrigue.

Mandy Oxendine is the story of two young light-complexioned North Carolina lovers who seek to enrich their lives through drastically contrasting means. Tom Lowrey leaves Mandy Oxendine and their secluded community behind to get an education in the North and become a teacher for African American children. During his two-year absence, Mandy concludes that she has been forgotten by Lowrey and also decides to leave home, but she makes the bold choice to live as a white woman when she settles down again seventy-five miles away. Lowrey tracks down Mandy near Sandy Run, a small town on the outskirts of fictional Rosinville, North Carolina, and secures a teaching job there. He must keep his distance from his beloved, however, as she is not only passing, but also being courted by a dodgy member of the decaying local white aristocracy. The drama that ensues highlights the vexing social position of light-complexioned, mixed-raced Americans in the postbellum South and calls attention to the extent to which race is socially constructed and, in some cases, an enactment.

Chesnutt is often characterized as a regionalist, and his first novel reflects key components of this late-century movement, despite other prominent literary influences, such as popular race and crime fiction.[5] The dialect, for example, is distinctly regional, particularly when Chesnutt gives voice to the many folk characters who populate the novel, characters whose voices help emphasize Lowrey's outsider position because of his education and more Anglicized speech. Chesnutt also takes pains to describe community customs accurately, such as the religious, educational, and vocational activities of the region, as well as the people of this community. In particular, he aspires to and achieves roundness in his portrayal of Mandy. Moreover, Chesnutt's keen attention to depicting his North Carolina setting accurately also points to the influence of regionalism on the novel, and this setting is central to the story's thematic development. The opening pages of *Mandy Oxendine* are rife with the sort of topological details that characterize the movement, which was in its heyday during the formative years of Chesnutt's literary career.

These physical features of the landscape take shape primarily through the eyes and reportage of the novel's third-person narrator, a figure who is like Tom Lowrey in many ways, particularly his carefully practiced speech, but who ultimately presents a worldview that is different from that of its two main characters. While Tom and Mandy struggle to navigate socially constructed categories of identity in various ways, the narrator refuses to sanction one strategy over another, concluding only that, whatever lifestyle they choose, "[t]hey deserved to be happy" (112). Moreover, the three primary figures—the narrator, Mandy, and Lowrey—are each clearly representative of how various genres compete in the book. For example, Chesnutt's narrator brings standard elements of regional fiction to the story by carefully recording the details of the North Carolina setting and by adopting a sympathetic stance toward his two main characters. Mandy fulfills (and then upsets) the role of the tragic mulatta, which is typical of race fiction. And Lowrey, whose character development is somewhat tenuous compared to Mandy's, becomes the central figure in the novel's similarly flimsy mystery plot. In addition, each of these figures also has a distinct relationship to the forest, which helps account for its evolving role as the story line progresses.

The first pages of *Mandy Oxendine* privilege the views of the narrator and suggest his awareness of and relationship to his surroundings, which constitute a fictionalized version of Cumberland County, a place where Chesnutt, himself a light-skinned son of free-born North Carolinians, lived as a child and later taught at various country schools. In the novel's opening scenes, the narrator painstakingly describes the ubiquitous trees of the terrain as he details Tom Lowrey's buggy ride from the Rosinville train depot to Sandy Run, the small community in which his school is located. It is in this passage that the reader also first senses Chesnutt's interest in the well-being of the natural environment. Chesnutt writes:

> Pines, pines, pines, covered the low, rolling hills and lined the roadside—long-leaved pines, scarred with turpentine boxes; short-leaved pines of later growth, fit for nothing but a poor quality of cord-wood. A scrubby blackjack undergrowth filled the space between the pines, except where it had been cleared away for easier access to turpentine boxes. The air was rich and heavy with the odor of the pines, and murmurous with their gentle swaying, and at times the cart moved noiselessly over a carpet of brown spikelets and fallen cones. In the hollows only, along the branches, the water-oak, small of leaf and dense of foliage, the honeysuckle, the fragrant bay-tree, the cypress—children of moisture—disputed place with one another in tangled profusion. (6)

This passage demonstrates Chesnutt's familiarity with the specific plant species in the forests of his setting, as well as his compulsion to describe carefully the state of the forest through the eyes of his narrator. In addition, it suggests Chesnutt's awareness of and interest in the appearance and health of the forest. The narrator's observation that man has "scarred" the trees with the addition of turpentine boxes suggests human culpability, and when he anthropomorphizes certain species as "children of moisture," he suggests their vulnerability at the hands of humans and their need to be protected. Chesnutt proceeds in a more directly critical vein as he goes on to write that an "unenlightened observer would think that so useful a friend as the pine would be treated kindly," and reveals that the "natives" nevertheless send their "women and children" out in to the forest regularly to cut saplings (6). By the end of Lowrey's buggy ride, the reader has a keen sense of the setting's plant species, as well as Chesnutt's concerns about the forest.

Chesnutt's warnings about the piney woods seem to have been warranted when one considers the dynamic environmental history of the region. According to Albert Cowdrey, "In many ways southern forests formed the centerpiece of the region's environmental history during the Gilded Age. From reservation to exploitation to the beginnings of scientific forestry in the United States, the woodlands exhibited the upheavals of a tumultuous time" (1996, 111). North Carolina had long been a center for the naval-stores industry, its longleaf pines a valuable commodity for the state during the first half of the nineteenth century. The production of turpentine and rosin added to their value and contributed to their widespread destruction due to harmful extraction tactics (Cowdrey 1996, 90). After the Civil War, northern investment and increased lumber production grew in the South, bringing much-needed income to the depressed region. However, even while the South's forests were being plundered, so were conservationist impulses burgeoning in the North, which would eventually trickle down to the region (119). By noting the precarious state of the pine forest in *Mandy Oxendine,* Chesnutt highlights a growing awareness among Americans at the end of the century that natural resources were limited and that conservation efforts were in the best economic interests of the public. This careful attention to his natural surroundings clashes somewhat with Mandy's and Lowrey's attitudes, however, and therefore helps Chesnutt establish a narrative voice that is distinct from those of his two main characters.

In addition to helping distinguish the book as regionalist—at least at its roots—the finely wrought geography of Chesnutt's setting, revealed through the eyes of his narrator, is important to the overall thematic structure of the novel, which pivots on the young couple's liminal societal position as African Americans who might choose to live as white residents. As Ryan Simmons observes, most of the book's chapters end in the "piney woods that separate the black and white communities of the town," which is "highly suggestive of Chesnutt's interest in the inarticulate, indeterminate borderlands between two cultures" (2006, 60). Furthermore, the piney woods are disrupted by another constant in the landscape of *Mandy Oxendine*: the Lumberton Plankroad, a "narrow road running as it did through unbroken forest" (47), which might be read as a physical manifestation of the color line. Cutting a swath through the forests of Lafayatte County, the road runs north past the small community of Sandy Run through the pine forest.

Although all residents, regardless of race and class, frequent the Lumberton road, it is also a place where social conventions are held to strict standards. For example, while Mandy can flirt with her white suitor Robert Utley along the road, she cannot allow herself to be seen conversing with Lowrey there. After a tense initial encounter, when Mandy and Lowrey talk in the novel, they do so primarily along the Sandy Run road, a "quiet path" that diverges from the Lumberton road and along which they believe they will remain unseen (42). Taken together, the pine forest and the Lumberton Plankroad serve as a buffer and a divider between the black and white communities, the division of which, Matthew Wilson notes, constitutes "a system of almost complete apartheid" in the novel (2004, 53). Thus, the forest is essential to the scaffolding of the story, in addition to the rural economy of the area. It is the lifeblood of this diverse rural community and is therefore a source of admiration for the narrator, who also notes its aesthetic value. Indeed, unlike Mandy and Lowrey, both of whom spend ample time within the piney woods, only the narrator is attuned to the "resinous quality of the air mingled with the perfume of the honeysuckle and the smell of running water" (8).

This type of celebratory approach toward the natural world was nothing new at the time and reflects the general public's increasingly nostalgic attitude toward the notions of wilderness and untouched nature around the turn of the century. Chesnutt builds on these descriptions in an unexpected manner, however, when he associates qualities of this Edenic natural realm with his heroine. The narrator goes so far as to attribute the most significant aspects of Mandy's demeanor to her time in the forest: "To the beauty nature had given Mandy, the companionship of the somber pines had imparted a tinge of sadness; the calm and solitude of country life had superintended repose" (27). She dwells within the woods, and they, in turn, are reflected in her unique personality. Even in her rare moments of happiness, Mandy's emotions are carefully interwoven with nature. While working in her garden one morning, she feels as though "[h]er spirit had caught something of the freshness and beauty of the morning" (65). She belts out a joyful song, and a mocking-bird picks up and repeats the "closing strain" (66). In accordance with this idyllic image, a stranger refers to Mandy as a "woodland nymph" when recalling a sudden encounter with her along the road (62), and although it's a flitting reference, it helps bring to full con-ceptualization the symbolic link between Mandy and nature established by the narrator. As Judith Fetterly and Marjorie Pryse point out, "Regionalist narrators use their location inside the region to advocate for an empathetic stance toward their subjects" (2003, 144). Chesnutt's careful linking of place and person—of the piney woods and Mandy—helps to promote an empathetic stance toward both.

Chesnutt continues to build on this connection between Mandy and the forest when he describes her racial makeup, which is, of course, central to the plot, for Mandy is one of those people for whom "[t]here was no external evidence of negro blood" (27). Her familial history, like that of the forest, is established as significant in the formation of her personality. In his article "The Free Colored People of North Carolina" (1902), Chesnutt seeks to dispel the notion that "the entire colored race was set free as a result of the Civil War" and calls attention to the 30,463 "free colored people" who lived in North Carolina in 1860, before the Civil War (205–06). In the novel, Mandy and Lowrey are said to have descended from this historically free population. In the same article, Chesnutt also high-lights the influence of Native American cultures, particularly the Cherokee and Tuscarora, in the racial makeup of this population. According to the legal doctrine of *partus sequitur ventrem,* he notes that "the child of a free mother was always free, no matter what its color or the status of its father, and many free colored people were of female Indian ancestry" (208). While describing Mandy, Chesnutt's narrator reveals that "the blood of three races commingled had resulted in a complexity of temperament very uncommon in sand-hill people of North Carolina" (27–28). Because of the historical and mythological—and albeit at times misleading—association between Native Americans and nature, Chesnutt also may be helping to account for and strengthening Mandy's symbolic ties to the forest by emphasizing her Native American blood.[6]

Mandy ruptures this association by violently denouncing the forest to which she is so clearly associated, however. Certainly, the narrator's characterization of Mandy as a "beautiful forest creature of great repose" hardly meshes with her language, attitude, and behaviors. She is a matter-of-fact young woman, an ambitious pragmatist who does not mince words and who privileges social advancement over love. Unlike the narrator, who celebrates the forest as both an aesthetic treasure and an economic resource worthy of careful consideration, Mandy views it more simply: as emblematic of the past from which she seeks escape. "[Y]ou lef' me in the woods, 'mongs' niggers, and tu'pentine trees, an' snakes an' screech-owls," she tells Lowrey, when he first appears in Sandy Run (22). "You lef' me 'mongs' niggers, an' I wouldn' be a nigger, fer God made me white [...] an' I *am* white" (23). In distancing herself from her African American heritage, she also rejects the backwoods setting of her former home, as well as the natural elements within, thereby animalizing the mixed-race members of her former community. Mandy's quickness to denounce her heritage, her unabashed racism, and the lack of guilt she feels for passing as white constitute some of this story's more radical elements.

If Chesnutt had hoped to make a name for himself as a serious writer of race fiction with this novel, then Mandy's boldness is likely what prevented him from achieving such renown. Hackenberry points out in his introduction to the novel that Chesnutt "wanted to write popular race fiction, a field dominated by white writers.[...]He also wanted to write fiction that presented nonwhites honestly—and thus change the racial attitudes of whites—but it was just as important that he earn a comfortable living from the sale of his books" (1997, xxi). In his journal, Chesnutt directly acknowledges his desire to surpass in quality the writing of Harriet Beecher Stowe and Albion Tourgée, both of whom were known for popular race fiction (Brodhead 1993, 125). Chesnutt argues that because he is a "colored man" with more extensive knowledge of the South and an intimate familiarity with the African American population, "their habits, their ruling passions, their prejudices," in addition to his insight into the "modes of thinking" of "the better class of white men," he is logically the more suitable author of such fiction. "[W]hy could not such a man, if he possessed the same ability, write a far better book about the South than Judge Tourgée or Mrs. Stowe has written?" Chesnutt posits (Brodhead 1993, 125).

Mandy's challenge to the southern caste system reinforces the influence of popular race fiction on the novel, yet Mandy simply does not fit the mold of what was expected of black characters by a mostly white readership. With this book, Chesnutt "tries to uncouple the adjective and noun, 'tragic' and 'mulatta,' which heretofore had been powerfully linked in the American literary imagination" (McWilliams 2002, 130), similar to attempts by earlier writers, including William Wells Brown with *Clotel* (1853), to fracture this association. And for all of its plot shortcomings, Chesnutt's novel achieves this rather progressive goal. Mandy is stereotypically beautiful and recalls Roxy of Twain's *Pudd'nhead Wilson* (1894) in her fairness and statuesque appearance. As a result, she also attracts the attention of numerous male characters, and she is repeatedly a potential target of sexual violence, which suggests the influence of the stereotypical figure of the "female light-skinned slave," whose "sexual vulnerability [...] is essential to propel the plot forward and to generate the reader's sympathy and outrage" (Raimon 2004, 5). Nevertheless, Mandy is hardly "tragic" in the full sense of the stock figure, as she is not agonized by her decision to pass as white or traumatized because of her liminal societal position. Although Mandy isn't exactly likeable—largely because of her quickness to find a white replacement for Lowrey and her initial rejection of Lowrey's affections when he returns—she is an admirable figure because of her fierce determination and sustained strength in the face of danger. Thus, Chesnutt both draws upon and manipulates the tragic mulatta trope by not punishing Mandy for denouncing her imperceptible African American blood or for attempting to ascend socially by passing. The book's attention to the difficulties associated with social advancement for determined mixed-raced people like Mandy and Lowrey endows it with elements of social commentary that are characteristic of race fiction, but Mandy's lack of torturous guilt about aspiring to miscegenation contrasts with the attitudes of similar characters—including Chesnutt's own Rena Walden, the protagonist of *The House Behind the Cedars* (1900), Chesnutt's first published novel, which also features a light-complexioned young woman who attempts to pass as white, though with decidedly more tragic consequences. Though to a lesser extent than in *Mandy Oxendine,* the geography of this book's setting contributes to Chesnutt's indictment of a southern society that upholds a caste system based on racial ancestry and helps demonstrate the imaginative link between geography and race throughout his work.

Indeed, in *The House Behind the Cedars,* setting is also important to the thematic structure of the book, the cedars of the title taking on symbolic significance in their capacity to act as a shield from an outside world in which racial tensions run high and a white appearance does not negate prejudice. The house where Rena Walden lives with her aging mother sits "on a corner, around which the cedar hedge turned, continuing along the side of the garden until it reached the line of the front of the house" (Chesnutt 1900, 275). It is located in a "neglected" and "uninviting" (predominately black) area of Patesville, North Carolina, yet it is an oasis of lush gardens and happy childhood memories, and, at one point in the novel, the site of an extravagant party open only to the community's lightest-skinned members. However, when Rena leaves this sanctuary for South Carolina, where she for a time joins her older brother John "Warwick" in passing for white, she suffers dire consequences, including the heartbreaking scorn of her wealthy white suitor when he discovers her secret. Ultimately, like in *Mandy Oxendine,* trees in this novel form a symbolic barrier, separating the light-skinned inhabitants from their darker neighbors and shielding Rena, a truly tragic mulatta, from the pain associated with the possibilities of passing and miscegenation. In *Mandy Oxendine,* however, the pines, which initially form a similar sort of buffer between white and black communities, eventually lose such significance, fading into the background as the novel evolves into a "whodunit" when somebody kills Mandy's white suitor as he attempts to assault her sexually in the forest.

Certainly, categorizing *Mandy Oxendine* becomes altogether impossible when Chesnutt adds a mysterious twist to an already-complex novel featuring elements of regionalism and race fiction. According to Hackenberry (1997), "His introduction of a popularizing device, the mystery form, two-thirds of the way into *Mandy Oxendine* dilutes its themes of injustice and thwarted opportunity" (xix). The device also contributes to the forest's transformation, as it becomes more thoroughly symbolically linked to the emotions driving the novel's violence. In the latter half of the book, Mandy confronts Utley about being engaged to his wealthy cousin and breaks off their liaison with the succinct explanation: "Yo'r road don't lay the same as mine" (72)—a statement that emphasizes the significance of the setting to the question of what constitutes socially sanctioned behaviors between people of not only different races but also different classes, as Mandy is passing for a poor white. Utley grows frustrated during continued attempts to seduce Mandy and finally "trie[s] to draw her deeper into the wood" (73) to assault her. Mandy struggles against him and is saved when "a dark form burst[s] from the woods" and tackles Utley (73). The next day, Utley's body is found "cold and stiff [...] in the shadow of the pines through whose branches like mourning plumes the wind soughed with a dirge-like undertone" (77).

At this point, the identity of the murderer becomes the central focus of a plot that initially revolved around the stifling impact of race relations on Mandy and Lowrey. Even Mandy does not know the identity of the man who had "vanished into the forest as quickly as he had come" (82), though she suspects it was Lowrey, a belief that reignites her love for him. He is the reader's prime suspect as well. First, Mandy is arrested and jailed for the crime, then Lowrey confesses and takes her place in jail and is nearly lynched for killing Utley, and finally the true murderer steps forth—Elder Gadson, an itinerant white preacher with a fanatical attraction to Mandy. As this murder-mystery plot races toward its climax, the forest takes on a foreboding ambiance that clashes with its earlier depictions established by the narrator. Even residents on their way to a nighttime church service project "weird shadowy shapes in the moonlight" (47), heightening the symbolic link between the forest and people's deepest secrets and desires.

Chesnutt's narrator strives to establish symbolic ties between the forest and the book's beautiful but threatened heroine, and Mandy severs such ties through her fierce denunciation of the natural world. Lowrey, however, clearly fulfills the role of symbolic representative of the forest as a liminal space between two worlds divided by a color line. White in appearance but unwilling to denounce his black heritage, Lowrey approaches the difficulties associated with being "so near the line" with a mild temperament. There is "something repugnant to him in the idea of concealment," and he refuses to feel "any special sense of shame or humiliation" on account of his "drop of dark blood" (46). His even-keeled depiction detracts from his interest as a character, however, and he seems to possess but a glimmer of Mandy's uniqueness and resolve. Fittingly, he is often seen in states of listless contemplation, traipsing through the piney woods, such as when he overhears a group of men who are idling on the jail's porch, joking about possibly assaulting their beautiful prisoner, and afterward "in the woods around it [Lowrey] wander[s] until late in the afternoon, a prey to the frightful visions conjured up by the coarse and heartless merriment of the group" (94). Unable to act on his anger, he retreats to the shadows of the woods that serve as a borderland between the culture with which he identifies and the culture coveted by his beloved.

Of course, this same forest is a place where many nightmares unfold before the novel's hasty denouement. Ultimately, all key (and notably violent) events in this story occur under the cover of the forest, heightening the tension between Chesnutt's gothic symbolism and rather forward-thinking concerns about the health of the piney woods. The piney woods are the site of not only Utley's death, for example, but also that of a young black student, Rose Amelia, who is so distraught by the thought of her beloved teacher being hanged that she runs madly through the forest until she dies face down in a swamp, either from exhaustion, from suicide, or from one of the fits to which she was prone. It is also the place where white townsmen bring Lowrey for a "necktie party" (103) in his honor, a scene that once again suggests the influence of race fiction upon the novel as well as Chesnutt's desire to shatter literary molds. Chesnutt depicts a raucous mob of men whose racist vitriol works them into a violent frenzy and leads them to put a noose around Lowrey's neck during what might be accurately described as a hate-fueled spectacle. Nevertheless, Lowrey, in both looks and behavior, contradicts the "hypersexualized and criminalized," "black as beast" metaphor that is typical of the "frightening drama of lynching" in literature (Gunning 1996, 3–4). Correspondingly, and just in the nick of time, the obsessive white preacher Elder Gadson, who has been called upon by the mob to offer a prayer before Lowrey dies, confesses to the crime. The lynching is called off by the men, one of whom pacifies his bloodthirsty companions by noting that Lowrey is, after all, a "pretty white nigger" (110). The next afternoon—out of the forest and in the light of day—the three confessors are brought before the town magistrate to tell their stories, including the truth about Mandy's racial heritage, which further decriminalizes Lowrey.

Without a doubt, the many competing literary influences that shape the plot detract from any continuity of environmental themes established early in the novel. And the ending's ambiguity regarding what the future will bring its two main characters—whether

Mandy and Lowrey will move to the North and embrace their African American heritage or go elsewhere and enter the "great white world" (112)—further obscures any message about what Chesnutt believed to be the best mode of social and professional advancement for people straddling the color line. Chesnutt promotes and intertwines themes of racial equality and environmental stewardship much more successfully in *The Conjure Woman*, however. Indeed, *Mandy Oxendine* reflects an environmental ethos in its nascent state that reaches much fuller development in his short story collection *The Conjure Woman* which has received some ecocritical attention because of its more consistent synthesis of humanitarian and environmentalist impulses. This ethos is different from that of some contemporary southern regionalists who romanticized their natural surroundings in large part because of their justified anxiety about the alterations and devastation industry would bring to the region after the Civil War. Indeed, Chesnutt's burgeoning environmentalism is rooted in folkloric traditions that conflate marginalized people and elements of nature and, in doing so, promote greater empathy for and protection of both. Conjure, or hoo-doo, combines elements of Caribbean and African spiritual practices with Christian ideas, and practitioners were believed to be able to access the powers of nature directly.

The presence of the conjurer in these stories and the absence of such a figure in *Mandy Oxendine* help account for *The Conjure Woman*'s more clearly and thoroughly established portrait of Chesnutt's environmental ethos. Aunt Peggy is one such fictional practitioner brought to life in Chesnutt's works by the former slave Uncle Julius, a storyteller who, as Lee Rozelle notes, "weaves human and ecological liberation together in his tales" (2006, 25). The physical well-being of Henry, from Chesnutt's frequently anthologized story "The Goophered Grapevine," for example, is directly linked to the health and growing cycle of a plantation's scuppernong crops when he consumes grapes that have been "goophered,—cunju'd, bewitch'" by Aunt Peggy and then drinks an elixir meant to counteract the gopher (6). Additionally, "Po' Sandy," the titular figure of another conjure tale, chooses to be transformed into a tree rather than be lent out by his master again and separated from his beloved wife Tenie, another conjurer. In a rather gruesome turn, Sandy (in tree form) is taken to the saw mill where he is chopped up, "sweekin', en moanin', en groanin'" all the while as Tenie looks on in horror (21). Whereas in *Mandy Oxendine* the community members enact cruelties against each other within the shadows of the forest, in "Po' Sandy" the mill workers enact physical violence against a person *and* the forest simultaneously, fracturing the symbolic connection between the two and establishing a more literal oneness. Both of these stories, by virtue of a conjure that fuses plant and human, challenge the commodification of people by linking the act to cash-crop agriculture or to the commodification of the forest—both of which had devastating environmental effects on the area in the latter half of the century.

Although Chesnutt may, on the surface, seem to be perpetuating a dangerous stereotype of the nonwhite as somehow closer to nature (as he in fact seems to do by linking the part–Native American character Mandy to the forest), a close examination of the conjure stories reveals this to be an oversimplification of his objective. By making southern slaves a part of the landscape that is being exploited, Chesnutt also asserts their natural right to exist in such a space. "Taken together," Jeffrey Myers explains, "the tales imply a necessity to recognize African American culture as intrinsic to the landscape that southern blacks inhabit, similar to the indigenous Native American cultures"; this is an "ecocentric way of viewing the self in the landscape that does not require mastery over nature or other people" (2003, 7). What Chesnutt exhibits in his beloved conjure stories, then, is decid-edly more complex than landscape nostalgia, as he seems to be asserting that the health of the natural world is inherently linked (or, in his tales, magically linked) to the well-being of its inhabitants. This interconnectedness between humans and nonhuman nature re-mains central to many forms of environmentalism today, as well as to our understanding of ecology. Ultimately, the folkloric magic that infuses his works allows him to conflate the human and nonhuman in a way that sets him apart from other regionalists who also sought to preserve, in writing, a natural world being threatened by industrial advances.

Chesnutt links his heroine Mandy Oxendine to the piney woods in a similar fash-ion, though it is one that is devoid of magic. This carefully established connection be-tween person and place points to Chesnutt's recognition of the problems associated with capitalist systems that perpetuate the subjugation of racial minorities, as well as the envi-ronmental effects of unchecked postbellum deforestation. Moreover, acknowledging this conceptual relationship between character and setting encourages readers to reconsider intersections between questions of race, regionalism, and the environment in turn-of-the-century fiction. At the end of the novel, when Mandy's racial heritage is revealed, she and Lowrey reunite and return to their "former home" (112), the backwoods community that she had so vehemently forsaken, to be married. In returning to Lowrey and to her rural homeland, she also apparently sheds her animosity for her African American heritage. This acquiescence fittingly corresponds with the resolution of the novel's mystery plot and the dissolution of the forest's symbolic association with human violence. Nevertheless, this resolution is tenuous at best, for what happens to Mandy and Lowrey *after* their marriage, which side of the color line they choose, remains a mystery, much to readers' dismay. Perhaps the only certainty is that this young couple faces an uncertain future—not at all unlike that of an American South on the cusp of great environmental and social change.

Notes

1. It is unclear exactly when *Mandy Oxendine* was completed, but Charles Hackenberry has concluded that Chesnutt likely finished the novel in late 1896 or early 1897 and suggested that the book may have been started as early as 1889 (1997, xv). The edition edited by Hackenberry is the first publication of the novel.

2. See "Other Nature: Resistance to Ecological Hegemony in Charles W. Chesnutt's *The Conjure Woman*" by Jeffrey Myers (2003) and Chapter 2 of *Ecosublime: Environmental Awe and Terror from New World to Oddworld* by Lee Rozelle (2006).

3. According to Ryan Simmons, for example, its rejection by publishers and the lack of evidence suggesting that Chesnutt attempted to publish the novel elsewhere are "not entirely surprising, since *Mandy Oxendine* comes across as an uncontrolled mess of a book" (2006, 58). Simmons goes on to suggest, however, that Chesnutt's "haphazard attempts to control readers' hearts and heads" may be symptomatic of a "sophisti-cated attempt" to work through difficult themes, rather than "immature development as an artist" (58). Other scholars have been more directly critical of Chesnutt's first novel. Charles Hackenberry calls atten-tion to the ways in which its "shift of focus, from a story of character and theme to a story of plot, strains the work" and "dilutes" more serious themes as it morphs into a mystery (1997, xix). Matthew Wilson also comments on the novel's "bifurcated" plot and considers the work to be a "test run" for Chesnutt's later race fictions (2004, 46). William Andrews argues that the book "lacks narrative density and sufficiently developed characters, plots, and themes" but concludes that the work was essential in the development of *The House Behind the Cedars* (1980, 146).

4. The events of *Mandy Oxendine* take place near the fictional city of Rosinville, North Carolina, which is likely based on Fayetteville, where Chesnutt's parents lived until 1856 and to which the family returned in 1866. His novel *The House Behind the Cedars* (1900) is set largely in Patesville, which also was modeled

on Fayetteville. Additionally, the Patesville area is the setting for the former plantation where Uncle Julius McAdoo lives in *The Conjure Woman* (1899). In *The Colonel's Dream* (1905), the central North Carolina city in which most of the novel is set is called Clarendon and is also presumably based on Fayetteville.

5. I employ Judith Fetterly and Marjorie Pryse's definition of regionalism not as a synonym for "local color" or as a subset of realism, but rather as one that "locates regionalism alongside realism and naturalism as a parallel tradition of narrative prose written roughly in the second half of the nineteenth century and at the turn into the twentieth" (2003, 4).
6. For a thorough examination of this phenomenon, see Shepard Krech's *The Ecological Indian: Myth and History* (2000).

Works Cited

Andrews, William. 1980. *The Literary Career of Charles W. Chesnutt*. Baton Rouge: Louisiana State University. Press.

Buell, Lawrence, Ursula Heise, and Karen Thornber. 2011. "Literature and Environment." *Annual Review of Environment and Resources* 36:417–40.

Chesnutt, Charles W., 1993. *The Journals of Charles W. Chesnutt,* edited by Richard Brodhead. Durham: Duke University Press.

——. 1997. *Mandy Oxendine: A Novel.* Edited by Charles Hackenberry. Urbana: University of Illinois Press.

——. 2012. "The Free Colored People of North Carolina." In *The Conjure Stories*, edited by Robert B. Stepto and Jennifer Rae Greeson, 205–211. New York: Norton.

——. 2012. "The Goophered Grapevine." In *The Conjure Stories,* edited by Robert B. Stepto and Jennifer Rae Greeson, 3–14. New York: Norton.

——. 2002. *The House Behind the Cedars.* In *Charles W. Chesnutt: Stories, Novels, & Essays*, 267–61. New York: Library of America.

——. 2012. "Po' Sandy." In *The Conjure Stories,* edited by Robert B. Stepto and Jennifer Rae Greeson, 14–22. New York: Norton.

Cooper, Joanna Penn. 2009. "Gothic Signifying in Charles Chesnutt's *Mandy Oxendine*." *MELUS* 34 (4):119–44.

Cowdrey, Albert E. 1996. *This Land, This South: An Environmental History.* Lexington: University Press of Kentucky.

Fetterly, Judith, and Marjorie Pryse. 2003. *Writing Out of Place: Regionalism, Women and American Literary Culture.* Champaign: University of Illinois Press.

Gunning, Sandra. 1996. *Race, Rape, and Lynching: The Red Record of American Literature, 1890–1912.* New York: Oxford University Press.

Hackenberry, Charles. 1997. "Introduction," in *Mandy Oxendine: A Novel,* by Charles Chesnutt, xi–xxviii. Urbana: University of Illinois Press

Krech, Shepard. 2000. *The Ecological Indian: Myth and History.* New York: Norton.

McWilliams, Dean. 2002. *Charles W. Chesnutt and the Fictions of Race.* Athens: University of Georgia Press.

Myers, Jeffrey. 2003. "Other Nature: Resistance to Ecological Hegemony in Charles W. Chesnutt's *The Conjure Woman.*" *African American Review* 37 (1) 5–19.

Nash, Roderick Frazier. 2001. *Wilderness and the American Mind.* 4th ed. New Haven: Yale University Press.

Raimon, Eve Allegra. 2004. *The "Tragic Mulatta" Revisited: Race and Nationalism in Nineteenth-Century Antislavery Fiction.* New Brunswick: Rutgers University. Press.

Rozelle, Lee. 2006. *Ecosublime: Environmental Awe and Terror from New World to Oddworld.* Tuscaloosa: University of Alabama Press.

Simmons, Ryan. 2006. *Chesnutt and Realism: A Study of the Novels.* Tuscaloosa: University of Alabama Press.

Wilson, Matthew. 2004. *Whiteness in the Novels of Charles W. Chesnutt.* Jackson: University Press of Mississippi.

E S S A Y

Recasting the Southern Turn: Alice Walker's *The Third Life of Grange Copeland*

by Shaila Mehra

After nearly a full century of literature dominated by themes of Northern migration and urban life, the phenomenon of the decisive black literary turn South since the late 1960s demands further analysis. Marked primarily by the work of women writers, the southern turn emphasizes a folk aesthetic based in oral traditions, black folk culture, and representations of organic racial community. The return to tropes and forms identified as premodern or preliterate signals an exhaustion with the failed promises of modernity. Literacy, migration, and uplift, heralded in the twentieth century as pathways to full participation in American civic life, did not succeed in producing full enfranchisement for all African Americans. Indeed, the retrenchment of racial inequality in the wake of the civil rights movement—a retrenchment marked by increased segregation in cities, impediments to school desegregation, the loss of jobs and the growth in income inequality, and the rise of the contemporary prison-industrial complex—illustrates a bitter end to the political project of modernity for African Americans. The literary turn to the South should thus be considered a tendency within black postmodern cultural politics to address the failures of modern life through representations of a space and time not tethered to modern values.

However, the turn to the South itself is hardly this clear-cut. In the work of Alice Walker, we see evidence of the complexity of this development in post-1960s African American literature. Born to rural Georgia sharecroppers and educated at Spelman, Sarah Lawrence, and on the battlefield of the civil rights movement in Mississippi, Walker is, without question, the catalyst enabling writers and scholars to reconsider making the South a site of creative and critical inquiry. Yet, as Thadious Davis has recently noted, Walker herself has not been at the center of the latest investigations into the postmodern turn south in African American art and literature. Davis attributes this to Walker's "naturalizing how so many scholars and artists approach the South today, and with that naturalizing a concomitant erasing of her very positionality in the process" (2011, 335). Recentering Alice Walker in and against recent critical understandings of the literary turn to the South demonstrates the complexity of her efforts to reimagine the region after the civil rights movement.

In innumerable ways, Walker made it possible for subsequent writers to embrace the South as a setting for their work. The contemporary canonization of Zora Neale Hurston's writings began as a result of Walker's tireless efforts to solve the mystery of Hurston's later years, mark her burial spot, and bring her work to African American and female readers. Locating the historical forces that denied black women "a room of their own," Walker's pivotal essay "In Search of Our Mothers' Gardens" (1974) traces how the richness of black women's creative endeavors imprinted themselves in everyday practices of cooking, quilting, and gardening. Through this essay, she trained a generation of artists and critics to see black female artistry beyond the boundaries of institutionalized art practices. Several of her novels are set in the rural South, including her most famous novel *The Color Purple* (1982). And through her nonfiction essays such as "The Black Writer and the Southern Experience" (1970) and "Coretta King: Revisited" (1971), she embarked on a full-scale effort to regenerate the possibilities of the South for African American writers. Today, scholars recognize all of these aspects of Alice Walker's work—making Hurston central to a reconstruction of black women's literary lineage, celebrating folk tradition and quotidian practices, and producing the South as a historically rich ground of African American literature—as essential factors in the Southern turn in postmodern African American writing.

Yet many of these same scholars find the move back to the rural South troubling. The decision of African American writers to set their work in small, isolated, racially homogeneous regions of the South marks an impulse to retreat from or displace postmodern crises of urban community onto imagined sites of harmony and collectivity. The South becomes the site where racial particularity and unique traditions are preserved, thus evading any risk of their dilution in an integrated space. The southern turn therefore produces a renewed pastoralism that places a discursively constructed South outside of history and of historical change; frozen in time, it remains immune to the transformations, as well as to the conflicts and crises, of modernity, making the South well-suited to protect cultural traditions from its incursions. In addition, the region is historically, for African Americans, a site of material hardship; however, the southern turn posits this hardship as the impetus for a distinct culture and opposition to the forces of modernity, integration, and universalism. For these reasons, many critics see the southern turn as a conservative gesture, one that generates a form of "segregation nostalgia" in which integration—a victory of twentieth-century black political organizing—is perceived as a detriment to black collectivity (Reed 1999, 129; Moses 2005).

The nostalgic gestures of the southern turn depend upon freezing the South in a state of premodern plenitude at the precise moment when it is undergoing massive modernization as economic growth leads to the wholesale redevelopment and expansion of cities.[1] However, the strength of the critiques leveled against this aesthetic move depends upon excluding or only narrowly considering those texts that do not conform to the premises of the argument. As a very early, even anticipatory, text in what would come to be known as the literary turn south, Walker's *The Third Life of Grange Copeland* (1970) resists, in important ways, much of the critique of subsequent southern literature by African American writers. By depicting family history as a mirror of national history, and by traversing the major historical shifts from sharecropping to migration to civil rights, the novel envisions a transforming South that is slowly being delinked from the legacy of slavery. In this transformation, Walker charts the new South as a region in which folk tradition and political modernization exist in dynamic and productive tension. As such, the novel places the pastoral ideal of the premodern South into tension with the material fact of historical change. The novel thus complicates and broadens the dominant critiques of the postmodern turn south. Rather than construct the rural South as an evasion of the transformations of modernity and postmodernity, *The Third Life of Grange Copeland* reveals how these transformations are changing the rural South itself.

The Southern Turn and Discourses of Crisis in Postmodernity

For critics of the literary turn south, the development of this turn is symptomatic of larger crises in postmodernity. As Madhu Dubey argues, if black modernist literature is characterized by a faith in the project of political modernity—including migration away from the South and its vestiges of slavery-based economy toward the industrial economy of cities—black postmodernist literature is characterized by skepticism about whether the project of political modernity has been both adequately realized and ultimately beneficial for African American people (2003, 2–5). Economic opportunity certainly did not reach African Americans equally. As blacks faced increased class stratification during and after the civil rights movement, along with a prominent national discourse on pathology fostered by the Moynihan Report, they confronted what came to be understood as a crisis of community. The supposedly natural intraracial links that could foster ongoing political organization around shared interests were beset by a series of economic and cultural forces that seemed to risk the coherence of black communality altogether. Black postmodern discourse is thus characterized by a concern for the fate of the notion of community. And, as a result, criticisms of the turn south in African American literature center on the discursive work these literary texts do to illustrate the crisis of community.

Hazel Carby and Madhu Dubey offer two of the most trenchant critiques of the southern turn in post–civil rights African American literature and culture. In "The Politics of Fiction, Anthropology, and the Folk," Carby identifies in the revival of Zora Neale Hurston in the late-twentieth century a move to "discursively displace" the problems of urban modernity onto an idealized, constructed literary South (1990, 76). She argues that, as Hurston preserves the folklore traditions of her native Eatonville in such texts as *Mules and Men,* she constructs "the folk" as an exclusively rural, southern population, juxtaposing this group against urban, northern and midwestern blacks (peasant and elite alike). In doing so, according to Carby, Hurston denies the scope and significance of the Great Migration's transformation of African Americans into a largely non-southern, urban population by reifying authentic black identity as rooted in rural, southern spaces and in oral traditions. Finally, Hurston displaces the attendant class antagonisms of the urban North onto a South represented as ultimately freed of those antagonisms and the disunities and tensions they foster. She thus demonstrates the contradictions embedded in the work of African American intellectuals as they try to represent "the folk."

In her recovery of Hurston's work in the 1970s, Alice Walker frames the characteristics of southern culture and community using the strategies that Carby critiques. Recounting an experience in which she shared *Mules and Men* with her relatives, she notes that as they were "reading the book themselves, listening to me read the book, listening to each other read the book…a kind of paradise was regained" (1983, 84). As the first- and second-generation descendants of the Great Migration, Walker's relatives find in Hurston—and, specifically, in reading Hurston *aloud*—a lifeline back to a seemingly lost southern heritage. In northern living rooms, they recreate an oral community associated with their roots in the rural South. Having disparaged what they did not forget of their heritage, these relatives come to affirm rural, southern, black folk tradition as their inheritance and indeed as a kind of "paradise… regained." Moreover, Walker writes that she sees in Hurston's work representations of "racial health; a sense of black people as complete, complex, *undiminished* human beings" (1983,

85). Hurston thus provides a direct and ringing refutation of discourses of pathology used to characterize black urban communities. In this anecdote, Walker seems to confirm the discursive construction of southern folk tradition as a site of plenitude, of authenticity, and of healing from the wounds of migration and displacement, and it is the act of oral transmission of folk tales that begins to bring these later generations of East Coast relatives back (at least imaginatively) to the South.

But for Carby, this construction of idealized community and shared heritage explicitly illustrates the twinned issues of uneven development and heightened visibility facing African Americans in postmodernity. As the justice system, the prison-industrial complex, and the disappearance of work function together to the extreme detriment of young African American men, prominent African American intellectuals must contend with the politics of representing the contemporary "folk," or the masses. Carby concludes: "The privileging of Hurston at a moment of intense urban crisis and conflict is, perhaps, a sign of [the] displacement [of contemporary conflict onto an idealized representation of the past]… Has *Their Eyes Were Watching God* become the most frequently taught black novel because it acts as a mode of assurance that, really, the black folk are happy and healthy?" (1990, 89–90). The inability to find ameliorative political solutions to the violence of systemic racial inequality in postmodernity leads, Carby suggests, to imaginative resolution through culture, and more specifically through the discursive production of a South outside of time, a location that provides authentic racial identity, folk tradition, and organic community as salves upon the wounds of postmodern urban crisis.

In a similar vein, Madhu Dubey argues that the literary-critical tendency to construct the South as a "pure elsewhere" to the urban North produces the region as a zone of resistance to the transformations of capital and sociality in postmodernity (2002, 368). Noting that the turn South in the 1970s coincides almost exactly with the reversal of the Great Migration beginning in the late 1960s, Dubey finds that, whereas Northern and Midwestern African Americans migrated largely to the burgeoning southern metropolitan areas, literary authors setting their work in the South—among them, Toni Morrison, Gloria Naylor, and Walker—choose to place their characters primarily in isolated rural regions marked equally by material deprivation and cultural richness.[2] The village of Shalimar in *Song of Solomon* and the island of Willow Springs in *Mama Day* are remote and racially homogeneous sites shaped less by political and social forces than by magical and supernatural ones. This aesthetic choice produces an extreme "discursive displacement" of urban crisis onto a location that appears to be its polar opposite geographically, temporally, and representationally. While Carby would argue that this displacement allows for an evasion of the seemingly intractable problems of urban crisis, Dubey nuances this view, noting that Morrison's and Naylor's southern folk aesthetic's emphasis on magic—conjuring, ghosts—betrays "the material impossibility of the literary escape it seeks" (2003, 145). In other words, the southern folk aesthetic that Dubey traces admits its fictionality through its very tropes, which are tropes of the unreal.

These criticisms of the southern turn identify the aesthetic's impetus to conservatism—literally to *conserve* an imagined past as a bulwark against the transformations of modernity and postmodernity. But the space of this conservative gesture—the rural South—is a site, historically, of deprivation and material lack for African Americans. Championing a space of inequality as a respite from the crises of the postmodern condition situates material lack as a ground for political opposition. Such championing is endemic to the postmodern cultural politics of difference, in which "the spaces that have been most conspicuously left behind by socioeconomic processes of modernization are widely construed as spaces of greatest cultural resistance to advanced capitalism" (Dubey 2003, 163). Such a politics renders racially othered groups and spaces as immune to or outside of the mediating forces of late capitalism. This "romance of the residual," as Dubey calls it, dangerously identifies oppositional politics with deprivation and thus requires ongoing deprivation to keep the oppositionality alive. It is a zero-sum form of political critique because any victory is fixed through loss, and material gains disqualify one from participation in the political sphere.[3]

While *The Third Life of Grange Copeland* ably represents the material deprivation of the rural South, it does so in order to contend with the fact of sweeping historical transformation. In other words, it does not steep itself in a "romance of the residual" so much as it depicts the rural South as residual in order to contrast emergent economic and political change within this very space. Moreover, through Grange's figurative three lives, Walker conceptualizes how individual actions contribute to such change. The novel seeks to present a method for engaging in political change from a place that can mobilize and transform, rather than conserve and romanticize, cultural traditions, and Walker's claim in the novel is that the rural South makes such engagement uniquely possible.

Theorizing Transformation in The Third Life of Grange Copeland

The Third Life of Grange Copeland is a novel about migration and return that considers the possibility of a utopian vision of sustainable life for blacks in the rural South. Over the course of the novel, the Copeland family's history represents the story of the American South in the twentieth century, beginning with slavery's descendent, sharecropping, and moving toward the civil rights movement and the possibility of full enfranchisement within American democracy. Utopian though it may be, Walker's South is not static. Rather, through the Copeland family, Walker represents the South as both the site and the enabler of intense historical change. If the major critique of the literary turn south is that it freezes the South in a past time in order to project onto it nostalgic visions of a simpler, organic racial community not readily attainable in the urban North, *The Third Life of Grange Copeland* provides ample challenge to this view.

Using Grange's life as the vehicle, the novel sweeps from the early twentieth century and a southern sharecropping economy barely removed from slavery, through the Great Migration to the industrialized urban northern metropolis, and back in a return migration to a rural South witnessing the growth of the civil rights movement.[4] In Grange's first life as a sharecropper in rural Georgia, he faces humiliating racist treatment, grinding poverty and hunger, and dehumanizing losses of dignity. Repeated humiliations lead him to become an alcoholic and to abuse his wife and children. At the end of his first life, he abandons his family to migrate north, and his thoroughly degraded wife kills herself and their youngest child, leaving Brownfield, their eldest son, an orphan. Grange's second life is spent in New York City, where dreams of financial opportunity in the industrial North give way to a reality of pimping and theft. As Grange is unable to gain economic footing and faces not only the ongoing control of whites over all means of production but also cold anonymity, he eventually acknowledges the untenability of life in the North. In

Grange's absence, Brownfield has replicated his father's life almost exactly—he works as a sharecropper, faces constant humiliation and mountains of debt, becomes an alcoholic, marries and ruins a respectable woman, abuses his children, and ultimately murders his wife, leaving his children orphaned. Upon learning of these events, Grange returns to Georgia, buys his own land, and assumes custody of his youngest granddaughter, Ruth. This third life synthesizes the experiences of his first two, in which disparate economic orders and geographical locations differentially shape Grange's character and worldview, preparing him for the task of ushering Ruth into adulthood.

Grange's three lives delineate epochal shifts that are defined by changing forms of labor. Walker depicts Grange's first life of sharecropping as barely removed from the logics of slavery. Through the surveilling forces of absolute white power and the burdens of ongoing, generational indebtedness, the agrarian mode of sharecropping perpetuates the ideology of white supremacy and possession of the labor—and, by extension, the bodies—of black southerners. Grange's second life follows the path of the Great Migration as he abandons the agrarian South for New York City's industrial economy and the secondary layer of labor—chauffeurs, household workers—that supports the burgeoning urban, white middle class of the industrial North. However, this second life is marked by disillusionment as he discovers that whites control all access to wage labor and that he must resort to petty crime in order to survive. In refusing to set up the industrial North as a foil to the agrarian South, Walker thwarts the trope of teleology in migration narratives. Not only does Grange continue to live in abject poverty in Harlem, but also the North's cold anonymity makes it even less hospitable than the rural South: "The South had made him miserable, with nerve endings raw from continual surveillance from contemptuous eyes, but they *knew he was there....*The North put him in solitary confinement where he had to manufacture his own hostile stares in order to see himself" (144–45). In Harlem, Grange must construct his own double-consciousness from a fantasized notion of white perceptions of him.

The absence of relationships, even of "miserable" ones, forces him to adopt an imagined negative white gaze against which he measures himself. Though Grange detests the loneliness and anonymity of the North, this absence of "continual surveillance" creates a space to see the white gaze as a construction that has adversely altered his own self-perception. In other words, in the absence of the negative white perception that shaped his view of himself as subhuman in the South, he has the space—geographic and mental—to begin to see himself differently. Whereas in the South the grinding poverty and hardships led Grange to take out his anger on his family, in Harlem he learns to direct his hate where he believes it belongs: at whites. This hatred liberates Grange: "There was no longer any reason not to rebel against people who were not gods. His aggressiveness, which he had vented only on his wife, and his child, and his closest friends, now asserted itself in the real hostile world" (155). His departure from rural Georgia provides him with a critical perspective on how the economic manifestations of southern racism, in the form of sharecropping, pervert the possibility of whole and healthy racial identity.

What brings him back to Baker County, though, is the news that his son, Brownfield, has murdered his wife and made Grange's grandchildren into orphans. Returning home to raise Ruth, he transforms into a nurturer of a young girl's life.[5] By taking Grange back to Georgia, Walker challenges Richard Wright's contention that the South is irredeemable, and she posits the South, not the North, as the actual telos of African American migration. Departing a figurative "economics of slavery" in the form of sharecropping for the modern, industrial North, Grange discovers in Harlem limited economic opportunity and the absence of communality, but he also learns that "necessary hatred" of whites gives him identity and will to live.[6] When that particular logic reaches its exhausted conclusion that "he could not fight all the whites he met… Each man would have to free himself, he thought, and the best way he could" (155), he returns "home" (156) where he can both preserve the next generation's "innocence" and negotiate for himself a sustainable position in the racialized economy of the post-slavery South. The South, rather than being irredeemable, becomes the site of Grange's redemption. Walker again manages to avoid the representational trap of romanticizing this redemption, however, by depicting the South not as a site of healing plenitude but as a geographic space in the grip of both economic and political transformations resulting from southern industrialization and of the civil rights movement.

In moving Ruth and the narrative itself into a post-sharecropping epoch, Walker, through Grange, presents her most trenchant political critique of the South. In Grange's accumulation of personal wealth and property, we see an assertion of his refusal to let himself and Ruth revert back to the static, predetermined, feudal economy of sharecropping. By depicting this process as a narrative possibility, Walker continues to assert the South's dynamism and intimatses that ongoing change and intimates that it is through this dynamism that the revolution of civil rights can take place. As Thadious Davis puts it, "Space, for Walker, is always in process and not closed, so that it is always outside of grand narratives of modernity" (2011, 344). In Davis's persuasive reading, Walker not only upends the logic that claims that the postmodern literary and critical turn south marks the rural South as premodern in order to effect a discursive displacement of the problems of urban crisis onto an idealized, pastoral representation, but she also identifies the region as itself postmodern through her stubborn refusal to romanticize and fix the space of the South as an unmediated site removed from the vagaries of capital. In attending to the complex economic transitions taking place in the South in mid-century, she presents multifaceted explorations of the diverse and changing social relations of the South.

Part of this complexity comes in Walker's representation of Grange's resettlement in Georgia. When Grange returns to Baker County, he marries an old lover in order to gain access to her money to purchase a small farm. He makes this farm, far off the road and isolated from the neighbors, an oasis free of the presence and influence of whites. The farm is a self-sufficient space for the family; Grange plants and harvests the family's food. He also grows cotton, which he refuses to let Ruth pick despite her protestations. To her, the cotton is soft and beautiful; she appears completely naive about the negative resonances of picking cotton for a former sharecropper like Grange. From the beginning of their time together, he will not allow her to repeat the labors of an enslaved person—he understands the historical context and the symbolic force of picking cotton. Preventing her from engaging in the labor associated with plantation slavery, he also thus controls the visuals by refusing to allow her to ride in the back of his truck, lest someone see her looking like "some kind of field hand" (125).

The farm is equity; Grange is building wealth that Ruth will inherit one day. While erecting a fence to mark his "propity" (173) he impresses upon her the necessity and legality of self-defense to protect one's private property. How are we to understand the celebration, in Grange's third life, of property ownership? The utopian ideal of black rural southern life presented in *The Third Life of Grange Copeland* involves property ownership, self-sufficiency, and the accumulation of family wealth, as well as Grange's distrust of all whites and many blacks, and his isolation from a key form of community in the church. In other words, Grange's third life repudiates the pastoral image of the rural South as a site both of organic racial community and resistance to capitalism and its mediating effects. Instead, his decision to purchase the farm suggests that property ownership and the accumulation of equity produce true independence. Moreover, for Grange, the acquisition of property allows for a welcome isolation. The farm, "far from town, off the main road, deep behind pines and oaks" (156), enables him to have "[i]ndependence from the whites, complete and unrestricted, and obscurity from those parts of the world he [chooses]" (141). Having obtained from his time in Harlem a critical understanding of how the negative white gaze shaped his racial subjectivity, he makes the farm a sanctuary. In it, he arms Ruth with the counter-knowledge of black folk culture and tradition as a bulwark against the same negative white gaze that he knows she will encounter.

Patricia Yaeger argues that property ownership bestows political power on subjects who, due to the residual effects of the slave system in southern culture, are still perceived as property themselves: "Even while the South lingered on the threshold of a fully commercial, mercantile economy, the ideological bonds defining personhood were already in place, defining selfhood in terms of the right to be nurtured by things that proved one's status (and offered more than a modicum of comfort) within the precincts of possessive individualism" (2000, 210).[7] In the sharecropping system that is depicted as an outgrowth of slavery in the novel, laborers and their labor continue to be owned by the landowner. As such, they reside outside the definition of personhood. This is why Grange's property ownership is presented as a moment of transformation in the novel—his move from being property to owning property upends the logic of slavery still dominant in rural Georgia. It also marks a profound economic shift in the South: while slavery was not a wage-labor economy minus the wages in the mode of modern capitalism, property ownership is central to modern capitalism. Grange's farm is wealth, it is equity, and it symbolizes the economic transformations that are, at the time of the novel's production, changing the Old South into the New South.

However, as Grange looks forward to a new era, two elements mark him as a residual character of a declining historical epoch. First is his farming. After midcentury, the South rapidly industrializes—southern cities grow at a rapid pace, demographers note decisive intraregional movement from rural to urban South, and industry itself chooses to locate in the South (lured, in large part, by southern states' insistence on pro-growth legislation and investment).[8] The agrarian economic mode that dominated the southern region for centuries is in active decline at the time of the novel's publication in 1970. As such, Grange's isolated, self-sufficient farm is ceasing to be the norm in the region. The second element is his treatment of whites as monolithically evil. He tells Ruth that whites killed her parents, that they enslaved her, and that they are her "natural enemy" (138–39). Grange feels responsible for teaching Ruth this line of racial knowledge because "[t]he hate…would mean her survival" (143). In the North, he learned that committing violence against whites bolstered his sense of his manhood and made him want to live. "Killing" the oppressor gave him back his humanity; it also was the only thing that would unite blacks politically. As Grange's third life is dedicated to protecting Ruth and ensuring her survival—and therefore, by extension, the survival of his family, his personal knowledge of the world's injustice, and the possibility of retribution or reparation—he feels it necessary to imbue her with an ideology of white evil.

The pressure Grange feels marks the significant historical divide between him and his granddaughter. Through the relationship between Grange and Ruth, Walker represents an evolutionary struggle between racial separation and integration. As Grange protects Ruth from Brownfield and ushers her into adulthood, a model of integration and racial trust that is aligned with the growing civil rights movement and with Ruth's youth supersedes his separatist model of race relations.[9] Whereas, to Grange, Ruth appears quite naive regarding white evil, to Ruth, nothing that Grange says about whites makes any sense. She is confused by Grange's insistence that whites killed her parents, because her father is still alive in prison—she cannot understand that by "whites" he means "white racism" because she does not yet know how to align individuals with ideology. Nor can she square his claim that "They brought you here in chains" with her "slightly rusty but otherwise unmarked ankles" (138). Grange draws connections between the past and the present—the "chains" of slavery signifying ongoing dispossession in the present, the current economic and political condition a direct articulation of the structural inequality slavery wrought on the nation. The "you" brought to America in chains, while not literally referring to Ruth, connects her immediately to her legacy as a descendant of slaves. Grange uses this imagery to collapse past and present; such a collapse, while evoking an affective sense of the burdens on African Americans in the rural South, nevertheless dehistoricizes the present. For Grange, contemporary events are conditioned by the past with little or no recognition of current forces. On the other hand, Ruth, in her dedication to the present, is just as blind as Grange to the workings of history in this southern space. As he notes, "she just couldn't see it" (139). Only the most literal claims make sense to a very young Ruth, and unable to understand the social and historical context of her family's history, she only sees on her ankles the absence of proof of Grange's claims about whites.

To Grange this is worrisome and frustrating, for his ability to protect Ruth and teach her self-defense depends upon her acknowledgment of white evil and thus of the world's order as he understands it. But her very literal understanding of daily life, coupled with some historical distance from the material effects of a debt peonage economy and, most importantly, the isolation and protection Grange's farm offers her, enables a fresh look at the races that allows her to begin to demystify whiteness, and thus to historicize it. When Grange encourages her to "be friends to every other of the downtrodden, especially if he's a man of color," Ruth points out that their white neighbors are equally downtrodden; they are so poor they must eat dirt, and "I don't see what their white has to do with it" (175). Against Grange's racialized worldview, Ruth sees similarities between blacks and whites along class lines. When Grange decides they should hide in the bushes to examine a nearby white family for "Ruth's further education," she discovers "that they were not exactly white, not like a refrigerator, but rather a combination of gray and yellow and pink" (181). Whites are not only not monolithic in Ruth's eyes, the descriptor "white" is not even accurate—whiteness consists of multiple colors and shades. As Grange tries to inculcate "the necessary hatred" in her, she continues to see distinctions and gradations that pose a challenge to his statements about whites, while also identifying whites' class-based commonalities with blacks. She wonders, "I mean, what I want to know, is did anybody ever try to find out if they's real *people*" and announces that "when I get big I'm going to find out. I want to see and hear them face to face" (182).

Here, Ruth and Grange represent opposing sides in a conflict over political ideology. Grange's entire personal system of justice, forged from crucial experiences in New York, centers on separatism and the black man's willingness to do violence to whites in the service of his own humanity and survival. The relationship between blacks and whites is purely adversarial and is based in Grange's experience of the historical realities of, first, Jim Crow segregation and debt peonage and, second, the absence of sustaining wage labor and lack of racial equality in the North. America's entwined racial and economic politics have created the conditions for Grange's adversarial worldview—to him, whites are both monolithic and utterly unchanging. When he suggests to Ruth that the only option for blacks is to depart the nation altogether, she counters that perhaps they can work to make the nation a place where they can feel "*at home*" and where it might be possible to forgive whites if they stop harming African Americans. Grange replies, "I honestly don't believe they *can* stop…Even if they could, it'd be too late. I look in my heart for forgiveness and it just ain't there" (210). Change itself is a hard-won battle, not a given, even for Grange. But, because he has dedicated his third life to preserving Ruth's innocence by providing her a refuge from the realities of segregated black life in the rural South, he has inadvertently given her the critical space to question his worldview altogether. As such, watching the Huntley-Brinkley report about school integration on television, she says she aligns herself with the students and claims there "Ain't nothing wrong with *trying* to change crackers" (233).

By situating the moment of this conflict between Grange and Ruth during the rise of the civil rights movement, Walker takes readers from the early years of the twentieth century when, in Alain Locke's words, the South was "medieval" (1997, 6), to the 1960s South of marches and sit-ins, and it indicates the contemporaneousness of the debate Grange and Ruth are having. Through the story of three generations of a single family, Walker presents a portrait of the historical transformations of twentieth-century America and how they begin to alter the political landscape of the South. At the end of the novel, four young civil rights workers travel to Grange's farm to encourage him to register to vote in the upcoming election. In disbelief that African Americans were even voting, let alone running for office, Grange "felt he had been caught sleeping, and that his nap had lasted twenty or forty years" (240).[10] Returning for a moment to the criticisms of the southern turn in African American literature, the primary argument is that it freezes the South in a nostalgic past moment, rendering it outside of the forces of history, in order to make the region a discursive escape from seemingly unsolvable social problems. By using family history to move the reader through the course of a century, Walker avoids making the largest critical mistake of the southern turn: her South is not frozen in time but is undergoing its own historic transformations as the civil rights movement seeks to move the region into political modernity.

While the novel leaves open the question of what Ruth's future will actually look like and what the civil rights movement will do for Baker County, that it ends with a moment of possibility not foreclosed by the fated "unseen force" that dictated the lives of previous Copeland generations indicates Walker's utopian literary vision for the rural South. Altered by historical transformations, it is in the midst of change. African Americans who are steeped in the folk knowledge of their ancestors, who recognize that their lives are continuous with those of diasporic blacks, with Africa, and with the global struggle for freedom, will stand at the forefront of this change. For them, the South can obtain other meanings. No longer just the site of their ancestors' subjugation, through the forces of economic and political change the South is shifting out of a frozen, feudal past and into a future where the modern African American subject can potentially live, partaking both of the cultural benefits of the southern homeland and of the political benefits of modernity. By charting the beginnings of an economic transformation in the South through the three lives of Grange Copeland, Alice Walker theorizes a historically dynamic South as a region where a vision of African American liberation is possible. In doing so, she attempts to disrupt the logic by which the South is used as a discursive displacement to evade the transformations of the postmodern city and the effects of those transformations on black community. Representing the South as a site in the grip of historical change destabilizes it, makes it unfit as a premodern, preliterate foil for the modern (and postmodern) North.

Conclusion

Alice Walker's rural South bears little resemblance to the characterizations of the literary turn south proffered by critics of the politics of southern regionalism. By shaping her narrative as an investigation into the dynamism, openness, and contingency of historical change, she situates rural Georgia as itself a postmodern space. She constructs this space as racially particular—Grange's many lessons to Ruth about African dance, diasporic history, and folk tradition mark his farm as a site of black history, culture, and identity—but does not base that particularity on its existence inside a structurally static, premodern South. In Walker's vision of the rural South, racial particularity can exist alongside and be negotiated through process of historical transformation. Indeed, the novel suggests that this negotiation will be part of Ruth's life work. As a result, *The Third Life of Grange Copeland* points to a way to preserve the analytical and critical function of racial particularity as a stance from which to question the dominant order without resorting to the segregation nostalgia with which the southern turn is often charged. By balancing so much movement, indeed by making movement and dynamism animating principles of southern black life, Walker's contributions to the literary turn south are emphatically not conservative, but radical. Walker's southern literature demands a reconsideration of recent readings of the southern turn. In her refusal to allow the rural South to act as inverse reflection of the postmodern urban North, she makes space for the region to be complex, fluctuating, and open-ended as it, too, moves inexorably into the future.

Notes

1. During the period of the 1960s and 1970s, not only did the Great Migration quickly reverse course, sending African Americans from the North and Midwest back to the South, but also simultaneously the South entered an active phase of industrialization and urbanization (Kasarda et al. 1991). Most of the return migration was to urban areas such as Atlanta and Memphis, not to rural enclaves, which themselves were rapidly losing population to these same urban centers. In other words, the conservatism of the southern turn inheres not only in its construction of the South as a pastoral alternative to urban crisis but also in its denial of the concurrent urbanization of the South.

2. Farah Jasmine Griffin makes a similar observation. In her account of the turn south at the end of a century dominated by northern migration narratives, she contrasts the reasons actual migrants gave for their deci-

sion to return to the South with culturalist accounts in art and literature. Migrants gave more varied and full reasons for the decision to leave northern and midwestern cities, citing everything from diminished economic opportunity to entrenched racial discrimination to crumbling urban infrastructures to the desire to reunite with family members who had remained in the South. By contrast, artists and writers uniformly cite cultural reasons for return migration—family, food, folklore, organic community, connection to a place of origin and to tradition—and Griffin comments that literary artists in particular downplay the effects of ongoing racism in the region, opting instead to depict the South as "racially monolithic" (1995, 181–82).

3. I want to clarify that Dubey is diagnosing (rather than enacting) this dynamic as a larger problem of "literary criticism that partakes of the broader tendencies of postmodern cultural politics" to romanticize disadvantage as the ground for authentic political claims (2002, 367).

4. In her study of black women's writing, Susan Willis emphasizes that the Great Migration was the most important social transformation in African American history because it effected an epochal shift from an agrarian to an urban society (1987, 3–6).

5. Harold Hellenbrand argues that this transformation "is the wish fulfillment of Walker's feminist conscious-ness," because through Grange's survival of racial hatred he has changed from a man who destroyed his family into a man who returns South to preserve and protect his family (1986, 124).

6. I refer here to Houston Baker's discussion of the "economics of slavery" as "the social system of the Old South that determined what, how, and for whom goods were produced to satisfy human wants" (1984, 26).

7. Houston Baker makes a similar claim in *Blues, Ideology, and Afro-American Literature*. Regarding Nanny, Janie's grandmother in *Their Eyes Were Watching God*, he states, "Nanny conflates the securing of property with effective expression. Having been denied a say in her own fate because she was *property*, she assumes that *only* property enables expression. *Their Eyes Were Watching God* implies that she is unequivocally cor-rect in her judgment and possesses a lucid understanding of the economics of slavery" (1984, 57).

8. Kasarda et al. note that from 1960–1985, the South gained two million manufacturing jobs, while the Frostbelt lost five hundred thousand such jobs in the same period (1991, 40). James Cobb documents how southern cities and states invested in infrastructure and subsidies in order to produce expansive economic growth in midcentury (1984, 27–50).

9. In *Talking to Strangers*, Danielle Allen identifies the civil rights struggles during the period of 1954-1965 (most pertinently, the moment of school desegregation in Arkansas) as "an epochal shift" that "does remain still undigested" (2004, 7). She argues that this unfinished moment in American history has led not to political friendship but to interracial distrust that "indicates political failure" (xiii). Ruth represents the sense of possibility in this moment—the possibility of interracial trust that could transform a Jim Crow society.

10. Walker's allusion to Washington Irving's short story "Rip Van Winkle" reinforces the representation of Grange as a residual character. Sleep suggests stasis or unchangeability, a condition arguably created through Grange's insistence on geographic isolation and individualist self-sufficiency. However, his "slum-ber" has prevented him from seeing how legal decisions such as school desegregation and voting rights have begun to undo the political landscape created by Jim Crow. As such, when he metaphorically awakens, he discovers that his own political and racial ideology, honed through his treatment in the Jim Crow South and the hypersegregated North, has perhaps become anachronistic. In Irving's story, Rip Van Winkle sleeps through the American Revolution. Walker's allusion suggests, though it does not triumphally assert, a similarly dramatic revolution taking place in the rural South.

References

Allen, Danielle S. 2004. *Talking to Strangers: Anxieties of Citizenship since Brown v. Board of Education*. Chicago: University of Chicago Press.

Baker, Houston A. 1984. *Blues, Ideology, and Afro-American Literature: A Vernacular Theory*. Chicago: University of Chicago Press.

Carby, Hazel. 1990. "The Politics of Fiction, Anthropology, and the Folk: Zora Neale Hurston." *New Essays on Their Eyes Were Watching God*, edited by Michael Awkward. Cambridge and New York: Cambridge University Press

Cobb, James C. 1984. *Industrialization and Southern Society, 1877–1984*. Lexington, KY: University Press of Kentucky.

Dubey, Madhu. 2002. Postmodern Geographies of the U.S. South. *Nepantla: Views from South* 3(2): 351–71.

———. 2003. *Signs and Cities: Black Literary Postmodernism.* Chicago: University of Chicago Press.

Griffin, Farah Jasmine. 1995. *"Who set you flowin'?": The African American Migration Narrative.* New York: Oxford University Press.

Hellenbrand, Harold. 1986. "Speech, after Silence: Alice Walker's *The Third Life of Grange Copeland.*" *Black American Literature Forum* 20 (1–2): 113–128.

Irving, Washington. 2006. *The Legend of Sleepy Hollow and Other Stories from the Sketch Book.* New York: Penguin Books.

Kasarda, John D., Hughes, Holly L., Irwin, Michael D. 1991. "Demographic and Economic Restructuring in the South." *The South Moves into Its Future: Studies in the Analysis and Prediction of Social Change.* Joseph S. Himes. Tuscaloosa: University of Alabama Press: 32–68.

Locke, Alain. (1925) 1997. *The New Negro: Voices of the Harlem Renaissance.* New York: Touchstone.

Morrison, Toni. 1981. "City Limits, Village Values: Concepts of the Neighborhood in Black Fiction." *Literature and the Urban Experience: Essays on the City and Literature.* Michael C. Jaye and Ann C. Watts. New Jersey: Rutgers University Press: 35–43.

Moses, Wilson J. 2005. "Segregation Nostalgia and Black Authenticity." *American Literary History* 17(3): 621–42.

Reed, Adolph L. 1999. *Stirrings in the Jug: Black Politics in the Post-Segregation Era.* Minneapolis: University of Minnesota Press.

Walker, Alice. 1983. *In Search of Our Mothers' Gardens: Womanist Prose.* San Diego: Harcourt Brace Jovanovich.

———. 1970. *The Third Life of Grange Copeland.* New York: Harcourt, Brace.

Willis, Susan. 1987. *Specifying: Black Women Writing the American Experience.* Madison: University of Wisconsin Press.

Woolf, Virginia. 1929. *A Room of One's Own.* San Diego: Harcourt Brace Jovanovich.

Yaeger, Patricia. 2000. *Dirt and Desire: Reconstructing Southern Women's Writing, 1930–1990.* Chicago: University of Chicago Press.

E S S A Y

Dramatizing the African American Experience of Travel in the Jim Crow South: *The Negro Motorist Green Book* in the African American Literary Imagination

by Michael Ra-Shon Hall

"With the introduction of this travel guide in 1936, it has been our idea to give the Negro traveler information that will keep him from running into difficulties, embarrassments, and to make his trips more enjoyable."
—*The Negro Motorist Green Book* (1949)

"That this change to complete Jim Crow happens at Washington is highly significant of the state of American democracy in relation to colored peoples today. Washington is the capital of our nation and one of the great centers of the Allied war effort toward the achievement of the Four Freedoms. To a southbound Negro citizen told at Washington to change into a segregated coach the Four Freedoms have a hollow sound, like distant lies not meant to be the truth."
—"My America" (1944), Langston Hughes

"Not until years had passed, and other, far, more sophisticated vacations had been taken—jaunts to Europe and Africa and Asia, paid for by credit cards and boosting us to a palmy level of worldliness we'd never dreamed of. Not until we Harmon children had gone our separate ways, and looked back suddenly to realize that this was the trip by which we would always judge all others. A journey that defined the ambiguous shape of our citizenship, when we moved across our country feeling as apprehensive as foreigners and at the same time knowing that every grain of dust was ours."
—*The Golden Chariot* (2002), Andrea Lee

Introduction

From 1936 to 1964 the *Negro Motorist Green Book,* the brain child of New York-based African American businessman and former postal worker Victor H. Green, served as a guide for African Americans both to lessen embarrassing situations in travel as well as to protect travelers from physical harm in the Jim Crow South and beyond. This travel guide, commonly referred to as the *Green Book,* assisted African American travelers during a period in US history when Howard Johnson, which operated restaurants and motor lodges, was the only national chain where black persons could eat and sleep, and Esso gas stations (now ExxonMobil) provided the only stations where African Americans could both refuel their cars and use public restrooms.

Contemporary playwrights have examined this moment in US history, when the *Green Book* served as a safeguard for African American travelers. In the critically acclaimed

The Green Book: A Play in Two Acts (2006), Atlanta native Calvin A. Ramsey presents the narratives of a *Green Book* salesman, a Jewish Holocaust survivor, and a soldier and his wife who converge on a "tourist home"—a house in which rooms are available for rent to transient visitors—in Jefferson City, Missouri, where they consider the value of this guidebook. His play offers a fictional window into a little known but important chapter in our shared American history. Andrea Lee's short musical, *The Golden Chariot* (2002), an abbreviated literary epic depicting African American leisure travel by automobile, also reflects on travel under Jim Crow, providing a comedic complement to Ramsey's play.

Together, these works by Ramsey and Lee chronicle two important dimensions of African American travel from the early 1900s through the 1960s. First, they illustrate the unique vulnerability of African American travelers during an era of Jim Crow segregation and discrimination and the resilience of African American travelers in finding ways to surmount impasses to physical and geographical mobility. Secondly, they foreground the role of the automobile not only as a signifier of class status but also as a limited means of avoiding the harsher aspects of Jim Crow era travel, as black travelers could hardly avoid stopping at gas stations, rest stops, and other accommodations, many of which did not welcome African American patrons. Ramsey's drama and Lee's comedy employ cultural specificity to affirm universal lessons about communal responsibility, individual agency and integrity, and ethics. More than literary abstractions, these works should be understood as creative expressions refracting not only aspects of the cultural history of racial restrictions on African American physical and geographical mobility, but also the ingenuity and fortitude demonstrated by modern African American travelers faced with legal impediments to their leisure travel.

Dramatizing the African American Experience of Travel in the Jim Crow South: The Green Book, A Play in Two Acts

The Green Book: A Play in Two Acts uses character dialogue to provide historical context on the situation of African American travel in modern times. The play opens with a brief telephone conversation between Dwight Green—a married, Harlem-based African American businessman in his forties, whose company publishes the Negro travel guide—and Langston Hughes. Green is arranging papers in his Harlem office when he receives a phone call from Hughes:

> Your friends there [in DC] are afraid to have you stay in their homes…? Because of the communist charges against you? That's a damn shame. Yes, Langston, I have an address for you. Let me grab a Green Book. Call this number. It's the Brown Family…Butterfield–60027. (Ramsey 2006, 5)

From the beginning, Ramsey highlights the utility of the travel guide as a practical means of securing accommodations for black travelers in the United States, even those of some status, whom one might not imagine being subjected to such difficulties. That is to say that in the conversation between Green and the poet Hughes, the reader notes that not even middle-class educated African Americans were immune to the regular insult of Jim Crow. Even more, the conversation presents the irony that the state calls Hughes to appear in the capital and defend himself as a loyal citizen even as the state's sanction on Jim Crow and its anticommunist crusade make it physically difficult for Hughes to travel and find accommodations in the capital. Indeed it's the communist charges that ultimately leave Hughes without a place to stay because, as an African American, his only recourse is to rely on friends' homes for temporary residence in DC. Ramsey's fictional representation of a phone conversation between Green and Hughes reflects not only Hughes's actual trip to Washington, DC, in March of 1953 to answer charges of communist affiliation before the Senate Permanent Subcommittee on Investigations chaired by Senator Joseph McCarthy, but also the poet and columnist's regular criticism of Jim Crow discrimination in the United States.

One of Hughes's articles, "Better Jobs for Women," which appeared in the *Chicago Defender* in 1946, caused controversy for its attack on Jim Crow inequalities that persisted in the US even after World War II. Hughes assailed the US government and southern transportations system for abiding discrimination domestically while US armed forces helped to combat injustices perpetuated by Nazis abroad. He contends that

> The wasteful, uncivilized, inconvenient and stupid Jim Crow travel system of the South still prevails. The Jim Crow car is a disgrace to America, and is an open and unashamed symbol of all the other Nazi-like inequalities to which Negroes are subjected. (1995, 32)

During an era when early struggles for civil rights had benefited from the leadership of such figures as James Weldon Johnson, W. E. B. Du Bois, Ida B. Wells-Barnett, Mary Church Terrell, Mary McLeod Bethune, Paul Robeson, A. Phillip Randolph, Walter White, and others, Hughes's focus on the Jim Crow car brings into sharp relief the hypocrisy of a nation that would enlist its sons and daughters in a fight abroad for freedom and democracy as it denied those same rights and privileges to its darker-skinned citizens at home. Describing Jim Crow discrimination and racial inequality in the United States, Hughes insinuates that America refuses both to acknowledge and to eliminate Nazis at home. After speaking with Hughes, Green asserts that it is "a crime, and a sin before God. Langston Hughes, the people's poet, can't find a place to stay in our nation's capital" (Ramsey 2006, 5). With this rhetorical gesture, Ramsey brings the issue of segregation and discrimination in public accommodations and travel to the literal and metaphorical doorstep of the nation.

Following the exchange between Green and Hughes, Ramsey includes a more extensive conversation between Green and one of his employees, Douglas Walker, to establish further a context for the play's plot. Walker, whose name merges the surnames of historic African American leaders Frederick Douglass and David Walker, has just returned from a successful tour in the South gathering information about businesses to include in the *Green Book*. This dialogue foregrounds the risks involved in travel for African Americans, common misperceptions about the South, and the value of travel to the acquisition of knowledge. After boasting of his success in the South, Walker admits that it was Green's example that had inspired him, despite reservations, to accept the assignment of traveling and gathering information in the South:

You mentioned that you never planned to work with The Green Book after college, but that things changed after you started reading the mail from people who bought The Green Book and how it had saved their families from harm on the open road. I think that…made me realize this was more than a job. (Ramsey 2006, 9)

A question that Walker's admission both raises and partially answers here is what was at stake for the Negro traveler in the South, and related to that question, what was the value of the travel guide? Hughes's 1944 essay "My America" offers a more visceral answer to these queries, making it clear that for African American travelers like Morehouse College professor Hugh Gloster, living under Jim Crow was not merely an embarrassment for both the rider and nation: often the lives of African American citizens were at stake.

· While riding as an interstate passenger, Professor Gloster was "ejected from a train… beaten, arrested, and fined because, being in an overcrowded Jim Crow coach, he asked for a seat in an adjacent car which contained only two white passengers" (303). Professor Gloster's forceful removal from the train was illegal, as Hughes notes, because "Jim Crow laws do not apply to inter-state travelers, but the FBI has not yet gotten around to enforcing that Supreme Court ruling" (303). Hughes goes on to show that attacks like the one on Gloster were not isolated incidents but reflective of a system of racial violence intended to control, or circumscribe, the mobility of black bodies, even when the law sided with those being "Jim Crowed." In addition to Professor Gloster's attack, Hughes reports that a probation officer of color, Fred Wright, on route from San Francisco to Oklahoma, was "beaten and forced into the Texas Jim Crow coach on a transcontinental train by order of the conductor in defiance of federal law" (303). Furthermore, an elderly clergyman, Dr. Jackson, while traveling south from Hartford, Connecticut, to the National Baptist Convention was "set upon by white passengers for merely passing through a white coach on the way to his own seat" (Hughes 1994, 303). Not only were black citizens regularly prone to vigilante assault while traveling on public transportation, particularly in the South, but at least in one instance a fatality occurred as a result of racial discrimination.

Pushing the issue of racial violence beyond the civilian population in the United States, Hughes (1994) emphasizes that similar attacks were perpetuated against uniformed black soldiers on public carriers, with one such attack resulting in "the soldier [being] dragged from a bus and killed by civilian police" (303). These narratives of Jim Crow racial violence in travel are precisely the kinds of incidents that prompted Victor Green to publish a guidebook for Negro travelers. Rather than sit idly by as increasing numbers of African Americans suffered discrimination, embarrassment, physical harm, and even death at the hands of white citizens, Green—like Harriet Tubman, William Still, Charles Sumner, and other abolitionists who served as conductors for the Underground Railroad—offered a means of protection by acting as a guide to a network of hotels, motels, rest stops, boarding houses, other accommodations, dining establishments, and leisure pursuits.

While Tubman and other abolitionists served as literal guides for escaped enslaved persons seeking refuge and a pathway to freedom in locales beyond the antebellum slave-holding South, Green created a guide to disseminate to African American travelers seeking protection while navigating a largely hostile postbellum America. Black travelers used this tool—a guide to a veritable geography of safe spaces—to reduce racist incidents while traveling in the South, across the country, and even internationally. In this way, early twentieth-century African American travelers negotiating a precarious national landscape appear to be the contemporary analogs of enslaved persons requiring a guide to escape the harsh realities of the South. In the case of both the enslaved person and the modern traveler, the South represented an unsafe geographical space plagued by the vagaries of white racial violence. Even more, the South was for both a place in which white persons used violence and intimidation to restrict and delimit the physical mobility of black persons. Put another way, for African Americans and their enslaved predecessors, the South geographically and culturally represented landscape and terrain hostile to anything akin to democratic freedom. In addition to historical context, Ramsey utilizes the conversation between Green and Walker to make concrete connections between the *The Green Book* travel guide and the cultural/historical experience of the Underground Railroad.

A major issue that surfaces in the exchange between Green and Walker is the difficulty of both traveling on the open road (at least not with the sense of freedom and democratic possibility captured in the "Song of the Open Road" by American poet Walt Whitman) and also finding food and safe, decent accommodations, such as restaurants and lodges. Specifically underscoring Hughes's reports of the deplorable and hypocritical treatment of black soldiers, Green reminds Walker of the situation for African American soldiers returning home from World War II. He states, "They have been home for almost five years now. They want all that America has to offer. They are sleeping in their cars, eating out of brown paper bags, and they are on the road. There are just not enough rooms for the thousands of our people traveling" (Ramsey 2006, 13). Green indicates a vast shortage of accommodations for a growing cadre of Afro-modern travelers that prompts Walker to reflect on a broader, informal network of boarding houses and guestrooms organized by African Americans as a response to that shortage

Communal responsibility and hospitality as mainstays of modern African American cultural history lie at the heart of the exchange between Green and Walker. Following Green's notation of the shortage of hospitable places available to the African American traveler, Walker expresses his own observation of this lack and his sense of an African American communal commitment to provide hospitality to known visitors and strangers alike. He explains, "In every Negro home I've been, I see a folding sleeping cot for that known and unknown traveler who is headed their way" (Ramsey 2006, 13). Walker's observation extends our understanding of African American hospitality and ingenuity beyond those places listed in *The Green Book* to include the many homes not documented in the travel guide, which remained prepared to receive the inevitable weary traveler unable (and unwelcome) to reside at white-owned hotels and motels. Walker's comment inspires Green to make a historical link adding, "The Underground Railroad was called Egyptland and in some ways, this is a modern day version of that" (14), a literary expression of the character's understanding of the connection between the cultural and historical experiences of enslaved persons escaping through the Underground Railroad and modern travelers using *The Green Book.*

Dialogue in the play not only establishes historical context for the situation of African American travel and a connection between *The Green Book* and the Underground Railroad, but also dispels popular misconceptions about the American South, affirming the importance of travel to knowledge. After Walker shares his reflection on the *Green Book,* indicating the significance and centrality of the travel guide to modern African American travelers, he admits his misconceptions of the South. Preceding his travels in the South, Walker believed southerners used corncobs instead of toilet paper and "was expecting to see Negroes hanging from trees" (Ramsey 2006, 9–11). Walker's statements reflect a view of the South commonly held in the early to mid-twentieth century (and often still today), whereby the South represents a backward geographic space in which the horrors of racial violence and primitive premodern conditions are amplified in the Northern imagination, both black and white. This misconception is one that the experience of touring the South helps to correct for Walker as he admits his previously held views of the South "were wrong." Walker's admissions not only foreground the value of travel to combating ignorance, reminiscent of Mark Twain's famous assertion that "travel is fatal to prejudice, bigotry, and narrow-mindedness" (Twain 1869), but his admitted fears about violence in the South reflect the concerns that lie at the foundation of the many incidents of racial assault Hughes reported in the *Chicago Defender.*

Finally, Ramsey uses the conversation between Green and Walker to address the limitations of automobile ownership for those middle-class African Americans for whom automobile ownership provided a means of avoiding the routine racial discrimination that characterized public transportation, particularly via bus and train, during Jim Crow. In addition to noting difficulties that African American travelers experienced in securing safe and hospitable accommodations, Walker makes a report to Green regarding gas stations in the South in which he expresses concern about the availability (or not) of full-service gas stations for African Americans:

> Well, there's good news and bad news. The Esso service stations will sell us gas, and we can use the restrooms there. But the Esso stations aren't in some of the smaller towns. Our people can buy gas at other stations, but are still not allowed to use the restrooms. This is not acceptable to me. (Ramsey 2006, 14)

Though Walker is clearly worried that gas stations in smaller towns do not permit African Americans to use their restrooms, an issue sure to inconvenience any traveler in need of relief after several hours on the road, he is optimistic that a national chain of gas stations does provide full service without discrimination to all travelers requiring relief. Walker's somewhat cynically optimistic report aptly captures the limitations of automobile ownership despite the opportunity automobiles presented African American families wishing to avoid Jim Crow in public transportation. Not only was automobile ownership an atypical luxury possession in black households, but, as Walker's report illustrates, not even automobile ownership could completely shield African Americans from discrimination in their travels. Gas stations at times served as reminders of the long reach of Jim Crow particularly in the rural South, and, as Green's response to Walker's report shows, they also provided opportunities to negotiate consumer power in the interest of civil rights gains.

Walker's report on the situation of gas stations hints at a historical relationship between Victor H. Green & Co., Publishers and Esso Standard Oil Co. and imagines the role consumer power and political lobbying played in achieving civil rights gains on Capitol Hill. As Green notes at the conclusion of Walker's report, "There's a Civil Rights bill[1] in Congress that's being shepherded through by Senator Hubert Humphrey of Minnesota, and Clarence Mitchell of Baltimore" and "Esso[2] has thrown their lobbyist behind this bill" (Ramsey 2006, 14–15). As the pages of *The Green Book* confirm, Esso gas stations (and a number of other white-owned businesses) responded to the growing power of the Negro dollar by fully servicing the needs of travelers without discrimination. Even more, Esso stations served as a venue through which the travel guide was sold and further disseminated to travelers who required its guidance.

Transformations in rights afforded to African American travelers as a result of lobbying the black dollar is not only imagined in Ramsey's play but also observed in the 1949 edition of the historic travel guide. In an article appearing in the 1949 edition "The *Green Book* Helps Solve Your Travel Problems," Wendell P. Alston, special representative for Esso Standard Oil Co., describes the unique problems faced by African American travelers but remains optimistic. His optimism anticipates the gains of boycotts organized by black consumers like the 1955–56 Montgomery Bus Boycott or the Southern Christian Leadership Conference's boycott of Winn Dixie stores much later in 1986[3]:

> More business men, representing increasing Negro enterprises, are traveling from city to city, and more white corporations cognizant of the mounting purchasing power of the Negro consumer, have Negro representatives in the field, a number of whom, like ourselves, spend half the year traveling. (Alston 1949, 3)

Ramsey's fictional rendering of a conversation between characters Green and Walker is more than dramatization—it is a representation of the actual relationship between white-owned businesses like Esso Standard Oil Co. and Victor H. Green & Co., Publishers. Reflecting not only on racial and ethnic paradigmatic restrictions characteristic of modern African American travel but also on the resourcefulness and inventiveness of individuals and communities to discriminatory impasses, the exposition provides a broad but detailed cultural/historical context for a series of events that unfold in the second half of the play. Walker's discussion of hospitality denied to African American travelers at gas stations in particular foreshadows dramatic events that occur in act II. Act I, scene 1 closes on Harlem to shift in the next scene to Jefferson City, Missouri, where another agent, Keith Chenault, is on assignment.

It is in act I, scene 2 that dramatist Calvin Ramsey sets the final stage for a complex set of interactions and circumstances that bring into relief the significance *of The Green Book* as a cultural/historical artifact. This complex set of interactions includes: 1) the encounter between Keith and a Jewish fellow traveler, Victor Lansky, an interaction that relies to some extent on connections between African American and Jewish cultural heritages (particularly shared traumatic cultural memories of racial and ethnic injustices); 2) the negotiations between Keith and Colonel Jones, a racist white businessman, which raise a moral issue about the limits of profit seeking at the expense of personal integrity and racial pride; and 3) the violent attack on Captain Smith as he seeks service at a gas station in Tennessee, which highlights the kinds of violence and embarrassment that *The Green Book* sought to prevent.

Ramsey foreshadows dramatic events leading to the play's climax largely through character development, particularly by unveiling characters' ethical stances, interior thoughts, and feelings. Scene 2 opens in the home of Dan and Barbara Davis, a forty-something African American couple who own a boarding house at which Captain George and Jackie Smith, both thirty years of age, and Keith Chenault, in his early twenties, are residing. The Smiths are preparing to leave the Davis' home to travel to Tennessee. In this scene we learn several things that are crucial to understanding the events that unfold in the second act: 1) Captain Smith is uneasy about traveling with his wife to his new post in Fort Benning, Georgia; 2) Barbara's sister, Shirley, is sending a new guest, Victor Lansky, to stay at the Davis's home; and 3) Victor, a white man, requires accommodations because he refused to reside at the Governor's Hotel due to its "No Negroes Allowed" policy (Ramsey 2006, 42). Dan and Barbara's teenage daughter Neena is distrustful of Keith because "he says things that sound like he doesn't like or respect Negro people" and Neena "saw his car at Colonel Jones's…the most racist and powerful man in this state" (50). Dan considers Neena's warning and ponders why Keith would pay a visit to a man of such ill will:

> The Colonel owns a string of hotels and gas stations all over the Midwest. Mr. "States' Rights" sees himself as a true patriot and Negroes as non-humans. There is not a single Negro in this town that respects that man. (Ramsey 2006, 51)

The family decides not to confront Keith about this issue, but, instead, to wait and see if Keith volunteers information regarding his visit to Colonel Jones.

In the final act of the play, Ramsey uses a sensitive conversation between Keith and Victor to relate his own artistic statement about racial and ethnic pride, communal responsibility, individual integrity, and something like a universal ethic. During this first of several complex interactions, two distinct and critical perspectives emerge between Keith and Victor. When Victor explains to Keith why he chose to stay at a black-owned establishment rather than remain at the Governor's Hotel, Keith replies: "Look mister. By your staying here you are taking a room away from a Negro. You're not doing us any favors by staying here" (Ramsey 2006, 77). Despite the moral fortitude demonstrated by Victor in challenging a racist practice, on a pragmatic level, Keith indicates that Victor's physical presence in one of few black establishments means fewer spaces for black travelers whose safety depends on the availability of such tourist homes. Still, Keith is surprised to learn that Victor has attended a lecture by W. E. B. Du Bois at Morgan State College as well as read about Du Bois in Negro newspapers, an interest that Keith does not share because he has little interest in being a "race man" (73–76).

Ramsey stages the confrontation between Keith and Victor to challenge our understanding of racial pride, communal responsibility, and personal integrity beyond a strict racial binary of black versus white. That is to say, what we learn about Keith and Victor illustrates not only how well-meaning white persons may inadvertently cause further complications in their quest to be morally upright, but also how self-interested black persons in their racial exclusiveness can make poignant, albeit defensive, observations about limited resources that should be safeguarded. Conversely, and with no less force, we also learn from the interaction between Keith and Victor how seemingly unaware white persons can inspire the most astute lessons about racial pride and communal responsibility—through their very commitments to interracial cooperation and solidarity—and how seemingly racially conscious and concerned black persons can allow individual greed and ambition to narrow their aims in ways that prove beneficial to the few but unintentionally detrimental to the many.

Inverting the critical potential of racial binary, Ramsey complicates his artistic vision further by having Victor also offer an assessment of Keith's actions and of their ethical consequences. Though Keith judges Victor to be unaware in his moral fortitude, he is intrigued to learn that Victor owns a copy of *The Green Book,* which Victor explains by noting that there was a time when displaced survivors of concentration camps in Germany "could have used a Green Book of their own" (Ramsey 2006, 87). Here, the critical perspective cuts the other way as Victor all but levels an indictment against Keith for exhibiting a lack of racial pride and commitment in his work and politics. Victor, whose dear friend is William Scott, a black photographer who once saved Victor's life from the horrors of a concentration camp in Germany during World War II, is shocked to learn that Keith has been making deals with a racist (and ex-military) businessman, Colonel Jones. In an attempt to convince Keith to reconsider his decision to negotiate with a racist businessman, Victor shares his experience of ethnic violence as a camp prisoner.

Ramsey's use of Victor as an authorial voice benefits from connections between Jewish and African American cultural heritages, and the ethics of racial and communal rights struggles fortifies the play's moral claims. After narrating a tale of his experience as a prisoner in a concentration camp, Victor queries Keith about the actions that Keith has taken to ensure that civil rights and liberties are protected and extended to African Americans. Keith replies that he is doing nothing because, "We have people that work on those kinds of things…we call them race men." Keith is insistent that he is not a race man but "a business man. That's my contribution. I am making something out of myself" (Ramsey 2006, 98–99). Dissatisfied with Keith's clear intention to reap the benefits of organized black struggle without enduring any of the hardships, Victor tells Keith that he reminds him of someone in the concentration camps: "We called him the collaborator…We meant it as someone who was a traitor to his people and himself.…You are very clever, just coasting along letting others do your share. All you want are the benefits" (106–107). Offering a scathing rejoinder to Keith's assessment of Victor as unaware and somehow unintentionally inconsiderate of racial politics and needs, Victor's assessment troubles Keith's own sense of himself as a man whose actions, ambitions, and investments contribute to broader racial and communal uplift.

Pushing the critical edge of inverted racial binary to its extreme, Ramsey reveals Keith to be not only morally corrupt but also hypocritical and lacking in personal integrity. At this tense moment in the conversation Keith pulls out the contract he signed with Colonel Jones and says, "You see this? I've been negotiating for two days, all day yesterday and today…cutting a deal with the most powerful man in the state" (Ramsey 2006, 109). Keith later reveals that he has signed a deal with Colonel Jones that allows African Americans to buy gasoline, purchase snacks, and use clean restrooms but at double the purchase price of white customers. Noting that Keith has just contradicted an earlier statement in support of segregation to protect Negro businesses, Victor discerns that Keith must be receiving a hefty commission for this deal and questions conclusively, "So you made a deal with the devil?" Keith agrees (109). Here, Ramsey fully turns the racial binary on its head, revealing Keith to be wholly self-serving and almost completely devoid of an active moral compass. Though Keith has spent a good deal of time insinuating that Victor's naivety is as harmful as it is well-intentioned, Keith has proven to be a greater threat to gaining and securing civil rights for African Americans than his assumedly unaware white counterpart. The point that Ramsey is making through Victor's critique of Keith is a simple, but potent message: there are well-intentioned white people and ill-intentioned black people, and any struggle for social justice must be aware of this reality in order to further its mission and fully realize its goals.

To exploit fully the substantial tension created by the verbal exchange between Keith and Victor, Ramsey has the most violent episode of the play occur in the midst of an already established conflict. The drama reaches its climax when Captain George Smith and his wife Jackie return suddenly after a violent encounter during their travels to Fort Benning. Jackie enters with a semiconscious George and screams as Victor approaches to offer assistance. "I don't want any white man to touch us," she exclaims. Victor judiciously steps back and Keith retrieves a *Green Book* and calls the number of Dr. Johnston, a black physician listed in the area (Ramsey 2006, 116–17). In an ironic, but not completely unexpected, twist we learn that George was attacked at a gas station owned by none other than Colonel Jones. A dispute ensued after Jackie returned from using the restroom to find George arguing with the station manager, who claimed that George owed him more money. The station manager made this claim as a result of the negotiations that Keith completed with Colonel Jones, a contract requiring double pay for black customers. Three white men, including the station manager, physically assaulted George, and Jackie, after rescuing George with a tire jack she had found in the car trunk, decided to return George to the Davis' home rather than continue to Fort Benning (118–21).

It is at this dramatic peak that Ramsey offers his unique perspective on black travel in the Jim Crow South and the level of unity, commitment, and moral fortitude required to combat the many injustices of this dark period in US history. Ramsey's perspective emerges through two moments in the denouement, or winding down, of the play. The first is a conversation between Barbara and Jackie in which Jackie reveals her fears and insecurities about being a frequently mobile soldier's wife, a fear that she has not shared with her husband. Barbara's response reveals Ramsey's assessment of the significance of *The Green Book* as a cultural/historical artifact and guide in the American experience:

> If there was a The Green Book that dealt with all aspects of living, not just travel, I would give it to Neena to spare her from pain and heartache. There is no such book. We have to live life and travel through it on our own and share the things we learn with others to make their journey a little easier. (Ramsey 2006, 125)

Not only do Barbara's comments comfort Jackie as she goes upstairs to see George, who is now awake and fully aware, but her comments also underscore the value of guidebooks of many sorts in helping us to navigate many aspects of our lives. She makes these comments, ultimately, to show gratitude for Green's foresight and leadership in creating *The Green Book* during a time when it was most needed. At the same time, however, Jackie's statements are also a lament since *The Green Book* in this instance did not prevent racial violence. Even more, her assertion that "[t]here is no such book," followed by an admission that African Americans must share life lessons with one another, reinforces the limitations of any guidebook to be a perfect resource and privileges shared experience as a more reliable guide for road and life travelers.

The second, and final, moment that defines Ramsey's artistic vision in creating this work is the interaction between Barbara and Keith. After Jackie ascends the stairs to join George, Keith comments almost dismissively that "he's going to be alright. I've seen plenty of cats in Harlem beaten up worse than that, and they shake it off, and in a few days are back on their feet" (Ramsey 2006, 127). Barbara's reply is exacting and commanding:

> This was no street brawl. They could have been killed. I have a feeling you know something about this double pay for gasoline situation. I have never asked anyone to leave my home, especially this time of night. But I will. I will not allow evil to enter into my home. You have a lot of opportunity to do a lot of good with The Green Book, but you also have the capacity to do a lot of harm. Whatever you have done, I want you to undo it before you leave this town. Whatever happened today with Jackie and George will be repeated over and over again until this mess is straightened out. Do you hear me? (128)

Barbara's authoritarian tone in her comments and commands to Keith make clear that it is not enough to have a material guide to ensure the safety of black travelers, but it is also necessary to have committed people of goodwill in order for that guide to realize its full purpose. After Keith agrees to dismantle the contract with Colonel Jones with a simple, "Yes ma'am," Barbara hands him an autographed copy of Du Bois's *Souls of Black Folk,* which she got for him at a lecture by Du Bois earlier that night. Dr. Johnston enters the home and Barbara leads him upstairs. Victor retires for the night, and the play closes with Keith standing alone with the autographed book. He slams the book into a wastebasket, walks away, stops, returns to retrieve the book, and exits the stage (Ramsey 2006, 128–29). Keith's unsettling and unresolved departure leaves the reader to speculate about the possibilities of his redemption.

Conclusion and a Coda: Some Reflections on The Green Book and Andrea Lee's The Golden Chariot

Ramsey's dramatic play *The Green Book: A Play in Two Acts* revisits a moment in the history of African American travel when black travelers required a tool with which to navigate an inhospitable and often hostile nation, particularly the Jim Crow South. Ramsey's play, more than literary abstraction, documents paradigmatic racial and ethnic impasses to African American mobility in a drama that, ultimately, employs the specificities of African American and US history to relate a more universal artistic and critical statement about communal responsibility, individual agency and integrity, and ethics. Providing a window into a little known and darker aspect of US history, Ramsey's play challenges us to consider how we might productively engage the past in ways that foreground the more universal potential of African American creativity without sacrificing those qualities of African American imagination which define it as such. In lieu of a conventional conclusion, I offer here an abbreviated treatment of Andrea Lee's *The Golden Chariot.* Foregrounding African American leisure travel by automobile, Lee's literary work complements Ramsey's two-act play, exploring the cultural history of African American travel beyond public transportation and extending our understanding of the role of guidebooks beyond a racially and culturally specific material artifact.

The Golden Chariot is a one-act "musical comedy, or traveling minstrel show," published by Andrea Lee in the Spring 2002 issue of *Zoetrope: All-Story,* the literary quarterly founded by Francis Ford Coppola in 1997. Lee's dramatic, musical comedy is set in August of 1962 and stars "a middle-class American Negro family and their brand-new 1962 metallicized Rambler Classic. [The whole family] head[s] on an epic summer-vacation trip across America, from Philadelphia to the Seattle World's Fair" (Lee 2002, 46–50). Like Ramsey's two-act play, published a few years later, Lee's musical focuses on a critical period in US history, when narratives of African American domestic travel reflected a broad struggle for freedom of mobility as a civil right. In fact, scene I of Lee's dramatic comedy begins with a central character—Dr. Earl B. Harmon—contemplating another guidebook African American travelers utilized to avoid humiliation, discrimination, and racial violence in their travels across the United States: the guidebooks of the American Automobile Association (AAA).

The exposition of Lee's musical comedy, much like that of Ramsey's drama, foregrounds paradigmatic racial and ethnic restrictions on African American mobility and the resilience demonstrated by travelers who utilized guidebooks as a means of avoiding the harsher aspects of modern travel in the Jim Crow South. As the family begins their trip, driving away from Philadelphia on the Pennsylvania Turnpike, Dr. Harmon (husband to Grace Harmon and father to his two sons, Walker and Richie, and to his daughter Maud) expresses gratitude for the AAA guidebooks with which the family travels safely:

> Oh, it's the AAA that gives us the bedrock of security, the courage to take this leap. American Automobile Association. The name inspires confidence. All of those A's, like the NAACP. The opposite of the KKK. The AAA guidebook tells us that it includes only hotels, motels, inns, TraveLodges, campsites, and guesthouses where, and I quote, no discrimination is made according to race, color, or creed. And there you are, there's the whole country open to us, like one big guesthouse. They can't slam the door in your face if they're in the guidebook. (Lee 2002, 48)

Positioning the AAA as an acronymic and organizational safeguard in direct opposition to the vulnerabilities and perils signified by the white racist and vigilante KKK (Ku Klux Klan), Dr. Harmon attributes the confidence that his family (and other African American families) enjoy in their travels to the AAA guidebook, which, like *The Green Book,* served as a navigational tool for African Americans traversing a racialized and precarious American landscape.

Events that unfold in Lee's musical comedy not only illustrate her interest, like Ramsey, in playing with racial binary to impart an artistic vision, but also situate communal responsibility as a significant concern for African Americans. The family's journey is not without incident as the younger son, Richie, complains in scene III that the family's old Kodak makes them seem "not even modern" in comparison to their friends and that all the girls in photo magazines "are white, the way all the girls in *Playboy* are, the way everybody is, everywhere in the movies, on TV, in everything we watch or read" (Lee 2002, 49). Richie's dismay at the lack of black visibility (and subsequent white hyper visibility) in media extends our conception of the negative effects of segregation to include segregated media on individual (and even communal) self-esteem and psyches. Having little (to no) access to images of blackness in popular media, in addition to owning an outdated means of capturing such images, disheartens the younger brother to the point of feeling premodern or primitive in relation to his white counterparts. For older brother Walker, individual integrity falls under question when he is not able to fulfill what he sees as his communal responsibility as an African American student in the midst of student protests for rights.

Walker's communal ethics resound with the ethos expressed by characters central to the artistic vision of Ramsey's play. Much after Richie's moment of dismay at feeling invisible in US society and media, Walker's displeasure with the family trip in scene V ultimately reflects an investment in collective action to achieve social justice as opposed to individual, and self-serving, pursuits. The oldest son renounces the road trip as a mistake, complaining, "The fight for civil rights is in the South, so we go west on a sightseeing expedition" (Lee 2002, 49). Walker expresses frustration that white students are traveling south to partake in SNCC-led student protests, while he returns home from college to work a summer job and vacation with his family. In contrast to the character Keith in Ramsey's play, Walker will not be content simply to better himself without contributing something to broader contemporary efforts to better the lives of others as well. Walker's frustration at not participating in the student-led fight for civil rights in the South is only exacerbated by his realization that even white students were journeying south to protest in solidarity with their black fellow students and activists. Similar to Ramsey's play, Lee's comedy plays with the black-white racial binary to highlight issues of communal responsibility, individual agency and integrity, and racial and ethnic pride.

Also like Ramsey, Lee frames her depiction of a middle-class, African American family's vacation by car in the context of Jim Crow racial discrimination and features a historic travel guide African Americans employed to safeguard their bodies and leisure enjoyment from the vagaries of racial discrimination and assault that defined African American travel in the United States from at least 1865 through to the 1960s. Unlike Ramsey's play, however, the problems that surface in Lee's piece have less to do with the backdrop of Jim Crow discrimination in travel, hospitality, and accommodations and more to do with internal dynamics of the Harmon family refracted against broader national concerns like the modern struggle for civil rights and the lack of black visibility in US society and popular media. That is not to suggest that the family does not experience moments of vulnerability in their travels. Indeed, moments of unease arise when the family stops at motels or national landmarks where, according to Walker, his father appears afraid that "he's going to hear that word 'nigger' which would sweep us right off the map of the U.S.A. Sweep his precious family right off to Oz, like a black tornado" (Lee 2002, 49). Though physical harm does not surface as an immediate concern for the family in Lee's comedy, the threat of white racial verbal assault lurks consistently in the background for the elder Harmon. Despite these moments, the family's trip proceeds relatively unimpeded by excesses of racial discrimination and conflict, resulting in a depiction of white racial violence not so much as an immediate physical threat as a recurrent psychological and traumatic memory of past injustices. That is to say that, unlike Ramsey's play, the threat of white racial violence in Lee's musical comedy appears more as a stain on the individual and collective cultural memory of African Americans than as an immediate possibility.

Complementing Ramsey's work of drama, Lee's short dramatic piece presents a perspective on African American domestic travel and tourism via automobile, a luxury for many African American families during the 1960s and earlier. Together, both plays represent works of African American literary imagination, which utilize material artifacts and historical research that not only ground the imagination in the specificities of African American cultural/historical experiences of modern travel, but even more, ably employ those cultural specificities to accomplish more universal critical and artistic statements. Offering a poignant example of the ways travel has inspired African American writers and literary works as well as the ways writers and creative works imagine and represent travel in the South and beyond as a (geographically specific) problem of modern mobility, my hope is that this essay inspires further exploration into the intimate relationship between modern travel, cultural history, geography, and the African American literary imagination.

Notes

1. Enacted by the 88th United States Congress on July 2, 1964, the Civil Rights Act aimed to protect voter rights from racial, ethnic, and other forms of discrimination via the unequal application of voter requirements. Even more, the landmark legislation empowered US district courts to intervene in cases of discrimination in public education and public accommodations (i.e. public facilities and institutions), including public transportation, among other safeguards. President John F. Kennedy in his June 11, 1963 civil rights speech made an explicit call for such legislation, and the bill gained traction with the sponsorship and support of such figures as Representative Emmanuel Celler, NAACP lobbyist Clarence M. Mitchell, Jr., and Senators Hubert Humphrey, Everett Dirksen, and Mike Mansfield. Following President Kennedy's assassination, the bill was championed and eventually signed into law by Kennedy's successor, President Lyndon B. Johnson.

2. The decision by Esso gas stations to cater to an African American clientele in segregated America resulted in part from the decision by Victor H. Green & Co., Publishers to sell travel guides to friendly white-owned businesses in addition to black-owned businesses. As Celia McGee (2010) notes in a *New York Times* article reflecting on the function of *The Green Book* during Jim Crow, Green insisted on marketing and selling "not just to black-owned businesses but to the white marketplace, implying that it made good economic sense to take advantage of the growing affluence and mobility of African Americans." As a result of Green's visionary distribution of *The Green Book*, "Esso stations, unusual in franchising to African Americans, were a popular place to pick one up" (2010).

3. Following the arrest of Rosa Parks, who refused to surrender her seat to a white passenger, the 1955–56 Montgomery Bus Boycott was a social and political protest campaign organized in response to the negative effects of segregation in the United States, specifically racial discrimination in public transportation in Montgomery, Alabama. The Southern Christian Leadership Conference's (SCLC) commitment to global human rights found its strongest expression in the civil rights organization's fight against apartheid in South Africa. In 1985, SCLC launched a successful boycott of Winn Dixie grocery stores for selling products grown or manufactured in South Africa. Its President, Joseph E. Lowery, described the chain's business in South Africa as an example of endemic racism in the company and as an affront to its African American customer base. For four months, beginning in September, picketers protested outside of stores in Georgia, Florida, Alabama, and North Carolina. Corporate leadership eventually agreed to cease all business with South Africa and pull any existing product from the shelves.

Works Cited

Alston, Wendell P. 1949. "The *Green Book* Helps Solve Your Travel Problems." In *The Negro Motorist Green Book*, edited by Victor H. Green. New York: Victor H. Green and Co., 3–4. From the Collections of the Henry Ford, Benson Ford Research Center, Dearborn, Michigan. University of Michigan at Dearborn. Accessed November 7, 2009. www.collections.thehenryford.org.

Hughes, Langston. 1944. "My America." In *What the Negro Wants,* edited by Rayford W. Logan. Chapel Hill: University of North Carolina Press, 299–307.

——. 1926. "The Negro Artist and the Racial Artist." *The Nation,* June 23. 692–694.

——. 1995. *Langston Hughes and the Chicago Defender: Essays on Race, Politics, and Culture, 1942–62,* edited by Christopher C. De Santis. Urbana: University of Illinois Press.

Lee, Andrea. 2002. "The Golden Chariot." *Zoetrope: All-Story* 6 (1): 46–50.

McGee, Celia. 2010. "The Open Road Wasn't Quite Open to All." *New York Times,* August 22. http://www.nytimes.com/2010/08/23/books/23green.html.

Ramsey, Calvin A. 2006. *The Green Book*: *A Play in Two Acts.* Atlanta: Calvin A. Ramsey.

Twain, Mark. 1869. *The Innocents Abroad, Or, the New Pilgrims' Progress: Being Some Account of the Steamship Quaker City's Pleasure Excursion to Europe and the Holy Land with Descriptions of Countries, Nations, Incidents, and Adventures as They Appeared to the Author.* Hartford, Connecticut: American Publishing Co.

E S S A Y

GEOCODING EDWARD P. JONES'S BLACK DC
IN HIS *NEW YORKER* SHORT STORIES

by Kenton Rambsy

T**he** relatively new arrival of Edward P. Jones as a well-known figure on the map of African American literary history is a testament to the notion that place and placement matters. Despite the fact that his first collection of short stories, *Lost in the City* (1992), received minimal coverage, Jones and his works garnered national attention after his novel, *The Known World* (2003), won the Pulitzer Prize. "I'm glad that *The New Yorker* has published four of the stories already," said Jones in an interview with E. Ethelbert Miller in 2006. "That tells me that maybe I'm on the right path" (Miller 2006). More than indicating that he was on the right path, what *The New Yorker* offered Jones was a platform in one of the most well-established and prominent publishing venues in the country. In *Media and Culture,* Richard Campbell, Christopher R. Martin, and Bettina Fabos explain, "The most widely circulated elite magazine is *The New Yorker.* Launched in 1925 by Harold Ross, *The New Yorker* became the first city magazine aimed at a national upscale audience" (2004, 276). Accordingly, *The New Yorker* served as the gateway that connected Jones and his works to a presumably affluent and intelligent reading audience.

Jones's *New Yorker* short stories, which were published between 2003 and 2011 and focus on predominately black neighborhoods in Washington, DC, offer unique and enriching opportunities for analyzing, or more accurately, "geocoding" an African American author's repeated treatments of a geographic region in a high-profile publishing venue.[1] Despite the long history and dense population of African Americans living in or near the nation's capital, specifically its predominately black quadrants, the city has a relatively small presence in scholarship on African American literature. Jones's *New Yorker* short stories reference quadrants and streets in Washington and thus enact a kind of geotagging or location-identification process that instills a sense of realism in his works to explain how locale impacts characterizations, raced-based character interactions, and plot development. What we might refer to as Jones's "literary geotagging," whereby he highlights racial-spatial dimensions of the nation's capital in his stories, and provides multiple renderings of Washington and diverse representations of black men and their experiences in a select geographic region. Jones's *New Yorker* short stories display his intimate knowledge of the geographies and demographics of the complex, vibrant, yet oft overlooked black neighborhoods of Washington, DC, that shape the racial identity and mobility of black characters, particularly male protagonists, who struggle against invisibility in one of the most political cities in the world.[2]

Jones's use of location-specific words contributes to how readers envision the city and his characters' various environments by setting his stories in well-known black neighborhoods to assist in constructing his plots and characters. In Jones's five *New Yorker* short stories—"A Rich Man" (August 2003), "All Aunt Hagar's Children" (December 2003), "Old Boys, Old Girls" (May 2004), "Adam Robinson" (December 2004), and "Bad Neighbors" (August 2006)—the narrators describe, in detail, routes taken by the characters, referring to cross streets, businesses, or notable buildings so that readers can gain a sense of the neighborhoods in which the characters reside. We might refer to the tendency of writers to pinpoint exact locales in an area as geotagging or literary geotagging, which likens their methods to the practice of utilizing electronic devices and social media to identify the precise locations of a person or group of people in a given geographic space. People who use social-media sites such as Facebook, Twitter, and Foursquare often use geotagging technology to make "friends," "followers," and general audiences aware of where they are or where places are located, as a means of establishing credibility by their association with these locations.

Jones's short stories seek to provide alternatives to popular depictions of the city's political life by offering glimpses of the everyday interactions of African Americans with the geography of the nation's capital. In an interview with Dan Rivas (2004), Jones explained, "I was in college and was shocked at the ignorance of my fellow students about life in DC They knew only that it was the seat of government." Commenting on *Lost in the City*, Jones further explained, "The stories, over two decades, came with my effort to set the record straight. DC is a place of neighbors where people do good and bad things to each other, just as they do in Dubuque and Seattle and Worcester." Jones was interested in offering a perspective that reflected his coming-of-age experiences as an African American in the city: "We lived in a black world and had little to do with white people in the rest of DC" (Rivas 2004). In his short stories, the daily lives of his characters and the central plots of his narratives reflect interactions between black people and as a result typically feature African American neighborhoods. Jones's identification of streets and landmarks—or, that is, his use of literary geotagging—helps him to achieve the task of presenting views of the District beyond governmental and national politics.

Jones uses a similar geotagging technique in his stories to map the geographies of black men in the nation's capital. In "All Aunt Hagar's Children," which takes place during the mid-1950s sometime after the Korean War, for example, the story's unnamed protagonist frequently wanders around his apartment near M and Sixth Street and also congregates with friends at Mojo's on North Capital near New York Avenue. In "Old Boys, Old Girls," the lead character, Caesar Matthews, rents a room on N Street after he is released from prison and frequently spends time at Franklin Park at Fourteenth and K Street. Jones's process of literary geotagging alerts his readers of his intimate knowledge of the city—especially of black neighborhoods. As a result, Jones gains credibility as a convincing storyteller of the region, as he provides fictive tales in real environments.

Perhaps even more notable is Jones's emphasis on navigation through the city given the historical segregation of people based on race and income.[3] The city of Washington is administratively divided into four quadrants of unequal size. Jones's *New Yorker* stories place a special emphasis on black male characters navigating the urban landscape in Washington, DC, primarily in the predominantly black northwest and southeast quadrants. For instance, all five of these short stories make reference to the characters either living in or passing through the northwest quadrant of Washington. Streets ranging from Fifth to Eighth appear frequently in the stories, with additional references to New Jersey and to New York Avenues as well as to M Street and to North Capital. These markers throughout Jones's *New Yorker* stories provide intricate details about the environments where the characters interact and reveals how despite the absence of city laws and ordinances barring black people from living and socializing in certain districts, a more pervasive economic and communal order dictates the movement of black people within Washington.

Jones's knowledge about Washington's geography and history leads him to construct characters that are similarly well-informed about the city. "All Aunt Hagar's Children" follows an unnamed twenty-four-year-old Korean War veteran, restless with his life in the city and anxious to leave on a gold-searching expedition in Alaska. He muses, "I was a veteran of Washington, DC and there was nothing else for me to discover" (Jones 2003a, 3). For the unnamed narrator, being a "veteran of Washington, DC," serves as subtle commentary on how race and economics will ultimately shape his future and limit him to traveling, living, and working along the same routes in which he grew up as a young boy. The narrator's frustrations stem from his knowing that in order to fully escape his environment, he must in many ways leave the city since black people seem to be relegated to specific areas of the city where he is most familiar. The narrator comments with intimate detail on his routes as he navigates the city and frequently mentions locations such as Dunbar High School, Kann's Department Store, and Shiloh Baptist Church, thus demonstrating that he is apparently knowledgeable about Washington in general, but more so about the city's northwest, majority black quadrant. Through detailed descriptions and references to landmarks, there is a symbiotic relationship where both the setting and protagonist are in turn made by each other.

The narrator's knowledge of Washington contributes to his communal worth, as he seems to be revered by other characters in the story owing to his experiences in other parts of the city, which by association give him special insight into relationships with people of different races and social classes. For instance, Miss Agatha, a close family acquaintance, remarks to the unnamed narrator, "Maybe workin' downtown mongst white folks grees with you" (Jones 2003a, 2). The unnamed narrator's knowledge of the "white world" through his employment provides him with more social authority in black communities, but even still, he does not possess the same respect in the majority-white areas of Washington because of the city's raced-based infrastructure. One could infer that the narrator's uneasiness about remaining in the northwest quadrant for the rest of his life and his eagerness to venture to Alaska stem from the knowledge that he acquired while working downtown and understanding the geographic and social barriers of the city. Even though the narrator travels outside of his northwest neighborhood downtown to F Street for work and mentions venturing into other quadrants to visit friends or other family members, he still seems to be most familiar and comfortable with the northwest district.

Conversely, in "Old Boys, Old Girls," Jones demonstrates versatility of narrative mode, applying the third-person perspective to explore the landscape of the city as opposed to writing in first person as he does in "All Aunt Hagar's Children." Jones traces the experiences of protagonist Caesar Matthews, who serves time in jail for murder and then adjusts to life after his sentence. With third-person narration, Jones can explain Caesar's interactions with the city from a more objective point of view. Once he is released from prison, Caesar is still confined to the Northwest district because of his inability or unwillingness to interact with other people as he takes up residence in a boarding house "in the middle of the 900 block of N Street, Northwest," begins a job at a restaurant called Chowing Down, and spends many evenings sitting in Franklin Park at Fourteenth and K (Jones 2004b, 9). Even though the unnamed narrator in "All Aunt Hagar's Children" did not have a criminal record like Caesar, they both are confined to the same neighborhoods because of a lack of economic resources and social capital to navigate or reside in other areas. Near the story's end, the identification of locations and street names dramatically increases as Caesar makes references to his immediate surroundings while reconnecting to memories of his boyhood home on Tenth Street, convenience stores he remembers on Eleventh and Q Streets, Immaculate Conception Catholic Church on Eighth Street, a bank near Seventh Street, and general remarks about Ninth and N Streets. In contrast to the stifling effect of geography on the unnamed narrator in "All Aunt Hagar's Children," the physical landscape of Washington helps to rehabilitate Caesar. The ex-con finds solace in reconnecting with physical locations from his childhood as he seeks to reintegrate himself into the northwest quadrant of Washington, DC. The neighborhood as a physical location is integrated into Caesar's personality and thus, intertwined with his past and future.

Jones further demonstrates his interest in linking characters to specific geographies in "All Aunt Hagar's Children" and in "Old Boys, Old Girls" by emphasizing, through literary geotagging, the relationship of race and class. The protagonists in "All Aunt Hagar's Children" and in "Old Boys, Old Girls" reside in the northwest district of Washington and travel along the same routes, signaling a commonality between the two, although the descriptions of how they interact with their environments varies. Even though they reside in the same neighborhoods, each character interacts with and interprets his neighborhood in a different manner: the unnamed narrator is ready to escape the confines of his childhood, while Caesar uses the district to reconnect with his past. The differences between these two characters highlight how Jones links the dispositions of characters with their mobility. Each character's knowledge of the city's neighborhoods seems to reflect how he interacts with fellow citizens and how he navigates the city.

Geography plays a major role in Jones's stories, as the neighborhoods where the characters reside and the social venues that they frequent correspond to aspects of their racial and cultural identities. The histories of segregation in the United States as well as the tendency of families, especially low-income families, to live in specific segregated locations over generations reflect the ways in which race and place are often linked. Places where people gather for social events or for leisure time are often culturally distinct and populated by specific racial groups depending upon the venue. For instance, in "All Aunt Hagar's Children," the frequently mentioned Mojo's appears to be a local eatery or bar in the predominately African American district on North Capitol. Similarly, in "Old Boy, Old Girls," Jones's descriptions of the prison in Lorton where Caesar spent a considerable amount of time as well as the boarding house on N Street where many African American who live in the District reside. Jones utilizes these locations and populates them with African American characters not by happenstance. Instead, he embeds his story with subtle societal traits to make the correlation between race and location more apparent.

As previously noted, Jones's five short stories in *The New Yorker* illustrate a diverse set of concerns and attitudes about people living in Washington, but how does Jones achieve his narrative objectives linguistically? Text mining facilitates the processes of quantifying specific words and phrases in Jones's stories and can lead to detailed accounts of how an author uses language to describe a concentrated area of a city and narrate stories in those locales. In the case of Jones, the particulars that he gives to locations contribute to his overall body of writing, which together offer an extensive and fairly detailed account of settings in Washington. Referring to a specific quadrant or using words such as "block" or "street," all assist Jones in describing the context of the environments in which his characters reside. Moreover, his language also helps to clarify the characters' interactions with various neighborhoods and sheds light on the people that inhabit those places.

Jones's inclination to map the city by identifying streets and landmarks differentiates his works from several canonical short stories, including "Sweat" by Zora Neale Hurston, "Battle Royal" by Ralph Ellison, "Sonny's Blues" by James Baldwin, and "Raymond's Run" by Toni Cade Bambara. In comparison to those writers, Jones offers a far more detailed presentation of the geographic spaces that his characters traverse. Furthermore, Jones pinpoints a far larger number of specific locations in his stories, presenting a view of Washington, DC, through storytelling, which has been relatively uncommon in the canonical history of African American literature. Jones's frequent usage of location-specific phrases reveals that he is distinguishing himself, in part, from other widely known black short story writers based on his devotion to detail-rich, geographically precise narratives about a single city. Hurston's and Ellison's frequently anthologized short stories are valuable for a number of reasons, but the writers do not describe locations and neighborhoods in towns in great detail. In Hurston's "Sweat," the town where the action of the story takes place is never identified; however, readers learn that the setting is a small Florida town that is "too far" from Orlando, which means a snake-bitten antagonist will not receive medical attention.[4] In Ellison's "Battle Royal," the setting is never identified beyond general descriptions as a southern town.[5] Additionally, neither Hurston nor Ellison ever use the word "street" in their short stories or identify specific roads, neighborhoods, or city landmarks. By contrast, Jones utilizes more than 311 words and phrases, including avenue, "southwest," "southeast," "northwest," "northeast," and "street" to highlight the particularity of the city. Jones makes actual cityscapes and neighborhoods of Washington central to the plot and character development in each story by showing how the location has a bearing on a character's personality and on the sequence of events in the short narratives.

Attention to specific words and how narrators use them can also influence the perception of location and how specific geographical regions function within the context of a given story. For Jones, the term "street" varies depending on the narrative style in a story such as in "Bad Neighbors" and "All Aunt Hagar's Children." In "All Aunt Hagar's Children," Jones uses a first-person perspective, and the unnamed protagonist navigates specific streets in the city, explaining at one point that "I took the long way—down Fourth Street, then along New York Avenue to Sixth Street" (Jones 2003a, 10). Conversely, in "Bad Neighbors," the third-person limited narrator uses the word "street" primarily to describe the "Eighth Street" neighborhood where the principal characters of the story live as well as their relationships to one another. "Even before the fracas with Terence Stagg," the narrator opens the story, "people along both sides of the 1400 block of Eighth Street NW could see the Benningtons for what they really were" (Jones 2006, 73). The narrator in "Bad Neighbors" uses the word "street" and other related terms primarily to describe a single block, while the narrator in "All Aunt Hagar's Children" utilizes the term to present broader areas of geographic space in Washington. Thus, Jones's use of different narrative modes alters how he presents varied city landscapes by providing different renderings of the northwest quadrant through different uses of the common word "street." The narrators' multiple presentations of the word "street" in Jones's *New Yorker* stories illustrate how a single word can alter the relationships between characters and their environments.

Indeed, the narrators play a crucial role in Jones's short stories as this persona ultimately dictates how words are used or emphasized to describe specific neighborhoods in Washington, DC. Each narrator demonstrates how the plot is intertwined with specific streets and dictates character interactions and movement. In "Bad Neighbors," threats of violence become central to the plot as the lead character, Sharon, is almost sexually assaulted by a group of college students near Thirty-Sixth Street around the Georgetown University Hospital. Her former neighbor, Derek, with whom she and other residents have had a strained relationship in the past, saves Sharon from her attackers. In this respect, location seems to push Derek and Sharon away from each other as well as to unite them. By focusing on the ideological differences of families on the Eighth Street northwest neighborhood, Jones reveals the diversity among black people living in the same district. Through the interactions between Sharon and Derek, Jones unsettles any monolithic or static views of "black people" in the city by revealing the intra-racial conflicts that exist between families on a common street. In short, geographic location or living in close proximity like Sharon and Derek does not necessarily suggest racial unity.

Location plays a pivotal role in the fiction of Jones as a way of critiquing intra-racial prejudices and stereotypes as well as extending his commentary to analyzing widespread discrepancies between black and white people. After rescuing Sharon from almost being molested, Derek decides to take her home. While on route, police race by them, probably responding to the incident from which they have just departed, and Derek remarks, "They gone pull that one patrol car they have in Southeast and the only one they got in Northeast and bring em over here to join the dozens they keep in Georgetown" (Jones 2006, 82). His comments about the police indicate his frustration with the lack of law enforcement in the southeast and northeast districts in contrast to Georgetown, which is located in the northwest quadrant of the city. Notably, Derek utilizes place-based references to offer a critique of inequality. The range of emotions conjured up by location reveals how in the context of this story the city's neighborhoods can both repel and attract Derek and Sharon from each other even though the two were once neighbors on Eighth Street. The narrative also provides opportunities for considering the operations of geotagging in the story. Geography, as evidenced through Derek's comments, contains racial and economic sentiments that often times escape the purview of law and order in the traditional sense. Honing in on the specific responses of African American characters and how they make distinctions between various districts in the nation's capital provides an artistic and cultural rendering of the particular ways that location shapes a person's responses to an environment based on one's racial identity and relationships with governmental power structures.

Jones's Washington settings have been the topic of discussion among reviewers who have commented on the significance of the reoccurring cityscape across the majority of his short stories. One such reviewer, Darryl Pinckney (2007), for instance, explains, "Washington isn't described in Jones's stories. It just is; a gathering of nostalgia-producing addresses, locations." In Pinckney's estimation, Jones's descriptions of the city are not fleshed out, but instead draw on his coming-of-age experiences and recollections of city life. Perhaps Pinckney is suggesting that Jones is so familiar with the neighborhoods that he does not feel obligated to delve into details regarding the significance of each intersection or cross-street in his stories. Jones's constant references to street names, cultural figures, and landmarks, however, draw on historical and social memories for each character. These memories reveal how a select geographic location conjures a range of emotions and thus becomes significant to the overall plot of each story.

John Harrison's (2006) review of *All Aunt Hagar's Children* likewise takes note of the centrality of Washington, DC, to Jones's characters in his short stories. He writes, "All of the stories are set in or en route to Washington, DC, and Jones's heavy reference to the street plan of DC leads me to recommend having a map of the area handy. Each story traces a journey—planned or unplanned, taken or failed—and an obvious root/route symbolism runs throughout the collection." In a footnote to his review, Harrison adds, "The only time I've been to Washington was for an 8th-grade field trip, and we decidedly did not visit the areas in question." The locations identified in Jones's stories are not tourist destinations. Instead, they are everyday neighborhoods or routes taken by black residents of the District. The many references to street names outside of the purview of tourists give range and depth to the readers' understanding of Washington. Jones's characters interact with the city in ways that display their immersion primarily in the northwest and southeast quadrants, and his use of literary geotagging provides impressions of the city that are geared toward the social interactions of neighbors and community members.

For some time now, scholars of African American literature have displayed keen interest in geographic location and migration.[6] Advancements in technology over the years, including the development of the Global Positioning System (GPS) and its many uses on social media and mobile devices, have made geotagging an integral feature of modern life. Literary geotagging might illuminate the positioning, location, directional, mapping, and geographic matters in the works of a writer like Jones, who is highly attuned to the specificities of streets, neighborhoods, and city landmarks. More attention to the kind of literary geotagging that appears in short stories, novels, poems, and plays by black writers can enhance our appreciation of the artistic renderings of real-life locations and their significance to the characterization of African American culture. In addition, a focus on literary geotagging brings us closer to explaining how the frequency of location-specific words contributes to how an author creates impressions of a neighborhood and gains credibility as a narrator.

Notes

1. Several canonical African American literary texts, including *Native Son* (1940), *Invisible Man* (1952), and *Song of Solomon* (1977), have concentrated on black male protagonists in multiple geographic regions, particularly Chicago, New York City, the Midwest, and the South. Accordingly, scholars have produced a substantial body of writings on these novels and the regions they have represented in their works.

2. Over the last fifteen years, Jones's work has appeared in *The New Yorker* more any other African American short story writer. His five stories, "Bad Neighbors," "Adam Robinson," "Old Boys, Old Girls," "All Aunt Hagar's Children," and "A Rich Man," were eventually collected in *All Aunt Hagar's Children* (2006).

3. Even though specific legislative measures to discriminate against African Americans were outlawed about forty years ago, Jones provides commentary about institutional factors that make discrepancies between black and white people apparent. For instance, in "Apart and Parcel: What Housing Segregation in D.C. Looks Like" Chris Dickersin-Prokopp (2012) explains, "The persistence of black-white residential segregation reflects the nation's inability to fully overcome the legacy of slavery, and it negatively affects education attainment, race relations, and productivity." He continues, "Despite nearly a century of legal and legislative struggles to integrate our blocks, segregation by race is still the norm in the District" (*Washington City Paper*). Despite seemingly advancing past separate-but-equal political and social ideology, factors still exist that contribute to widespread housing discrimination. Even though black people cannot be barred from participation

in the economy and public sphere because of constitutional rights, institutional barriers and unequal access to education and employment place economic obstacles that still segregate a majority of black people based on class status and income. These issues, which disproportionally affect black people in comparison to their white counterparts, have the ability to dictate the neighborhoods and environments in which one lives.

4. We might conclude that the story is set in Eatonville, Florida, since a town cofounder, Joe Clarke, makes an appearance as a minor character in Hurston's story. See Valerie Boyd, *Wrapped in Rainbows: The Life of Zora Neale Hurston* (2004, 20–22).

5. At the end of Ellison's novel *Invisible Man,* readers learn that the "Battle Royal" took place in an Alabama town (Ellison 2004).

6. Farah Jasmine Griffin's *"Who set you flowin'?"* examines migration patterns of African Americans during the early twentieth century. Her work positions migration narratives as a central genre of African American cultural traditions.

Works Cited

Baldwin, James. 2004. "Sonny's Blues." In *The Norton Anthology of African American Literature,* edited by Henry Louis Gates and Nellie Y. McKay. New York: Norton.

Bambara, Toni Cade. 1972. "Raymond's Run." In *Gorilla, My Love.* New York: Random House.

Boyd, Valerie. 1970. *Wrapped in Rainbows: The Life of Zora Neale Hurston.* New York: Scribner.

Campbell, Richard, Christopher R. Martin, and Bettina Fabos. 2004. *Media & Culture: An Introduction to Mass Communication.* Boston: Bedford/St. Martin's.

Danticat, Edwidge. 2001. "Seven." In *The New Yorker,* October 1. http://www.newyorker.com/archive/2001/10/01/011001fi_fiction.

Dickersin-Prokopp, Chris. 2012. "Apart and Parcel: What Housing Segregation in D.C. Looks Like." *Washington City Paper,* August 31. http://www.washingtoncitypaper.com/blogs/. citydesk/2012/08/09/apart-and-parcel-what-housing-segregation-in-d-c-looks-like/.

Eggers, Dave. 2006. "Still Lost in the City." *The New York Times,* August 27. http://www.nytimes.com/2006/08/27/books/review/Eggers.t.html?pagewanted=all&_r=0.

Ellison, Ralph. 2004. "Battle Royal." In *The Norton Anthology of African American Literature,* edited by Henry Louis Gates and Nellie Y. McKay. New York: Norton.

Griffin, Farah Jasmine. 1995. *"Who set you flowin'?": The African American Migration Narrative.* New York: Oxford University Press.

Harrison, John. 2006. "All Aunt Hagar's Children By Edward P. Jones." *The Quarterly Conversation.* (Spring 2006). http://quarterlyconversation.com/all-aunt-hagars-children-by-edward-p-jones-review.

Hurston, Zora Neale. 1995. "Sweat." In *The Complete Stories.* New York: HarperCollins.

Jones, Edward P. 2003a. "All Aunt Hagar's Children." *New Yorker,* December 22. http://www.newyorker.com/archive/2003/12/22/031222-_-ction1.

———. 2003b. "A Rich Man." *New Yorker,* August 4. http://www.newyorker.com/archive/2003/08/04/030804-fiction.

———. 2004a. "Adam Robinson." *New Yorker,* December 20. http://www.newyorker.com/archive/2004/12/20/041220fiction.

———. 2004b. "Old Boys, Old Girls." *New Yorker,* May 3. http://www.newyorker.com/achive/2004/05/03/040503-

———. 2006. "Bad Neighbors." *New Yorker,* August 7. http://www.newyorker.com/archive/2006/08/07/060807-fiction.

Miller, E. Ethelbert. 2006. "Edward P. Jones talks about 'The Known World' and his Washington, D.C., short stories." *Howard County Poetry and Literature Society.* May 9. http://www.youtube.com/watch?v=W5sPWxFiVZI.

Pinckney, Darryl. 2007. "Black Wisdom." *The New York Review of Books,* March 9. http://www.nybooks.com/articles/archives/2007/mar/29/black-wisdom/?pagination=false.

E S S A Y

IN-BETWEEN BLACK SELF AND WHITE DESIRE: MOBILITY AND LIMINALITY IN ANN PETRY'S *THE STREET*

by Ashley Bourgeois

T he final pages of Ann Petry's 1946 novel, *The Street,* find Petry's defeated protagonist, Lutie Brown, on a train bound for Chicago, finally abandoning the son she has tried throughout the novel to protect. As she questions the possible good it has done to "teach people like [her] to write," she foresees no positive prospect for the race, and condemns not only her son but the entire black race to both illiteracy and inferior social status. Trying to "figure out by what twists and turns of fate she had landed on the train," Lutie lays the full weight of blame on the "god-damned street" (Petry 1946, 435). Petry blames the street, too. In an interview with James W. Ivy just after *The Street*'s publication, Petry asserts that she intended to "show how simply and easily the environment can change the course of a person's life." She wants readers to know "why the Negro has a high crime rate, a high death rate, and little or no chance of keeping his family unit intact in northern cities" (Ivy 1946, 48–49). In her statement, Petry points to the deterministic elements of her narrative, which set it squarely within the tradition of naturalist fiction; Lutie's world of racial injustice and sexist oppression constitutes the determined environment that represents the "best-known aspect of the genre" (Howard 1985, x). Early critical reception of *The Street* aligns the narrative with Richard Wright's *Native Son,* and critics deem Lutie, like Bigger Thomas, a doomed character, powerless to act upon her own fate. That Petry seeks to expose the horrors of African American urbanization in the first half of the twentieth century is readily apparent and well-justified by readers and critics alike; but as she details Lutie's efforts to detach from the black community, Petry also explores a desire for space that stands to threaten racial solidarity. While I do not discount the naturalist elements working against Lutie, decentering the naturalist paradigm allows readers to investigate different ways in which "space," what Michel Foucault (1986) refers to as the "great obsession" of the twentieth century, functions within the text. An investigation of Lutie's relationship to space allows readers to recognize her free-will decisions that denote the rejection of her black family and community. If loyalty represents a "commitment to those who share a common fate" (Fletcher 1993) Lutie's active dismissal of that commitment to her race is underscored by her desire for, and active pursuit of, white spaces throughout the text.

Feminist critics contributing to theories of spatiality note the ways in which space operates in relation to intersecting identities of race, gender, sexuality, and class. Mary Pat Brady, in *Extinct Lands, Temporal Geographies: Chicana Literature and the Urgency of Space,* claims that women of color write with a "sense of urgency about the power of space, about its (in)clement capacity to direct and contort opportunities, hopes, lives"; this same sense of urgency characterizes the ways in which these authors emphasize the need to "contest power" within these spaces (2002, 9). Similarly, Claire Drewery notes that certain spaces hold not only the "ominous threat of exclusion" for women but also possibilities for creativity and subversion (2011, 13). Discrete spaces then, unlike the unyielding determinist environment, hold a contradiction, and in this way the production of space contributes to social processes, becomes itself a social process, "active and generative" as opposed to fixed, "inert and transparent" (Brady 2002, 7). Within the fictional realm, spaces of oppression and/or opportunity can seemingly act alone upon a character, but to the extent that these same spaces potentially inspire the actions of that character, spaces become relational, working with the character, to develop a social meaning that either contributes to positive social change or upholds an oppressive social order. The production of space requires the interaction of its inhabitant. Throughout the nonlinear narrative that brings spatiality to the forefront of *The Street,* space acts upon Lutie to effect desire, but as a relational process, it negates any notion of her helplessness. Without negating the power of space to affect her subjectivity, this analysis integrates spatial concepts of mobility and liminality to frame Lutie's rejection of black spaces, both tangible and intangible in favor of an unattainable, white ideal. In seeking this ideal, Lutie fails to identify black spaces as sites from which members of black families and communities claim and contest power.

The Street follows Lutie Brown, a single black mother seeking a better life for her son, Bub, in 1940s New York. When her husband Jim can't find work, Lutie provides for her family, working as a maid and nanny for the Chandlers, a blue-blood family living in Connecticut. As she absorbs their conversations and attitudes, Lutie is increasingly obsessed with the "good life" defined by material wealth and commits herself to attaining it. When her husband leaves her for another woman, Lutie fears the moral education that her son might receive from his father and from his "blousy girlfriend"; but seeking a place of her own she finds that all she can afford is a crowded upstairs apartment in a dilapidated building on 116th street in Harlem. While living there she meets a parade of characters including Jones, the building superintendent; Min, his live-in girlfriend; Mrs. Hedges, the strange madam who observes all corners of the street from behind her open window; and Boots, the "bad boy" musician and draft dodger who offers Lutie a singing job extended by Junto, white owner of the local hangouts. When Lutie spurns Jones's sexual advances, his revenge involves a scheme to corrupt Bub; and when Bub is unfairly apprehended, Lutie goes to Boots for money. Unbeknownst to her, Boots and his white boss, Junto, have been scheming themselves—each determined to have Lutie sexually. Motivated by both self-defense and pure rage, Lutie murders Boots and walks away convinced that she can do nothing to help her son. Ultimately she leaves him waiting for her at a children's correctional facility as she boards a one-way train for Chicago.

Petry's narrative voice twists and turns throughout *The Street,* following Lutie through myriad spaces throughout the text. Readers attempting to visualize Lutie's geographical movement will locate her all over the city; not only does she move from three different homes and hold at least three different jobs, she frequents the bar and is often en route, or in between spaces, onboard a train or subway. Lutie's mobility stands in direct contrast to Petry's secondary characters, whose stories are also told in relation to space. Jones's "cellar" craziness is attributed to time spent in small, tight places on boats and in basements; Boots is demoralized as a porter on Pullman cars, where spatial proximity to white patrons serves to reinforce his racial inferiority. Working for Junto, even his luxurious car can't afford him real freedom to move: Boots's mobility is subject to the white man's whims. Mrs. Hedges escapes death by fire by pushing herself, with much difficulty, through a window space too small. Though it doesn't consume her, the fire leaves her hard, powerful body scarred and doomed to a confined space behind her window, from where she keeps eye over the space of the street beyond. Only Min's mobility stands to challenge Lutie's. Although she spends what seems to be the majority of the narrative trapped within Jones's apartment, taking up "the least possible amount of space," her desire to keep that space finally motivates her movement beyond it, as she enlists the help of Mrs. Hedges, the local "Prophet," and finally the moving man she cozies up to (Petry 1946, 24). For these secondary characters, interactions with space are informed by their desire to remain tethered to the black community, while Lutie's are most often motivated by a desire to move beyond it.

Lutie's mobility—her ability to move from one place to another—is not only indicative of her agency, but also, her privilege. Mary Pat Brady asserts that for women of color, mobility exists as a "carefully restricted privilege [...] Curtailing women's mobility makes it more difficult for them to take advantage of the economic opportunities that shape spatial production and to challenge systems of social reproduction" (2002, 134). To the extent that all women on the street face the horrors of urban segregation, they are far removed from the realm of white privilege. And yet, even within the most marginal of communities, there exist hierarchies of privilege; the street is no exception. When in *Their Eyes Were Watching God,* Zora Neal Hurston's character Granny refers to a black woman as "de *mule* uh de world" she correctly assesses a hierarchy based upon gender and race (1937, 14). But even among poor black women there exists a hierarchy of privilege in relation to a multitude of intersecting identities. Lutie occupies a privileged position in relation to her female counterparts within the text based upon her range of mobility.

If, as Brady asserts, mobility exists *as* a privilege, it is also true that access to mobility is *a result of* privilege. Lutie's ability to occupy the many spaces that she does is based at least in part upon her own set of privileges, which can be identified as family, beauty, and education. When Lutie's mother passes away, it is Pop who insists that she finish high school. She is married immediately following graduation, and while her beauty may ultimately be read as a curse that intensifies the gendered oppression and sexual abuse that she endures from men both within and beyond the African American community, beauty helped Lutie to secure, at least for some time, "a big handsome husband of her own" (Petry 1946, 41). When Mrs. Hedges views Lutie's hair and "smooth, unscarred skin" longingly, she is reminded that she will "never have any man's love" (246). When Lutie takes her job with the Chandlers, Jim watches the two-year-old Bub and following her separation from Jim, when Lutie returns to school and administrative work, Pop is there to watch young Bub. While it's true that Lutie must look for work because "the white folks [didn't] like to give black men jobs that paid enough for them to support their families," without her family to provide childcare service along the way, the education and job choices that provide Lutie with greater mobility would not likely be available to her (388). Lutie's spatial interactions, increased by greater mobility, inform her rejection of black community in favor of white space. In her analysis of Sandra Cisneros's *Woman Hollering Creek and Other Stories,* Brady asserts that women's movements are directly related to their "range of desires," and we can see Lutie's increasing desire for white domestic space attributed at least in part to her movement (and determined nonmovement) between spaces (2002, 134). In her case, mobility affords her increased exposure to the "other" lifestyle—both in terms of the white Chandler home and its commodity representation in the advertisement for the white kitchen that she encounters on board the train. It is the desire for, and pursuit of, these spaces that fuels the rejection of her husband, father, and son, and informs her dismissal of black domestic space. When Lutie takes a job working for the Chandlers, it is out of necessity. Although Mrs. Pizzini, her local grocer, warns against it, claiming, "Not good for the woman to work when she's young. Not good for the man," her advice is a luxury Lutie's family cannot afford (Petry 1946, 33). The determinist elements working against her family demand that she look beyond her home: Jim can't find work and they must provide for a young son. However, it is not her decision to work for the Chandlers, but her decision to remain at the Chandlers more often than necessary that contributes to the disintegration of her family.

Although as she settles into life with the Chandlers, Lutie finds herself at different turns both in awe of and repulsed by the family, she ultimately "absorbs" some of their same spirit—particularly, their views on wealth and ambition. When Lutie begins working for the Chandlers, her schedule affords her one day a week to be home with her own family. She remembers that at one point during her stint there, she actually hated the Chandlers' street, and longed to go home to her small frame house to be with Jim and Bub. But as soon as she lets the Chandlers' philosophy about money infiltrate her letters home to Jim, she stops going home to that small house, nearly altogether. When Mrs. Chandler suggests that she visit home once a month, to make for four days at a time with her family as opposed to one every week, Lutie adjusts her schedule accordingly. Then, Lutie cuts even those once-a-month visits in an effort to save money; independently she makes the decision to go home to her family only every other month, totaling only six visits home a year. Mrs. Chandler's suggestion does not infringe upon any of Lutie's actual time spent with family; it merely serves to rearrange it. Lutie's decision to skip visits, however, cuts her family time in half. Her unwillingness, not inability, to move between domestic spaces more frequently is indicative of her desire for the white space she serves, even in spite of the violence and emotional turmoil she witnesses there, including Mr. Chandler's alcoholism, Mrs. Chandler's philandering, the suicide of a relative, and an elaborate family cover-up. According to Brady, the "regulation of space reinforces the regulation of desire and pleasure" (2002, 135). In other words, in a controlled environment, a person becomes limited in his or her ability to envision terms of personal satisfaction; what provides pleasure within a given space often becomes desirable by all those who inhabit it. In her decision to remain at the Chandlers', Lutie self-regulates her spatial situation to some extent, rejecting the desires and pleasures that her time spent at home may afford her in favor of being surrounded by material wealth.

Critics who address Lutie's separation from her husband tend to treat her as the unfortunate victim of Jim's indiscretion, almost always employing passive terms to describe the situation that she encounters upon coming home to find her husband with another woman. Richard Yarborough admires Lutie's "tremendous drive to get ahead" when he describes the situation (1981, 63). In "Buried Alive: Gothic Homelessness, Black Women's Sexuality, and (Living) Death in Ann Petry's *The Street*," Evie Shockley recounts how Lutie *loses* the "little house where she had once lived in a conventional nuclear unit with her son and husband when her husband's adultery precipitated a permanent separation (in lieu of a prohibitively expensive divorce)" (2006, 445). Critics fail to mention, however, that what "precipitates" Jim's adultery may well be Lutie's dismissal of him; she does not so much "lose" her family as she gives it up.

By rejecting the black family space, Lutie denies herself a sense of belonging that might inform her decisions. In "African American Family Life: An Instrument of Culture," Wade W. Nobles notes the provision of family as necessary "support systems that were unavailable in other majority group institutions" (2007, 74). Black family contributes to "legitimacy of beingness" by providing members with a source of "connection, attachment, validation, worth, recognition and respect." Nobles classifies this "legitimation of beingness" as one of five "family strengths" associated with the African American family, which makes black individuals more "capable of responding to complex, vague and unfamiliar experience" (82). Long after her separation, when she reflects upon black women who work, Lutie recognizes the vicious cycle of oppression that plagues black families. Still, she misunderstands Jim's reaction to her absence. She imagines he "couldn't stand being shut up in the little house in Jamaica" the same way she can't stand her own apartment, and admits that while living on the street she at least has the privilege of a job "that takes her out every day" (83). Lutie assumes that Jim's problem was their small house, and yet that's where she finds him when Pop calls her home, seemingly happy while watching his new woman cook. Jim has remade the same "conventional family unit" that he had lost when Lutie left. His need is not the space—it's the need to have her in it. While she rightfully identifies ways in which the dominant economic order seeks to humiliate black men and destroy the black family, Lutie never admits that depriving Jim of herself contributes to the demoralization of both.

Many critics laud Lutie's drive for success and upward mobility, but if her ultimate aim is in fact, as Petry suggests, "keeping her family intact," Bub is the last remaining member to whom she is responsible, and the member who suffers most at the hands of Lutie's mobility. Not only does Lutie similarly deprive Bub of herself when she leaves him alone so that she can take care of Little Henry Chandler, but she denies him the same legitimation through family when she decides to leave Pop's place—where she goes for refuge upon leaving Jim. While she forgives the Chandlers their myriad transgressions, she is too quick to uproot her son from his extended family, citing reasons related to Pop's drinking and blousy girlfriend, Lil. Lutie's concern for her son's welfare is undeniable, and yet her decision to isolate them both from her family does not serve his best interest. According to Lutie, the "thing that really mattered was getting away from Pop and his raddled women, and anything was better than that. Dark hallways, dirty stairs, even roaches on the walls. Anything. Anything. Anything" (Petry 1946, 4–5). Of course "anything" on the street, turns out to be worse for her son and herself. In "The Effects of Evil in Ann Petry's *The Street*: Invoking Biblical and Literary Tradition," Annie Perkins notes that when Lutie moves, because she disapproves of her father's lifestyle, Bub loses "a home where he is cared for and, equally important, supervised" (2004, 339). Despite their shortcomings, Pop and Lil provide Bub with the family and sense of belongingness he needs. Left home alone on the street, Bub falls under the unwelcome supervision of Jones, who seeks out time with the boy first to endear him to his mother and finally to enact revenge against her.

At home with Bub on the street, Lutie is often too preoccupied with money to commit any real time or attention to her son. While she has the extra cash to send Bub to the movies and visit the Junto for a beer herself, she disregards opportunities to bolster relations with him. Perhaps most astonishingly, she discounts his fears regarding the very same space that she herself detests. Several times she notes her own disdain for the apartment, her inability to remain there because the walls are pushing in on her, and yet, she goes out nights to pursue a singing career, leaving Bub alone in the space. While it's true that as a single mother without a budget for after-school care, she must leave Bub home alone in the afternoons, she stretches her time away from him for money, just as she had in her position with the Chandlers. Whereas Pop might have watched him while she was out, in the new space, he is alone. Lutie's treatment of Bub stands in stark contrasts to the care she showed Little Henry following his uncle's suicide: when she found "his small face so white, so frightened [...] she very nearly cried. None of them had given him a thought; they had deserted him as neatly as though they had deposited him on the doorstep of a foundling hospital." When she took him into her arms, she assured him her arms were a "solid safe place *where he belonged,* where he was safe" (Petry 1946, 48). When Bub tries to tell his mother what it's like for him to be alone in the dark, Lutie's face is "shut tight with anger and her voice so hard and cold" that he decides against it (316). While Lutie accepts Little Henry into motherly arms, Bub is shut out, or rather shut into the dark space of the apartment, and his mother's regular absence foreshadows her final desertion.

Only weeks after moving onto the street, Lutie's longing for physical space culminates in her estimation of the white kitchen that she encounters in an advertisement while on the train. Again, mobility fuels her range of desire. The ad depicts a gorgeous white couple: "They were standing in front of a kitchen sink—a sink whose white porcelain surface gleamed under the train lights. The faucets looked like silver. The linoleum floor of the kitchen was a crisp black-and-white pattern that pointed up the sparkle of the room. Casement windows. Red geraniums in yellow pots. It was, she thought, a miracle of a kitchen" (Petry 1946, 28). In "The Opacity of Everyday Life: Segregation and Iconicity in *The Street*," Meg Wesling (2006) understands Lutie's desire for the kitchen as an affirmation of her ability to succeed in the domestic sphere, but if the kitchen in the advertisement represents desire for the domestic, it is specifically the white kitchen, the white domestic sphere, and the white lifestyle that she associates with it, that Lutie desires. According to Kimberly Drake, Lutie believes that if she can "recreate the 'clean' bourgeois home (including its isolation), she can find the satisfaction [that she] associates with the white middle class" (2011, 102). But Lutie loathes her own kitchen. Leaving the market for home one day she walks "slowly, avoiding the moment when she must enter the apartment and start fixing dinner" (Petry 1946, 63). Certainly her dilapidated kitchen holds no joy for her—nor should it necessarily; but the space serves as a meeting place for her and her son, and Lutie denies that potentially creative black kitchen space in favor of an unattainable one. She allows the white kitchen, as she attests, to "change her whole life," blaming it, as she does also the street, for her ultimate demise (56).

Considered within both gendered and racial contexts, the kitchen space is ambiguous in its representation of power. Much feminist theory identifies the kitchen as a site of oppression and isolation for women; as part of the domestic realm to which women are relegated, the kitchen limits female mobility and fosters their exclusion from more public spaces. But as Hazel B. Carby (1989) argues in her seminal work, *Reconstructing Womanhood: The Emergence of the Afro-American Woman Novelist,* the domestic space can serve to empower the African American woman attempting to shake her image as a hypersexualized slave. Even within the context of slavery, however, the kitchen held subversive potential. In "To Tell the Kitchen Version: Architectural Figurations of Race and Gender in Harriet Jacobs's *Incidents in the Life of a Slave Girl* and Harriet Wilson's *Our Nig*," Katja Kanzler (2006) explores the kitchen as a liminal space. She notes than in its geographical positioning on the southern plantation, the kitchen functioned as a literal barrier, an in-between place separating the white house from the slave quarters; but it was also an in-between space for the way it functioned as both a site of oppression and subversion for slaves (par. 15). Kanzler recalls how, for Frederick Douglass, the kitchen "accommodates scenes that flesh out the exploitation of slave labor, the violent abuse of slaves, and the dynamics of the slave community that regularly assembles in that room" (par. 18). Betty's kitchen, in *Incidents in the Life of a Slave Girl,* Kanzler argues, can be read more emphatically as a "symbol of resistance, outlining ways in which slaves appropriate the spaces slavery assigns them" (par. 26).

This discussion of the slave kitchen demonstrates, in a specific space, the potential for oppression and subversion that both Mary Pat Brady and Claire Drewery address in their accounts of gendered spaces. Although the slave kitchen was not spatially appropriated for the black community, it functioned in part as a black communal space, and serves to inform the "black" kitchen Lutie both occupies and rejects within the text. This kitchen, both potentially subversive and communal, stands in stark contrast to the Chandler kitchen, which Lutie describes as being just like the one in the ad on the train. Glistening and seemingly unlived in, Lutie has bought into white commercialism in exchange for the "African spiritualness" that W. E. B. Du Bois (1903) describes in *The Souls of Black Folk* as that which might deny the intense drive for material wealth. Langston Hughes (1926) similarly cautions against running away "spiritually from [the black] race" in "The Negro Artist and the Racial Mountain," and bemoans "this urge within the race toward whiteness, the desire to pour racial individuality into the mold of American standardization, and to be as little Negro and as much American as possible."

Lutie's desire for whiteness informs and substantiates what other critics refer to as her naivety and misguided adoption of an unlikely, white male role model in Benjamin Franklin. Walking home from the grocery store one day she aligns herself with the prominent historical figure, "thinking that if Ben Franklin could live on a little bit of money and could prosper, then so could she" (Petry 1946, 64). According to Drake, "in accepting a white model of identity, Lutie disowns both her culture and her community, placing herself in vulnerable isolation" and notes that her faith in the "self-made man" story of Ben Franklin causes her to "ignore her own instincts and the teachings of her grandmother, both of which are essential parts of her identity" (2011, 104). Lutie rejects an intangible space in the voice in her dead grandmother—a voice Lutie both recalls and ignores throughout the novel. In *Who set you flowin'?* Farah Jasmine Griffin notes that Lutie "makes a conscious effort to disassociate herself from her grandmother's influence" and in doing so, dismisses a "safe space embodied in the ancestor—a space grounded in oral tradition and emerging from an African past" (1995, 115). In "Patterns Against the Sky: Deism and Motherhood in Ann Petry's *The Street,*" Marjorie Pryse contends that Petry simply allows Lutie to "make the wrong choices, follow the wrong models" rather than questioning her decision to dismiss her grandmother's voice (1985, 123). Pryse goes further to suggest that *Petry* should have realized the potential for Granny in the novel and notes that instead, the author allows her protagonist to choose as her model Benjamin

Franklin (124, my emphasis). But it is Lutie, not Petry who ignores Granny's potential, and Petry, rather, who reminds us over and over of the active decisions Lutie makes to ignore her. In terms of psychical spatial positioning, we might associate Lutie's rejection of her grandmother's voice as the moment of separation from the cultural space of African-ness and her entry into a liminal state, suspended between racial identification.

Liminality refers to the occupation of the space in between. As Drewery notes, "liminality" is a term resistant to definition. The term's Latin root, "*limen*," translates to "threshold," and so the liminal condition is one preoccupied with negotiating and trans-gressing boundaries, often characterized by indeterminacy or ambiguity. In "Looking for Liminality in Architectural Space," Catherine Smith (2001) defines the liminal space as transitional, standing in between as neither one thing nor another, but a "thirdspace" involving two points of opposition or interrelation. In Lutie's case, her own sense of intan-gible liminality resides between white and black worlds; she is suspended, in some sense, between who she objectively is, and who she wants to be. According to Victor Turner, liminality as a social status happens along a continuum, an uncomfortable yet subversive condition situated between "successive states of being" within a given social structure. For Turner, the liminal position holds promise of a breakthrough, a sort of upward mobility, with transcendence as the ultimate goal.

As Lutie tries, without success, to secure upward mobility, trains and subways rein-force time spent in the "in-between," both physically and figuratively. It's during her time en route that Lutie finds retreat from her black identity, and enters into a sort of post-racial, liminal space. When on board to meet her new employer, Lutie ponders how Mrs. Chandler will recognize her, but almost the instant she arrives, a young blond woman ap-proaches her, smiling and saying hello. When Lutie looks around, she realized "she needn't have worried [...] there wasn't another colored person in sight" at the station (Petry 1946, 36). Lutie had forgotten the black skin that served to "other" her. She forgets and is re-minded again of her black identity, when she and Mrs. Chandler take the same train to New York: "On the ride they would talk—about some story…in the newspapers, about clothes, or some moving picture. But when the train pulled into Grand Central, the wall was suddenly there" (51). While they inhabit the liminal, in-between space of the train, Lutie believes she and her mistress to be friends, but when they arrive to fixed destina-tions, Lutie is once again the help. Resentful, Lutie argues with herself: "Would it hurt Mrs. Chandler just once to talk at that moment of parting as though, however incredible it might seem to anyone who was listening, they were friends? Just two people who knew each other and to whom it was only incidental that one of them was white and the other black?" (51). It is because of the color of her skin that she cannot remain friends with Mrs. Chandler beyond the confines of the liminal train space. Her skin is a determinist element of heredity—she cannot change its color, nor the social reaction to it, nor the sense of oppression that it invites. But on the space of the train, Mrs. Chandler's white eyes can overlook Lutie's color, and so the production of that space as an equalizer depends upon the interactions of those who inhabit it.

If Lutie yearns to defy the racial difference as it exists between herself and white Mrs. Chandler, she wishes to emphasize difference as it exists between herself and her black counterparts within the text. The stairwell of her building on the street serves as a differ-ent type of liminal space. While the train promotes feelings of racial equality for Lutie, the stairwell implies her imposed superiority to her black counterparts. Not only does the liminal space of the stairwell act to distance Lutie physically from the tenants below her on the street, she attempts to create psychological distance from those blacker than her. By describing these characters according to color, Lutie attempts to create a space for herself that is not among them. Drake notes that when Lutie refers to Min, Jones's live-in girl, as "small and dark," Petry makes a subtle comment on Lutie's colorism (2011, 114). What Drake fails to mention is the way in which Lutie identifies all of her social contacts according to color. Upon seeing Mrs. Hedges for the first time, she notes she is "very black" (Petry 1946). Walking behind Jones, the superintendent to see the apartment, she notices that the rod of the flashlight in his hands is "almost as black as his hands" (12). During her first encounter with Boots, she notices his scar that stands out "sharply against the dark brown of his skin" (152). By emphasizing black difference, Lutie attempts to move beyond the liminal space, drawing herself closer to the white society she deems more desirable.

In "Beyond Protest: The Street as Humanitarian Narrative," Clare Eby rightly observes that Lutie's immediate acquaintances "strike her as insignificant, inimical, or even lacking humanity" (2008, 34). Lutie's inability to credit her race with humanity may be the grumblings of a larger African American community. In 1944, (just two years prior to publication of *The Street*) Swedish economist Gunnar Myrdal published *An American Dilemma, Vol. 2: The Negro Social Structure,* in which he notes that those members of the African American community willing to "admit Negro inferiority…in fact [commit] treason to the race" (765). When Lutie sizes up her closest social contacts, she most often envisions animals. Mrs. Hedges is a snake, and Boots, a cat. Walking behind Jones, Lutie expects to see "horns sprouting from behind his ears…[and] a cloven hoof" that will "twitch" as he plods down the stairs (Petry 1946, 20). By ridding these characters of their humanity, Lutie assumes their inferiority, even despite the obvious identities they share in terms of race, class, and in the cases of Mrs. Hedges and Min, gender.

As she attempts to remove herself from the black community, Lutie enters into a sort of in-between, or liminal, psychological space; but this liminal position does not afford her the "breakthrough" Turner alludes to in relation to social status. Although Drake (2011) claims that Lutie "transcends aspects of her own culture, ideologically or physically crossing the boundaries that separate [herself] from whites," (93) Lutie's black skin remains a boundary that separates her from the white world, a boundary impossible to cross. She cannot "become white," nor can she envision a black role model who embodies her class desires. Her successful transcendence and reincorporation into black society would entail upward mobility, and the assumption of a superior class position within that structure. Instead, her choices throughout the novel only succeed in consigning her to the inferior social status she wished so badly to avoid.

In "Skin as a Trope of Liminality in Anne Enright's *The Gathering*," Ana-Karina Schneider discusses the skin's liminal quality, and although she does not deal with racialized skin, she does point to the ways in which the skin has implications for understanding individual subjectivity:

> Reference to skin invites analysis of skin as liminality, contact zone, an index of identity, but also a signifier in constant quest for recognition of its signifying power

and of its referent. Skin presupposes a self-other, inside-outside dialectic that defines interpersonal relations as much as the production of subjectivity. [...] As it participates in identity negotiation, skin both establishes and destabilizes one's sense of self. [Skin] is a space to traverse, both through and across, not a place to dwell in or on. (2013 6–13)

Like any other seemingly fixed or "natural" space, the scope of the skin's social meaning depends upon social interactions. When she considers "why people with white skins hated people who had dark skins," Lutie decides it is perhaps just a "shock" and concludes that "dark skins are smooth to the touch; they are warm from the blood that runs through the veins under the skin; they cover bodies that are just as well put together as the bodies that are covered with white skins" (Petry 1946, 71). Despite her seeming refusal of any inferiority based upon color, Lutie's skin contributes to a certain destabilization of self as she fails to understand its ability to define her interpersonal relations, particularly with white people. Lutie's skin as an "index of identity" becomes an unwelcome reminder of her inability to transcend race, because in the "self-other" it presumes, she locates both her subjective, white desire and black, racialized identity.

As Lutie navigates a liminal space between subjective desire and racial identity, she fails to grasp the positive potential of her blackness. In *The Souls of Black Folk*, Du Bois outlines his concept of double consciousness, which speaks to the a difficulty the African American individual faces, attempting to resolve a two-ness contained within him: a black self and an American self that are at once the same, but different:

It is a peculiar sensation, this double-consciousness, this sense of always looking at one's self through the eyes of others, of measuring one's soul by the tape of a world that looks on in amused contempt and pity. One ever feels his two-ness,—an American, a Negro; two souls, two thoughts, two unreconciled strivings; two warring ideals in one dark body, whose dogged strength alone keeps it from being torn asunder" (1903, 38).

Du Bois, like Schneider, grapples with an inside-outside dialectic; one feels his "two-ness" within himself, but also because there is an "other" presence that observes him, a white "world that looks on." While Schneider contends that the skin is "not a place to dwell in or on," Du Bois suggests that it is because of the undeniable reality that the world does dwells upon black skin that African Americans experience this difficult struggle defined as double-consciousness; white eyes fail to cross the threshold of black skin to encounter a similar American identity that lies beneath. Still, for Du Bois, this notion of occupying two spaces held possibility, just as for Turner, occupation of the in-between, or the liminal space, held promise of a social breakthrough. Du Bois recognizes and appreciates the African American longing to "merge his double self into a better and truer self." Yet "[i]n this merging he wishes neither of the older selves to be lost. He would not Africanize America, for America has too much to teach the world and Africa. He would not bleach his Negro soul in a flood of white Americanism, for he knows that Negro blood has a message for the world" (1903, 39). Ultimately, Lutie loses sight of this African message and fails to merge into a "better, truer self."

In "The Walking Wounded: Rethinking Black Women's Identity in Ann Petry's *The Street*, Carol Henderson agrees with Houston Baker's claim that "the critic [is] responsible for proposing alternative ways to view African American female expression in the literary imaginary" (2000, 267). Focusing on the "shapeless form" and "seared body" of Min and of Mrs. Hedges respectively, Henderson avoids any real discussion of Lutie, but makes a strong argument for reevaluating of the ways in which female characters "express themselves through interactions with their environment" (267). Ultimately, Lutie is resolved to her black self through enactment of black violence and as Eby notes, by the novel's end, she doubts her own humanity as she has doubted the humanity of those black selves around her. Slipping from a faulty liminal space, Lutie is forced to realize that the street is not, as she once suspected, a temporary fix, but her final destination. Her relocation to Chicago, the second largest urban city outside of New York, indicates the repetition of life on the street that will confirm her most dreaded social status.

Despite Lutie's vague intimations of her own accountability in the final pages of the narrative, critics eager to exonerate her foreclose any consideration of her interactions with space throughout the text, and of the ways in which those interactions incite desire. By exploring Lutie's free-will decisions related to mobility, readers might locate two distinctive, but not conflicting, messages at work within Petry's text. Lutie needn't be helpless or blameless in order for Petry to succeed in her attempt to show how the environment "can change" one's life; she does that. However, the author simultaneously suggests that the ways in which environment can do so are not always and only thoroughly determined by external forces. Through Lutie, Petry exposes the dangerous position of race/space relations—the process by which oppressed individuals, already shoved into spaces of unbelongingness by a dominant society, can contribute to the sense of unbelongingness that segregates them from their own communities—communities necessary to their survival.

Works Cited

Brady, Mary Pat. 2002. *Extinct Lands, Temporal Geographies.* Durham: Duke University Press.

Carby, Hazel. 1989. *Reconstructing Womanhood: The Emergence of the Afro-American Woman Novelist.* New York: Oxford University Press.

Drake, Kimberly S. 2011. *Subjectivity in the American Protest Novel.* New York: Palgrave Macmillan.

Du Bois, W. E. B. 1903. *The Souls of Black Folk.* Boston: Bedford/St. Martin's, 1997.

Drewery, Claire. 2011. *Modernist Short Fiction by Women: The Liminal in Katherine Mansfield, Dorothy Richardson, May Sinclair and Virginia Woolf.* Burlington: Ashgate.

Eby, Clare Virginina. 2008. "Beyond Protest: The Street as Humanitarian Narrative." *Melus* 33 (1): 33–53.

Fletcher, George P. 1993. *Loyalty: An Essay on the Morality of Relationships.* New York: Oxford University Press.

Foucault, Michel. 1984. "Of Other Spaces, Heterotopias." <http://www.foucault.info/doc/documents/heterotopia/foucault.heterotopia.en.html>.

Griffin, Sarah Jasmine. 1995. "Who set you flowin'?": *The African American Migration Narrative.* New York: Oxford University Press.

Henderson, Carol E. 2000. "The 'Walking Wounded': Rethinking Black Women's Identity in Ann Petry's *The Street*." *Modern Fiction Studies* 46 (4): 849–67.

Howard, June. 1985. *Form and History in American Literary Naturalism.* Chapel Hill: University of North Carolina.

Hughes, Langston. 1926. "The Negro Artist and the Racial Mountain." <http://www.english.illinois.edu/maps/poets/g_l/hughes/mountain.htm>.

Ivy, James W. 1946. "Ann Petry Talks about First Novel." *Crisis* (53): 48–49.

Kanzler, Katja. 2006. "To Tell the Kitchen Version: Architectural Figurations of Race and Gender in Harriet Jacobs's *Incidents in the Life of a Slave Girl* and Harriet Wilson's *Our Nig. Gender Forum* 15 Genderforum.org.

Myrdal, Gunnar. 1964. *An American Dilemma, Vol. 2: The Negro Social Structure.* New York: McGraw-Hill.

Nobles, Wade. 2007. "African American Family Life: An Instrument of Culture." In *Black Families,* edited by Harriet Pipes McAdoo. Thousand Oaks: Sage Publications.

Pryse, Marjorie. 1985. "Patterns Against the Sky: Deism and Motherhood in Ann Petry's *The Street.*" In *The Critical Response to Ann Petry,* edited by Hazel Arnett Ervin. Westport: Praeger Publishing. 2005.

Schneider, Ana-Karina. 2013. "Skin as a Trope of Liminality in Anne Enright's *The Gathering.*" *Contemporary Women's Writing.* <http://cww.oxfordjounals.org/early/2013/01/04/cww.vps028.short>.

Shockley, Evie. 2006. "Buried Alive: Gothic Homelessness, Black Women's Sexuality, and (Living) Death in Ann Petry's *The Street.*" *African American Review,* 40 (3): 439–60.

Smith, Catherine. 2001. "Looking for Liminality in Architectural Space." *Limen* 1 <http://limen.mi2.hr/limen1-2001/index.html>.

Wesling, Meg. 2006. "The Opacity of Everyday Life: Segregation and Iconicity in *The Street.*" *American Literature* 78 (1): 117–40.

Yarborough, Richard. 1981. "The Quest for the American Dream in Three Afro-American Novels: *If He Hollers Let Him Go, The Street,* and *Invisible Man. The Critical Response to Ann Petry.*" Hazel Arnett Ervin, ed. Westport: Praeger Publishing. 2005.

E S S A Y

(DIS)PLACED BODIES:
REVISITING SITES OF SLAVERY IN OCTAVIA BUTLER'S *KINDRED*

By *Maja Milatovic*

Displacement is a form of survival
—Trinh T. Minh-ha

In an interview with Randall Kenan (1991), Octavia Butler discusses her visit to Talbot County, Maryland in the early 1970s where she went to do research for *Kindred* (1979), her novel on antebellum slavery. She also visited Washington and took a tour of Mount Vernon, the well-known estate of the first president of the United States, George Washington, which, according to Butler, was the closest she could get to a former plantation. Commenting on her experience, Butler concludes:

> Back then they had not rebuilt the slave cabins and the tour guide did not refer to slaves but to "servants" and there was all this very carefully orchestrated dancing around the fact that it had been a slave plantation. But still I could get the layout, I could actually see things, you know, the tools used, the cabins that had been used for working. (Kenan 1991, 496)

Mount Vernon's slave quarters opened to visitors in 1962. Since that time, the quarters have been extensively renovated and researched, including numerous changes in the discourses surrounding their legacy.[1] However, at the time of Butler's visit, there remained a troubling silence surrounding the site of exploitation and revisionist redefining of slave cabins as servants' quarters. Confronted with the difficulties of accessing relevant historical information on slavery in Maryland during her visit, Butler turned to antebellum slave narratives and to fiction as a way of reimagining the realities of slavery. Combining her speculations on the hidden lives of Mount Vernon slaves and the insights gained from slaves' own testimonies, Butler wrote *Kindred,* evoking plantation life while simultaneously questioning the possibility of this retrieval.

Kindred captures the political tensions and turbulent social changes of the post-civil rights period, which witnessed a renewed academic interest in the legacy of slavery and its representations with a specific focus on slave narratives as valuable historical testimonies. This period also saw the flourishing of the neo-slave narrative genre with numerous African American writers, creating fictive representations of the period of slavery using the form and conventions of the antebellum slave narratives. As Ashraf Rushdy (1999) argues, writers of neo-slave narratives mark the moment of a newly emergent black political subject by employing ideologically charged texts and their structures and returning to the form in which African Americans first expressed their political subjectivity (6–7). Revising, extending, and challenging the forms and conventions of slave narratives, neo-slave narrative writers actively counter the amnesia and appropriation surrounding the legacy of slavery in the post-civil rights era.

Staging a literal return to the period of slavery through the time-travel trope, *Kindred* poses numerous questions relevant for its contemporary context such as accountability and privilege, and intersections of race, class, and gender politics. The novel's protagonist is a 1970s black woman named Edana (Dana) Franklin, who is married to a white man, Kevin Franklin. Seized by a mysterious force, Dana suddenly gets transported to antebellum Maryland. There she learns that she must save her white slaveholder ancestor Rufus from harm long enough for him to rape and impregnate her foremother Alice and start Dana's family line, thus ensuring her own survival. Whenever Rufus is in danger, Dana gets "abducted" back into the past to come to his rescue. Complicating matters even more, her white husband joins her on one of these trips. Together, they must perform the roles of a master and slave to survive. Incidentally, Kevin gets stranded in the past for five years without Dana, where he struggles to survive without compromising his antiracist social values.

Focusing on the protagonists' movements through space and time and their interracial relationship, this article argues that their displacements challenge and destabilize the couple's notions of race, gender, and their individual and collective histories, while pointing to the remnants of the slave past in the present and challenging the possibilities of historical retrieval. I use the term displacement for its associative possibilities, connoting an enforced departure, a contingent shift of bodies and minds, destabilization of certain frames of reference and encompassing a notion of loss. Within this context, the critically marginalized character Kevin underscores *Kindred's* preoccupation with interracial intimacies and white male privilege, which transcends time and space.[2] Kevin's proximity to the white slaveholder Rufus and his evolution as an antiracist white male reveal an incisive critique of whiteness and its constructions. Furthermore, Kevin's interracial relationship with Dana points to the the sociohistorical mutability of race and gender as the couple moves between their contemporary California home and antebellum Maryland. The sites of slavery are therefore conceptualized beyond the temporal and geographical to include the body as a site of trauma as well. The protagonists find themselves physically and psychologically transformed through their direct encounter with a traumatic slave past, inhabiting different positionalities depending on the time and space they happen to occupy. Although written in the 1970s, *Kindred* is a visionary work whose focus on an interracial relationship and its preoccupation with whiteness speaks to numerous current issues such as colonization, dispossession, authenticity, and intersectional politics. After more than four decades, the novel remains a relevant fictional challenge to post-racial discourses, revealing the role of privilege in attempts to historicize racism, sexism, and the effects of slavery and colonization.

Focusing on contemporary protagonists and continuously questioning their frames of reference, *Kindred* points to specific and often subtle forms of oppression whose origin Butler locates in slavery. Within the context of depicting plantation life, *Kindred* closely parallels the form of a slave narrative in its themes, structure, and other conventions, but also revises it by subverting its rules and introducing innovative and frequently controversial elements. Marc Steinberg (2004), for instance, labels *Kindred* as an "inverse slave narrative" since its protagonist is born into freedom but becomes enslaved by traveling back into the past (467). This definition of *Kindred* captures its preoccupation with temporal and spatial displacements or bodies moving through space and time with unforeseeable consequences. *Kindred's* nonlinear structure and disruptive narrative pattern departs from the linearity found in certain conventional slave narratives and their teleological plots starting with similar premises of birth, followed by a life in slavery filled with experiences of violence, abuse, and exploitation and ending in eventual freedom. This particular progression charts the protagonists' path in the context of the abolitionist struggle, sentimental tradition, and putative expectation of a white readership in mind. Although inverted, *Kindred* also maps the path of a protagonist who travels back to antebellum Maryland where she herself becomes enslaved. However, this journey is anything but linear; *Kindred* further complicates this notion through staging irregular, sudden, and repetitive journeys to the antebellum past. Dana is taken from various parts of her own home at any time and drawn back to wherever Rufus happens to be. These spatial irregularities are also complemented by temporal disruptions that seem difficult to explain or predict. What appears like an instant in Dana's contemporary time can seem like years in antebellum Maryland. This discrepancy makes Butler's notion of time travel more challenging as it resists interpretation and serves to destabilize linear figurations of the past as well as challenge simplified portrayals of lives under slavery.

Establishing a connection between the mysterious force and the white slaveholder, Dana is taken to the past whenever Rufus is in danger. Therefore, Dana's displaced body itself is transformed into a site of slavery, indelibly marked by the experience of commodification. Referencing that particular aspect, Lisa Woolfork (2009) sees these abductions as white male privilege transcending time and space (25). Just like white slaveholders commodify and control black women's bodies in the past, the force causes Dana to lose her own willpower and agency in her present as she is summoned back to save a white slaveholder's life. The force that suddenly seizes Dana and transports her into the antebellum past is never fully explained and can be relegated to the realm of the fantastic or supernatural.[3] Although Dana is unable *willingly* to prevent her own spatial and temporal shifts to the past, Butler introduces an element of control: namely, whenever Dana's life is in danger, she is transported back to her present. This miraculous escape is also connected to Dana's *own* feelings of fear and threat, which eventually diminish as she realizes that the everyday brutalities she experiences might not necessarily kill her. At one point, Dana tries to escape the plantation but is caught and brutally punished. Rufus's father Tom Weylin kicks her in the face, resulting in a scar and a missing tooth. Then he ties her up and begins beating her: "He beat me until I tried to make myself believe he was going to kill me. I said it aloud, screamed it, and the blows seemed to emphasize my words. He would kill me if I didn't get away, save myself, *go home!*"(Butler 1979,176). However, Dana knows that this was only punishment and that she would survive it. She soon realizes that bringing herself *willingly* into a situation of imminent death can facilitate her return to the present. When Rufus hits Dana for imploring him not to sell one of his slaves, she is determined to take control and leave him in the past. In effect, Dana calmly slits her wrists in warm water and escapes to contemporary California, knowing that the threat of impending death from bleeding will prompt her escape. Underlying this act of taking control is bodily repossession or reappropriation or resisting to white slaveholding commodification of the black female body. Willingly removing her physical self from the slaveholder's presence and exploitation, Dana mirrors the runaway slaves' escape to the North and their subsequent disruption of the slaveholders' economic system, resulting in the reduction of their slave numbers.

Dana's transgressiveness as a character and her resistance to racist and sexist assumptions is revealed from her first encounter with Rufus, who initially mistakes her for a man. The first time that Dana returns to save Rufus, he is only a little boy drowning in a river. He sees her through the time-travel gap moments before she appears to save him and describes the scene in the following words: "I saw you inside a room. I could see part of the room, and there were books all around—more than in Daddy's library. You were wearing pants like a man—the way you are now. I thought you were a man" (Butler 1979, 22). Rufus's comment on Dana's appearance and context are significant of her ability to inhabit multiplicity and resist white, male classification. Seeing Dana surrounded with books through the time-travel gap reveals a radically different context to the one in which Rufus lives where she would be enslaved. The fact that Rufus is able to see her in her home before she is abducted to join him forms a specific temporal and spatial link between their realities, giving Rufus more information about the future and about Dana's particular position. In fact, Dana gets mistaken for a man numerous times throughout the narrative for wearing pants and displaying confidence. These conflations anticipate numerous other conflations occurring in the novel, once again reinstating the intricate connections between the past and the present, or rather, the remnants of the past in the present.

The transformative effects of spatial and temporal displacements are particularly evident in Dana's contemporary context and her relationship with her white husband Kevin, who joins her on some of her travels. The couple's experiences in antebellum Maryland bring into question their contemporary power dynamics, their reluctance to engage with issues of race, and the repercussions of Kevin's unacknowledged privilege while demonstrating numerous correspondences between the antebellum past and their present. Furthermore, Kevin and Dana's interrelated experiences of displacement reveal more complex issues that *Kindred* touches upon, such as interracial desire, challenges to racist and sexist discourses, and the sociohistorical mutability of race and gender categories. Displacing her protagonists temporally and spatially, Butler is able to explore the effects of oppressive ideologies perpetuated and legitimized in slavery and its pervasive effects on contemporary black and white individuals. Significantly, Dana meets Kevin while working at a casual labour agency, a location that instantly establishes a link to the slave past when Dana refers to it as the "slave market." However, she immediately refutes the comparison, concluding that "it was just the opposite of slavery" (Butler 1979, 52) in that the workers pressured by need choose to do low-paid and demeaning jobs in order to survive. The ease with which the workers as well as Dana compare the job market to slavery indicates certain commonalities in terms of exploitative and dehumanizing jobs, but it also underscores their distance from the realities of enslaved individuals. Juxtaposing the past and the present through this comparison, Butler criticizes the ease with which historical traumas are co-opted to describe current experiences. More specifically, Butler identifies the risks of marginalizing and trivializing the effects of slavery in an unequal and divisive contemporary society. Warning against appropriation, Butler's linking of the past and the present urges for a more accountable approach to the lived realities of enslaved individuals.

Situated in the seemingly progressive 1970s, Kevin and Dana's relationship is continuously challenged by the radically different social positions they occupy as well as by their shared refusal to discuss privilege and issues of racism and sexism. Butler makes this distinction in social status between Dana and Kevin very early on, anticipating the extreme form this inequality will assume in antebellum Maryland. Both Kevin and Dana want to become writers and seem to start from the same position of working low-paid, exploitative jobs to sustain themselves while they write. Although the couple meet in the casual labor market, Kevin is able to quit after publishing his first novel while Dana continues to struggle. Butler relentlessly questions the unearned, unmeritocratic aspects of Kevin's privilege since his race and gender place him in a favorable position. The fact that the protagonists are both writers serves to illustrate this point: Dana finds herself in a socially unfavorable position, while Kevin as a white man, already has a good "head start." Although it can be argued that Kevin is simply a better writer than Dana, their writing talents remain incomparable as they do not rest on equal grounds for evaluation. More specifically, in a society that privileges white men over black women, Kevin has legitimacy and connections enabling him to succeed, which are not afforded to Dana.

Kevin's sense of entitlement demonstrates numerous correspondences between him and Rufus, the slaveholder, and establishes additional links to the antebellum past. When Kevin and Dana move in together, Kevin suggests that she should throw *her* books away as they do not fit into his flat. This gesture points to the fact that Kevin finds his own work more important and expects Dana to sacrifice her books, erasing her subjectivity in the process. Another similar incident occurs when he suggests that Dana should quit her job, as he would help her find something better. Kevin fails to perceive Dana's reluctance, as this option would make her economically dependent on him. In fact, Kevin does not find her loss of independence problematic, as he seems to welcome the opportunity to steer her career and facilitate her job change without considering her own wishes first. Finally, when Kevin proposes to Dana, he tells her: "I'd let you type all my manuscripts" (Butler 1979, 109), once again showing his disregard for Dana's own work. Kelly Wagers (2009) suggests that "despite Dana's surface objections to this secretarial role, her record of Kevin's public success repeatedly, usually uncritically, figures his work as more legitimate than hers" (31). While it is evident that Kevin certainly considers his work more important, Dana questions that assertion. She suggests that Kevin should throw away *his* books instead, refuses to be dependent on Kevin's support and to quit her job at the agency, and ultimately refuses to type his manuscripts. Kevin's request for her to type his manuscripts anticipates the events that would occur in the slave past, when "Dana's literacy undoes her" (Steinberg 2004, 472), as Rufus uses her writing skills to manipulate and exploit her. Namely, Dana refuses to write Kevin's manuscripts in their present; however, she consents to writing Rufus's letters in the past. The link between the two is established through the notion of white, male privilege. Despite Dana's protests and her strong sense of individuality, she does not pursue the issue of Kevin's sense of entitlement further. When placed in extreme antebellum circumstances, however, she consents to Rufus's demands. Her creativity is thus subjected to white men, either through their sense of entitlement or through slavery's commodification.

Kevin's privilege is also reflected in his ability to choose and establish control over his own body as he *decides* to join Dana on her trips to antebellum Maryland. Contrasting Dana's lack of control over her own displacements, Kevin is not influenced by the mysterious force. Determined to share Dana's experience, even if it means risking his own life, Kevin holds on tightly to Dana and they are both taken to antebellum Maryland. Kevin's trip to the past is therefore dependent on Dana as he needs to hold on to her in order to be transported. Dana's displaced body becomes yet another link between Kevin, who needs her to return to the past and Rufus, whose survival is dependent on Dana saving him from harm. In other words, the black female body serves as a vehicle for the white man's access to history as well as a vehicle for his survival.

Bringing their contemporary issues to antebellum Maryland, the couple's dynamics drastically change as they are forced to perform the roles of a slave and slavemaster to survive. It is precisely in the role of a slaveholder that Kevin's problematic attitudes and his proximity to Rufus become most apparent. For instance, when Rufus asks Kevin whether Dana belongs to him, he replies: "In a way. She is my wife" (Butler 1979, 60). Similarly to his assumption that Dana would gladly type his manuscripts, Kevin does not pause to question his assertion of marital ownership. Therefore, the property relations that commodify the black female body during slavery are reflected in Kevin's notions of marriage and the wife figured as a form of possession.[4] Apart from an evident doubling with Rufus, Kevin is frequently conflated with various violent white men throughout the narrative. For instance, he gets mistaken for an abusive spouse in their contemporary period. Seeing Dana's bruises and wounds acquired in antebellum Maryland, Dana's cousin assumes that Kevin is beating Dana and even tells her: "I never thought you'd be fool enough to let a man beat you" (Butler 1979, 116). The misogyny and violence against women in antebellum Maryland is therefore connected to the present, once again linking Kevin and Rufus's social positions of domination. Dana's wounded body serves as a witness to this systematic abuse, read differently depending on time periods. The damaging conflation of her loving husband, Kevin, with a violent, abusive spouse and the cousin's ready conclusion testifies to the misogynistic legacy of violence and the silences surrounding it in the contemporary period. Another conflation occurs during Dana's first trip, when a white patroller attempts to rape her. As she is suddenly transported into her present, afraid for her life, she confuses Kevin with the patroller and scratches his face. Dana also sees Kevin in Rufus's father, Tom Weylin, comparing his eyes to Kevin's: "His eyes, I noticed, not for the first time, were almost pale as Kevin's. Rufus and his mother had bright green eyes. I liked the green better, somehow" (Butler 1979, 90). This preference for Rufus and his mother's eye color demonstrates Dana's unconscious distancing from her husband as their previously unaddressed issues of privilege, race, and gender begin to surface.

Kevin's romanticized views of the past further contribute to the couple's distancing, reflecting the ease with which he is able to locate himself in dominant historical narratives. In a conversation about antebellum Maryland, Kevin states that this would be a great time to live in and adds: "I keep thinking what an experience it would be to stay in it—go West and watch the building of the country, see how much of the Old West mythology is true" (Butler 1979, 97). Dana angrily responds to his comments: "West... That's where they're doing it to the Indians instead of the blacks!" (97).[5] The Old West in this context becomes a site of contestation, perceived differently by the displaced protagonists. Kevin's version of history is one of historical erasure according to which the colonizers braved the unknown and created a nation "out of wilderness." From this narrative, numerous idealized accounts of the Wild West and the Frontier emerged, controlled and dispersed by the colonizers. As a white man, Kevin is able to identify with this account of national myth-making and to assert freely his romantic wish to explore the Old West without giving the horrors of colonization any thought. Contrastingly, Dana points out the silenced narrative of forced assimilations and removals of Native Americans during the antebellum period. Angrily countering her white husband's assertions and historical amnesia, Dana allies herself with the voiceless Native Americans and connects them with black people in a shared context of dispossession and enslavement. Through this example, Butler highlights the destructive effects of historical amnesia, which resulted in the creation of national myths omitting the voices of those who suffered under slavery and colonization.

Kevin and Dana's prolonged stay in the past transforms their bodies into sites of wounding as well as survival in diverse and mutually constitutive ways. In particular, Kevin's antebellum experiences result in his disillusionment and allow him to evolve as a character. As Ashraf H. A. Rushdy (2001) suggests in his analysis of white privilege in *Kindred,* "Butler's point is that whiteness is primarily an ethical issue" (120). Indeed, Kevin's development explores the ethical implications of being a white person in a society that legitimizes the enslavement and exploitation of black people. The concern about ethics and accountability is voiced by Dana, anxious about Kevin's stay in the past: "A place like this would endanger him in a way I didn't want to talk to him about. If he was stranded here for years, some part of this place would rub off on him. No large part, I knew. But if he survived here, it would be because he managed to tolerate the life here. He wouldn't have to take part in it, but he would have to keep quiet about it" (Butler 1979, 77). Dana's comments point to the difficulty of making an ethical choice in extreme circumstances; in order to survive, Kevin would have to adapt and keep silent about his attitudes toward slavery. However, he is implied in the system legitimizing slavery due to his race. During one of their visits, the couple accidentally separates and Kevin gets stranded in the past for five years. When finally reunited with Dana, she reflects on his weary, aged appearance: "His face was lined and grim where it wasn't hidden by the beard. He looked more than ten years older than when I had last seen him. There was a jagged scar across his forehead—the remnant of what must have been a bad wound. This place, this time, hadn't been any kinder to him than it had been to me" (184). Dana's final line works as a comparison and highlights the mutually constitutive aspects of their antebellum experiences.

Correlating Kevin's and Dana's ordeals, Butler makes a point that slavery marks everyone involved in diverse ways. From her first trip to the past, Dana is continuously vulnerable as a black woman; she is nearly raped and gets whipped, beaten and bruised. Marked by the slavery period himself, Kevin's ragged appearance and the scar across his forehead correspond to Dana's wounds and scars. While Dana's body suffers far more hardships, vulnerabilities, and cruel punishments leaving her wounded and scarred, it seems that Kevin *witnesses* more brutalities than Dana during his five-year stay.[6] While Dana reveals she "heard stories" of various brutalities done to slave women and their children, Kevin relates that he had seen a woman "strung her up by her wrists" by her master who "beat her until the baby came out of her—dropped onto the ground" (Butler 1979, 191). Therefore, through scarring and witnessing brutalities done to other black women, including his own partner, Kevin evolves as a character. Responding to Dana's ethical concerns, Kevin reveals that he had been helping slaves escape. Consequently, he is able to reflect on his own implication in power structures that privilege some and disadvantage others as well as his accountability. Recognizing these privileges in the past enables Kevin to identify the ways in which oppressive practices of the past inform the present. Ultimately, Kevin becomes more reflexive about his contemporary context, about constructions of whiteness and race discourses, and about his interracial relationship.

The violent ending of *Kindred* sees Dana and her foremother Alice countering the slavemaster's will using their bodies as sites of resistance. Alice commits suicide by hanging herself after Rufus lies to her that he sold their children. Finding out about Alice's death, Rufus seeks comfort from Dana, calling them "two halves of a whole" (Butler 1979, 257). The fact that this conflation comes from Rufus is significant, as it demonstrates a clear link between Dana and Alice as enslaved black women submitting to his authority. However, Alice and Dana share a bond that goes beyond Rufus's conflation of them. Namely, both women resist Rufus by reclaiming their bodies. According to Angelynn Mitchell (2001) Alice takes her life, exercising "her right to choose death, freedom of a different sort, over bondage" (64). Alice's choice ultimately removes her from Rufus as she takes control over her commodified body and ends her life. This act mirrors Dana's wrist cutting as an act of resistance to Rufus's authority and possessiveness. Both women take control of their bodies and remove themselves from the slaveholder's possession.

Although these acts of resurgence establish proximity between the two women, it is Dana's final act of resistance to the white slaveholder that differentiates her from Alice. Acknowledging her contemporary frame of reference, Dana kills Rufus after he tries to rape her. Moments before sinking the knife into his side, Dana briefly hesitates: "He was not hurting me, would not hurt me if I remained as I was. He was not his father, old and ugly, brutal and disgusting. He smelled of soap, as though he had recently bathed. For me?" (Butler 1979, 260). Reading Dana's hesitation, Elizabeth Ann Beaulieu (1991) suggests that "in this passage, we see the remaining vestiges of Dana's maternal feelings for Rufus. How can a mother, surrogate or otherwise, kill the child she has nurtured?" (127). Although Dana meets Rufus for the first time when he is only a child and feels protective toward him, her feelings toward the adult Rufus emerge from a particular conflation with Kevin rather than maternal sentiment. Hesitating moments before killing him, she differentiates Rufus from his abusive, "disgusting" father and reflects on his cleanliness. Taking into account Dana's discomfort concerning the lack of hygiene, germs, and unsanitary conditions of the nineteenth century, it is evident that she associates cleanliness and washed bodies with her contemporary reality. Therefore, she is intimately connecting Rufus's scent to her husband's and contemplating submission based on this particular conflation. She ends her internal dialogue with an abrupt and decisive "No," concluding: "A slave was a slave. Anything could be done to her. And Rufus was Rufus—erratic, alternately generous, and vicious. I could accept him as my ancestor, my younger brother, my friend, but not as my master and not as my lover" (Butler 1979, 260). Differentiating herself from a slave, Dana understands that within the context of property relations, the categories of brother, friend, and lover are no longer applicable. Caroline Rody (2001) aptly argues that through killing Rufus, Dana "avenges her victimized foremothers" (75). Following this argument, Dana severs ties with Rufus and chooses her enslaved ancestors as her kindred, acknowledging the sacrifices and the compromises they had to make in order to survive.

The metaphorical act of severing ties with slavery and her white slaveholding ancestor leaves permanent reminders on Dana's body, attesting to the impossibility of historicizing past traumas and to the effects of white privilege spanning generations. In the final moments before escaping, Rufus grabs Dana's arm, pulling her back. The time-travel gap closes around Dana's arm, ripping it away from her body. Interestingly, *Kindred* begins proleptically with Dana's loss of arm in the prologue and ends with it, figuring the narrative as cyclical rather than linear. The first line of the prologue contains an ambiguous term: "I lost an arm on my last trip home. My left arm" (Butler 1979, 9). The word "home" is multifold in this context, as it remains uncertain whether Dana means her ancestral home in antebellum Maryland or her contemporary home in California. Reflecting on Dana's loss of arm in an interview with Randall Kenan (1991), Butler states: "I couldn't really let her come all the way back. I couldn't let her come back whole and that, I think, really symbolizes her not coming back whole. Antebellum slavery didn't leave people quite whole" (498). Dana's loss of *wholeness* represents the culmination of progressive bodily brutalization that occurs throughout the novel in the form of scars, bruises, wounds, and whip marks. No one is spared from this marking of the body as all characters carry permanent scars, bearing witness to their experiences. Even though he is mortally wounded, Rufus exercises his will one final time, refusing to let Dana go. His sense of entitlement costs Dana her arm as the time-travel gap closes on her limb. Rufus's refusal to let go also signals the treatment of the slave during slavery, stripped of their rights to own their own bodies. The wall of Dana's home closing in on her arm as Rufus clings to it works as a figurative break with the past, leaving her with indelible scars. Similarly to Kevin's scar, Dana's body becomes a site of both marking and loss.

Permanently marked by their experiences, the Epilogue sees Kevin and Dana question their own implications as a black woman and a white man in the seemingly "free" contemporary society. Safely back in their present, the couple decides to return to the sites of slavery in Maryland and Baltimore to discover what happened to Dana's ancestors and to the Weylin plantation. They find out that the slaves burned the house to hide Rufus's murder, in a last act of community support and resistance. However, they locate no conclusive records on what happened to all of them, including Rufus and Alice's children. Wondering why she came to Maryland and Baltimore again, Dana touches the scar Tom Weylin's boot left on her face as well as her empty left sleeve. Kevin offers a response: "You probably needed to come for the same reason I did….To touch solid evidence that those people existed. To reassure yourself that you're sane" (264). Similarly to Butler's visit to Mount Vernon, Maryland and Talbot County, Kevin and Dana are unable to construct a coherent linear narrative and retrieve information, left only with speculations on what happened to Rufus and the family. Touching their scars as forms of tangible evidence, their marked bodies become testimonies to their experiences, as permanent reminders of both suffering and survival. Left with only speculations, the couple has no guidelines on how to restructure their lives and to make sense of their experience. Consequently, they must accept certain historical omissions and the inability to fully account for the lives of enslaved individuals.

Emphasizing its skepticism about fictionally reimagining slavery, *Kindred*'s ending offers no particular closure and leaves numerous questions unanswered. Both Kevin and Dana remain silent about certain aspects of their experiences. For instance, Dana never tells Kevin what exactly happened during her last moments with Rufus: "Kevin would never know what those last moments had been like. I had outlined them for him, and he'd asked few questions" (Butler 1979, 64). Kevin is also vague about his five-year stay in the past, the brutalities he witnessed, and how he got his scar. Their silences demonstrate that certain experiences of enslaved individuals still remain untold and can never be expressed with words, reimagined through fiction and explained away through linear histories. Although the inconclusiveness at the end of the novel might point to a more pessimistic vision of the past and the present, I would argue that it signals a potential for healing while remaining cautious about appropriating, explaining away, or marginalizing the legacy of slavery.[7] Bound by a particular experience, Dana and Kevin must recreate their own ontologies based on newly acquired perspectives on their individual and collective histories. Imagining an interracial couple's return to the past through spatial and temporal displacements and leaving them physically and psychologically marked, Butler offers a progressive critique of whiteness, national myths, and dominant historical narratives, pointing to the violent effects of erasure and appropriation. In a multicultural and multiethnic society where inequalities endure and where the legacies of slavery, colonization, and their representation persist as burning issues, *Kindred* remains an important and visionary work of fiction that gestures toward rebuilding dialogic relationships with the past while acknowledging the challenges of its reconstruction, urging for a careful reconsideration of the ways in which that very past continues to inform the present.

Notes

1. The most recent refurbishment of Mount Vernon's slave cabins happened in 2010 as a result of two decades of research and over ten months of intensive work aimed at uncovering and reconstructing the lives of slaves at the plantation. According to a report by Voice of America, a number of descendants of George Washington's slaves attended the opening celebration of the restored quarters, reflecting a new way of engaging with this legacy. One of the attendees was Rohulamin Quander, who insightfully commented: "Renovating the slave quarters is a significant gesture of recognition for the hundreds of enslaved African-Americans—men and women—who lived there" (Elmasry 2010).

2. Guy Mark Foster (2007) discusses this critical gap in his astute reading of *Kindred*'s contemporary context and consensual interracial desire. Reflecting on the relevance of critical engagement with Dana and Kevin's relationship, Foster suggests that *Kindred*'s faithful depiction of a black victimology narrative, centered around a black woman, "distracts readers critical of literary and cultural narratives of interracial intimacy that deviate from conventional portrayals" (143). Furthermore, Foster finds that critical analyses that focus on the historical narrative of interracial rape marginalize the consensual interracial desire represented by Kevin and Dana's marriage (148). He also argues that the novel's depiction of a non-pathologized interracial relationship between a black woman and a white man anticipates many of the insights derived from critical pedagogies of whiteness (153). While Foster situates his discussion on white privilege and Kevin and Dana's interracial intimacy in the contemporary period, I examine their experiences in the past and present as mutually constitutive, explored through sites of slavery figured through their marked bodies as well as spatial and temporal displacements.

3. Sandra Y. Govan (1986) also argues that the agency that moves Dana is never clear since she never understands how it happens (88). The lack of *scientific* explanation for the time travel is also one of the reasons Butler (Kenan 1991) insists that *Kindred* is a fantasy instead of a science fiction novel, claiming that "there's no science in *Kindred*" (495).

4. Commenting on this particular passage, Marc Steinberg (2004) suggests that Butler uses Kevin to "extend into the present a classic type of human ownership in western civilization—the marital exchange" (469). Although Kevin is not a negative character who would *consciously* consider his wife as his property and would possibly be shocked to be compared to a slaveholder, Butler uses him to critique unquestioned assumptions that come with his position of privilege, the ideas that he seems to take for granted and continuously problematizes them.

5. Anne Donadey (2008) argues that the one brief allusion to the Indians in the novel constitutes its weakness since it presents the United States in black and white terms only and finds that its view of race has aged given the "multicultural makeup of the country in general" (78). This assumption conveys the idea that Butler's intention was to represent experiences of African Americans as the essential United States experience. It also posits Butler's views of race as fixed and dichotomous. Contrary to Donadey's argument, I argue that Butler's focus on slavery and its effects goes beyond presenting history in black-and-white terms. Apart from exploring the particular legacies of slavery, Butler critiques whiteness and points to the socio-

historical mutability of race and gender, which are crucial to contemporary issues such as colonization, dispossession, authenticity, racial constructedness, and white privilege. Those are anything but "aged" and remain imperative diverse contexts and discussions.

6. Missy Dehn Kubitschek (1991) sees this particular difference as Kevin requiring "a greater shock to move him to action" (43). Protected by his gender and race, Kevin can never inhabit Dana's antebellum reality despite being placed in the same time period. While Dana might not have *witnessed* such brutalities, she experienced trauma on her own body because of her race *and* the particularity of her gender.

7. Beverly Friend (1982) sees this inconclusiveness as part of Butler's pessimistic and didactic vision: "Men understand how the world is run; women do not. Victims then, victims now" (55). However, Butler moves from such dichotomies in the very exploration of power relations and privileges that accompany the interracial couple. Both are permanently marked by their experiences and both survive, returning to the place of trauma. The silences and gaps can also be read as potentialities and Dana's amputated arm points to a reinvented life with a disability, which requires certain adjustments. Butler ends the novel with an unresolved sense, not of victimization, but of possibility.

Works Cited

Beaulieu, Elizabeth Ann. 1999. *Black Women Writers and the American Neo-Slave Narrative.* Westport, Connecticut: Greenwood Press.

Butler, Octavia. 1979. *Kindred.* Boston: Beacon Press.

Donadey, Anne. 2008. "African American and Francophone Postcolonial Memory: Octavia Butler's *Kindred* and Assia Djebar's *La femme sans sepulture.*" *Research in African Literatures* 39 (3): 65–81.

Elmasry, Faiza. 2010. "Harsh Life of Washington's Slaves Revisited." *Voice of America.* Accessed November 29. http://www.voanews.com/content/harsh-life-of-washingtons-slaves-revisited-111032034/163434.html.

Foster, Guy-Mark. 2007. "Do I look Like Someone You Can Come Home to Where You May Be Going?": Re-Mapping Interracial Anxiety in Octavia Butler's *Kindred.*" *African American Review.* 14 (1): 143–64.

Friend, Beverly. 1982. "Time Travel as a Feminist Didactic in Works by Phyllis Eisenstein, Marlys Millhiser and Octavia Butler." *Extrapolation* 23 (1): 50–55.

Govan, Sandra Y. 1986. "Homage to Tradition: Octavia Butler Renovates the Historical Novel." *MELUS.* 13 (1/2): 79–96.

Kenan, Randall. 1991. "An Interview with Octavia E. Butler." *Callaloo* 14 (2):495–504.

Kubitschek, Missy Dehn. 1991. *Claiming the Heritage: African American Women Novelists and History.* Jackson: University Press of Mississippi.

Minh-ha, Trinh T. and Nancy Chen. 1992. "Speaking Nearby: A Conversation with Trinh T. Minh-ha." *Visual Anthropology Review* 8 (1): 82–91.

Mitchell, Angelynn. 2001. "Not Enough of the Past: Feminist Revisions of Slavery in Octavia Butler's *Kindred.*" *MELUS.* 26 (3): 51–75.

Rody, Caroline. 2001. *The Daughter's Return: African American and Caribbean Women's Fictions of History.* New York: Oxford University Press.

Rushdy, Ashraf H. A. 1999. *Neo-slave Narratives: Studies in the Social Logic of a Literary Form.* New York: Oxford University Press.

——. 2001. *Remembering Generations: Race and Family in Contemporary African American Fiction.* Chapel Hill: The University of North Carolina Press.

Steinberg, Marc. 2004. "Inverting History in Octavia Butler's Postmodern Slave Narrative." *African American Review.* 38 (3): 467–476.

Wagers, Kelley. 2009. "Seeing 'From the Far Side of the Hill': Narrative, History and Understanding in *Kindred* and *The Chaneysville Incident.*" *MELUS.* 34 (1): 23–45.

Woolfork, Lisa. 2009. *Embodying American Slavery in Contemporary Culture.* Urbana and Chicago: University of Illinois Press.

"GOD'S DOMINION": OMAR IBN SAID'S USE OF ARABIC LITERACY AS OPPOSITION TO SLAVERY

by Akel Ismail Kahera

It is He who has made the earth subservient to you. Walk about its regions and eat of His provisions. To Him all shall return at the Resurrection.

Are you confident that He who is in heaven will not cause the earth to cave in beneath you, so that it will shake to pieces and overwhelm you?

—from *Surat al-Mulk, Qu'ran,* as quoted in *The Life of Omar Ibn Said* (1831)

Omar ibn Said, Courtesy of Davidson College Archives.

Omar ibn Said's *The Life of Omar Ibn Said, Written by Himself* (1831) occupies a unique position within the slave narrative tradition. As the only surviving Arabic autobiography written by a slave from the United States, the *Life* juxtaposes a religious exegesis based on the textual authority of the Qur'an with a first-person account of Omar's life. Only recently rediscovered, having been found in a trunk in a Virginia attic in 1995 and sold to a private collector after being lost since 1920, the manuscript has sparked renewed interest in writings by enslaved Muslims in America, and in particular Omar's literacy in Arabic and his religious training. Omar's *Life* is a hybrid narrative: it is a slave narrative, a spiritual narrative, and a quasi-conversion narrative. This essay examines two critical moments in Omar's life—his Arabic writings on the walls of a Fayetteville, North Carolina, jail during his imprisonment and his ambiguous relationship to Christianity later in life. Omar's meditation on the Qur'anic chapter *Al-Mulk,* which means "Dominion" or "Sovereignty," encapsulates the contradictions between these narrative modes, challenges the religious sanction of slavery, and undermines the practice of granting slaveholders dominion over other human beings.

While the paucity of primary sources has made scholarly research of antebellum Muslims rather difficult, scholars have pieced together the story of enslaved African Muslims in America from a variety of sources. In the 1940s, the oral history narratives published by the Works Progress Administration generated a cycle of renewed inquiry, which led to the discovery of Muslim forenames and surnames among many Muslim descendants. Allan Austin's *African Muslims in Antebellum America: A Source Book* (1984) is perhaps the earliest attempt to record and study the lives of enslaved Muslims. Austin's subsequent publication, *African Muslims in Antebellum America: Transatlantic Stories and Spiritual Struggles* (1997), revealed that the Hausa, the Mandingo or "bookmen," and the educated Fulani from West Africa were part of the slave population. Similarly, Sylviane Diouf's *Servants of Allah: African Muslims Enslaved in the Americas* (1998) posits an impressive catalog of descriptions of cultural and political life, which depicts African Muslims throughout the Western hemisphere as well-read, well-traveled, cosmopolitan, multilingual, courageous, and resourceful, seizing opportunities even in unfamiliar surroundings (1998).[1] Those who wrote a variety of texts all used Arabic as their vehicle of communication and Islam as their vehicle of liberation (Diouf 1998, 39). Ronald Judy's *Dis-forming the American Cannon: African-Arabic Slave Narratives and the Vernacular* (1993) shifts scholarly attention to the richness of vernacular texts in order to highlight the knowledge and acumen of educated enslaved Muslims.[2] This body of scholarship has made it possible to evaluate Omar's narrative in a renewed way, as demonstrated in Ala Alryyes' *A Muslim American Slave: The Life of Omar Ibn Said* (2011), a critical edition of Omar's writings that includes multiple translations of Omar's *Life* alongside a facsimile of the original Arabic manuscript and a number of critical essays and commentary on Omar by a range of scholars. In particular, Alryyes provides critical annotations with his translation of the *Life* that highlight the significance of the Qur'an to the *Life* and that call upon scholars to examine more closely the centrality of Omar's Muslim faith to any study of his life and work.

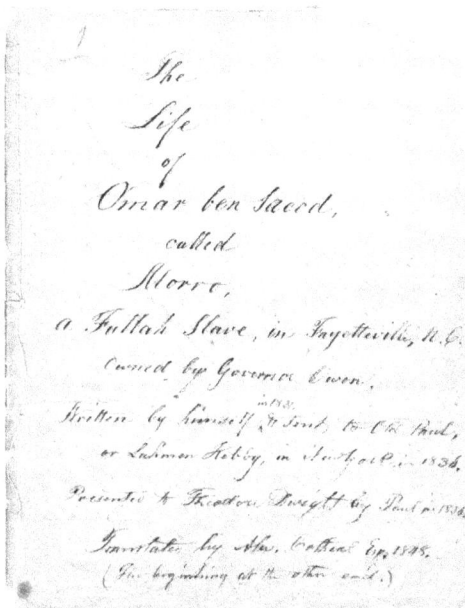

This additional English-language title page of Omar ibn Said's autobiography offers details about how his story was disseminated. Courtesy of the Omar ibn Said Institute.

Omar's Life and the Power of the Qur'an

Omar was a Fulani Muslim tribesman of Futa Toro, modern day Senegal. Born around 1770 and part of a community where the diffusion of knowledge was fully imbedded in the social milieu and geographic landscape, Omar received twenty-five years of religious schooling and made the *hajj*, or pilgrimage to Makkah, kept the fast, prayed regularly, and had on occasion engaged in jihad, or "striving." While the details of Omar's jihad are unclear, it is worth noting here that classical jurists had distinguished four ways by which the believer could fulfill his jihad obligation—by the heart, the tongue, the hands, and the sword (Willis 1967). After teaching for six years in the Futa Toro, Omar began a new venture as a trader, a known practice among the educated Muslim clerics of West Africa (Alryyes 2011, 3). Fulfilling the obligation to teach and trade earned West African clerics the title of *marabout*.[3] The *marabout* would normally travel from one locale to another, teaching religious studies and engaging in business transactions at the same time. Omar was captured in 1807 by slave traders and shipped to Charleston, South Carolina. He recalls, there

> came to our country a big army. It killed many people. It took me, and walked me to the big Sea, and sold me into the hand of a Christian man (*Nasrani*) who bought me and walked me to the big Ship in the big Sea.
> [W]e sailed in the big Sea for a month and a half until we came to a place called Charleston. (2011, 61–63)

After his first owner died in 1808, Omar was sold to an especially harsh man known only by his last name, Johnson. Johnson exacted extreme physical labor from Omar, who describes himself as "a small man who cannot do hard work" (2011, 63). In 1810, Omar found the means to escape but was later caught and jailed in Fayetteville, North Carolina after he is discovered having "entered [one of]the houses to pray" (63). As Omar recounts, "I saw a young man.… He spoke to his father that he saw a Sudanese man in the house… another man riding a horse with many dogs took me walking with them for twelve miles to a place called Faydel. They took me to a big house [building]" (63).

While imprisoned, Omar wrote his first Arabic petition on the walls of his jail cell. Unable to speak English, he could not say who he was, or where he had come from: but, finding coals in the ashes of his cell Omar filled the walls of the jail with pious petitions from the Qur'an. Omar effectively put the power of the Qur'an to use in order to condemn his treatment while drawing on the mass appeal for his release generated by the local fascination with his Arabic writing on the cell walls. Using the jail as a literary space of protest, Omar turns to the power of writing in order to continue to protest his multiple forms of captivity and petition for his own freedom. Omar's literacy should be understood as inextricable from his religious knowledge: he not only became fluent in Arabic through his religious education but also would have understood the power of authorship and literacy as vital to human existence, as stated in the Qur'an: "Proclaim! And the Lord is Most Bountiful—He Who taught (the use of) the Pen" (96:3-4). The petitions may have been unreadable to the local population, but, even as a strategy for attracting attention to his plight, the petitions worked: the strange Arabic handwriting on the prison walls drew the notice of the citizens of Fayetteville, and he was released after spending sixteen days in confinement. This liberation from jail depended, however, on his re-enslavement: he was purchased by John Owen of Bladen County, a general of the southern militia, and the influential Owen family took Omar to their estate, where he lived for the rest of his life.[4]

Omar's early Qur'anic petitions on his jail cell walls led the Owen family to take a special interest in this learned slave's religious education, which led to increased public interest in his religious practices. In 1822, when Omar was more than fifty years old, the family purchased two key texts for him—a translated copy of the Qur'an as well as an Arabic Bible. His encounter with Christianity may be gleaned from his narrative:

> I am Omar, I love to read the book, the Great Qur'an.
>   General Jim Owen and his wife used to read the Bible, they used to read the Bible to me a lot. Allah is our Lord, our Creator, and our Owner and the restorer of our condition, health and wealth by grace and not duty. (Ibn Said 2011, 73)

As public interest in Omar's story grew, many influential individuals, groups, and institutions—including Frances Scott Key, the American Ethnological Society, the American Numismatic Society, and the American College in Beirut, Lebanon—speculated about his religious identity and largely presumed his conversion. An entry in the *African Repository* in June 1869 confirms this presumption; of Omar, it concludes, "His false belief has been supplanted by a true and living faith in Jesus Christ."[5] Twentieth-century critics and historians alike have assumed or heavily suspected Omar's conversion to Christianity before his death, citing as evidence his possession of this Bible, his writing of the Lord's Prayer and the twenty-third psalm, and conflicting interpretations of Omar by southern whites (who were apparently convinced that he was a Freemason and equally convinced of his conversion to Christianity). In writing about Omar and other educated slaves, critic Patrick Horn notes, "These often-neglected narratives offer insights into the truly multiethnic, transnational nature of American literature; the lives they describe are those of educated travelers and active agents in their own destinies who rely on various tactics to overcome adversity" (2012, 46). Although Horn describes enslaved Muslims as "educated travelers and active agents," he unquestioningly affirms nineteenth-century assumptions about Omar's conversion to Christianity: "Omar's subsequent conversion to Christianity rendered him a celebrity of sorts, and his story was recounted in several religious magazines and pamphlets" (49). Horn argues for Omar's conversion using secondary sources, such as religious magazines and pamphlets, but also notes that "Omar's account stops short of explicitly professing faith in a Christian God or explaining the reasons for his conversion" (50).

Ghada Osman and Camille Forbes provide a new platform for rethinking Omar's complex spirtual identity when they assert, "Omar strategically both identifies and disidentifies with the Christians/Westerners by whom he was surrounded and influenced… through his specific uses of Qur'anic references, he maintains a distinction between himself as Muslim and the Westerners/Christians with whom he interacts" (2004, 332).[6] The claims that Omar converted to Christianity disavow the many declarations he made in his own writings, which suggest that he remained a Muslim; more importantly, however, even critical accounts attentive to the complexity of Omar's relationship to Christianity fail to account for an important Arabic rhetorical strategy of concealing one's true faith—a strategy known as *idtirar* (and *taqiyyah*) in Arabic—which is an important feature of all of Omar's writings as he sought to defy a web of power relations and social pressures. One instance of this strategy of concealment may be detected in Omar's use of the *basmallah*—the phrase beginning nearly every chapter of the Quran and translated fully as "In the name of God, the Most Gracious, the Most Merciful"—before writing the Lord's Prayer and the twenty-third psalm. Thus, while Omar's precise spiritual identity later in his life is left to speculation, it is most likely more complicated than a simple conversion narrative would presume. He may have yielded to missionary pressure more in appearance than in fact; he may have appreciated the beauty of these scriptures but not their substance; he may have accepted either or both religious doctrines, as a syncretic form of worship not unlike the forms in many parts of the antebellum South, where slaves combined African indigenous belief with Christianity. Perhaps Omar had momentarily hoped that if he served his master who rescued him from prison, caused no trouble, and honored his master's religion, then he might be treated better. If such possibilities cannot be proven true or false, then it is equally important to recognize that neither do Omar's manuscripts show proof of his conversion.

Yet the question remains, for whom had Omar written these documents? Certainly the Owen family could not read Arabic, and his texts were not readily accessible among the plantation slaves who had the capacity to read them. In fact, they were not addressed to anyone in particular. It would appear that Omar was engaged in purposeful deception and self-preservation, using Arabic as a language of dissimulation to guard or preserve his life in a time of danger. It is possible that Omar also realized that he might make something reasonably comfortable out of an apparently helpless situation. He was not free, and he obviously did not want to be resold. The Owen family did not require him to perform hard labor in his remaining years in the involuntary servitude.

Omar's Exegesis of Al-Mulk

Omar's *Life* takes into account various complex relations of the elements of faith and practice. He begins the narrative with the sixty-seventh chapter of the Qur'an, *al-Mulk*. It begins with the *basmalah*, which, as noted above, precedes nearly every chapter in the Qur'an and is a common invocation in Muslim communal doctrine. *Al-Mulk* takes into account complex human relations of power, including dominion, authority, sovereignty, and control. Omar employs these verses—and indeed the whole chapter of *al-Mulk*—as a mechanism for transferring power from the supporters of slavery to God, who holds dominion over all humankind. And it is this acknowledgment of God's absolute power that enables Omar to undermine Christian justifications for slavery and empower himself to rise above the sufferings caused by enslavement.

The use of *al-Mulk* as a prologue to the narrative is a strategic part of the text's excoriating message against the institution of slavery. Within the first lines, *al-Mulk* points to the problem of human ownership: "Blessed is He (God) in whose hands is the dominion; and He is able to do all things" (67:1). Omar wisely raises the problem of his servitude within the prologue, citing *al-Mulk* to lay bare the linkages between his servile condition and the knowledge of his faith and the power of his creator. It is here that Omar reveals his secret thoughts about his captivity, about the tensions between master and slave as well as his plan to overthrow the system of oppression *spiritually*. Indeed the repetition of custody, control, ownership, and absolute power turns up throughout the thirty verses of the Qur'anic chapter in very pointed terms. *Al-Mulk*'s exegesis highlights these terms in order to challenge the power of the servile estate and practice of servitude.

Influential Muslim theologian and philosopher Fark al-Din al-Razi said that *al-Mulk* stands for the power, might, and authority of God both in the visible and invisible world (Asad 1993, 879). It would seem that Omar's reading of *al-Mulk* could counsel revolt by laying bare the sharp disparity between God's authority over humankind and the institution of slavery, in which some humans claim absolute authority over others. According to Muhammad Asad in his *Message of the Qur'an*, "The fundamental idea running through the whole of *al-Mulk* is man's inability to ever encompass the mysteries of the universe with his earthbound knowledge and hence his utter dependence on guidance through divine revelation" (1993, 879). The etymological and lexigraphical meanings of the term *al-Mulk* (which include derivations meaning "property" and "a deed of ownership") contribute to the hermeneutic complexities of its inclusion in the narrative. Prominent Qur'an scholar Al-Zamakshari (1075–1144 CE) states that *al-Mulk* means "God's dominion," which occurs in the first verse of the chapter. But *al-Mulk* has also been designated as "the Saving One," *al-Munjiyah*, and as "the Preserving One," *al-Waqiyah* (Asad 1993, 879). These terms point to the dichotomy of servitude and to Omar's juxtaposition through subversive means, and stress the unfathomable quality of God's existence and power.

"The Saving One," *al-Munjiyah*, and "the Preserving One," *al-Waqiyah*, have direct reference to Omar's oppressed condition, providing an opening through which his redemptive voice emerges. With regards to Omar's oppressed condition, nodal Qur'anic verses one and two explicitly mention death and life: "Blessed be He in whose hands is Dominion; And He over all things Hath Power: He who has created death and life that he may try which of you is best in deeds" (1781–90). Yusuf Ali's exegesis notes that "*mulk*" means "dominion," "lordship," and "sovereignty," and that "*mulk*" and "*malakut*" are from the same root. "*Malakut*" refers to "lordship" in the invisible world, but "*mulk*" refers to the visible world (Qur'an, 1781 n. 5555). Ali notes that death before life makes reference to another Qur'anic chapter, 2:28: "Seeing that you were without life [literally dead], and He gave you life; then He will cause you to die, and will bring you back to life again" (1781 n. 5556).[7] Particularly evident are references to man's punishment in verses six and seven of *al-Mulk*: "When they are cast into that [hell], they will hear its breath indrawing [sobbing] as it boils up....[I]ts keepers will ask them, has no warner ever come to you?" When we consider Omar's case against slavery and the servile estate, the interpretation of *al-Mulk* is influential in his condemnation.

What these descriptive terms share is Omar's interest in asserting God's dominion and His immanent punishment for those who are evil or wicked in their treatment of others. The message is explicitly stated in verses sixteen and seventeen of *al-Mulk*: "Do you feel secure that He who is in heaven will not cause you to be swallowed up.... Or do you feel secure that He who is in Heaven will not send against you a violent tornado; So that you shall know how terrible was my warning." *Al-Mulk* also speaks of one's dependence on the Creator, addresses the aspirations of the human soul, and tells of the need to arrive at charitable meaning to understand better the human condition and the idea of creation.

Among a host of eschatological themes, *al-Mulk* speaks of Allah (God) as the eternal, omnipotent creator of the universe, upon whom all life depends. After all, *al-Mulk* takes into account the relation between God and His servants and the emotional struggle to renounce the torment of the grave.

Omar's appropriation of *al-Mulk* introduces the reader to the teleological compression of space and time—the never-ending struggle of life and the ultimate condition of death—in a way that defies the human control over life and death under slavery. His use of *al-Mulk* counsels obedience to Allah and a rejection of the institution of slavery. Indeed, the emancipatory thrust of *al-Mulk* inherently points to Omar's knowledge and to his spiritual realism. The Qur'an also refers to God as *Maaliki yawm-id-deen* (Master of the day of Judgment). *Al-Malik,* with the definite article, is one of the divine names of Allah (*the asma-Allah al-Husana*). This rhetorical gesture of using the Qur'an in an autobiographical narrative is not an established convention in Arabic literature. Although it resonates with the mystical piety common to Sufi literary traditions, it also underscores the centrality of Omar's exegesis of *al-Mulk* to his narrative by a slave who nonetheless uses religious knowledge and literacy to contest the conceptual underpinnings of his enslavement.

By using *al-Mulk* to contrast his servile condition as a slave to all humanity's servile condition to Allah, Omar reveals and undermines the mendacity of slavery.[8] It was precisely his recognition of this fact that gave him the opportunity to escape from the torture and subjugation of his mental and physical condition. According to one *hadith*—an authentic report transmitted from the prophet—*al-Mulk* endows the reader with an elevated rank, summoning people who care about him and warding off suffering, affliction, and distress. Understood in this way, Omar's description of the servile spaces he encountered, his captivity, and his attempt to escape provoke several dichotomies comprising of freedom and bondage, self and identity, power and knowledge, center and periphery, and life and death. *Al-Mulk* need not be reserved solely for Qur'anic exegesis, for it transfers most immediately to the second part of the *Life*, which introduces Omar's personal history. Indeed, the prologue, narrative, and epilogue coexist and work together to extend the meaning of his servitude and explain the power of his intellectual poise.

Omar's protest against the servile estate may have coincided with the ideological purge of many abolitionist sympathizers in the South. Even if the narrative was meant to bolster the antislavery complaint, it is clear that Omar's use of the pen highlights the overwhelming interest that he was able to solicit from the plantation aristocracy in North Carolina.

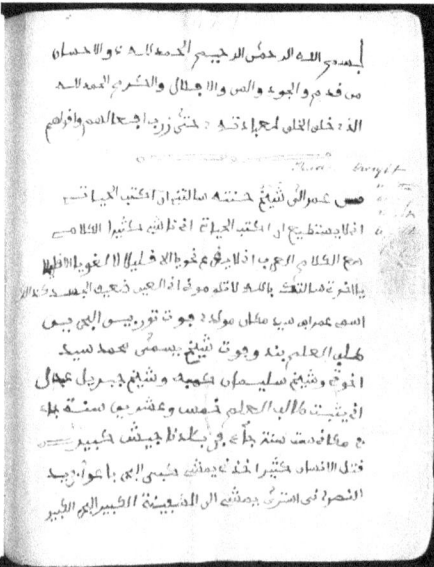

A page from Omar Ibn Said's autobiographical manuscript. Courtesy of the Omar ibn Said Institute.

Conclusion

The Life of Omar Ibn Said, Written by Himself provides an occasion for rethinking rhetorical strategies of spirituality in challenging the dichotomies of servitude and freedom. The narrative represents ibn Said as both a savant and as a slave who used Arabic and Qur'anic rhetorical strategies of protest and concealment to endure his captivity, which reemphasizes the power of writing in precarious, life-threatening circumstances. In his use of rhetorical strategies and tropes, ibn Said continuously negotiates between his faith and his enslavement. His persistent attention to *al-Mulk* as a source transforms the Qur'anic chapter into evidence against the institution of slavery, boldly exposing the unlawfulness of such practices at a spiritual level. By turning the narrative into an epistemological tool against the logic and legality of slavery, ibn Said provides a new framework for understanding the human experience. In light of the current flourishing research perspectives on his life and writings, future studies of the *Life* will contribute, in a wholly transdisciplinary way, to the reevaluation of questions that place the narrative squarely at home with some of the most important texts of its time.

Notes

1. Amongst the most memorable African Muslims in America are Ibrahim Abdur-Rahman, Yarrow Mamout, Lamine Kebe, Bilali Mohammed, and Salih Bilal. Muslim captives included devoted *marabouts* (teachers), *talibs* (student novices), *imams* (prayer leaders) the whole community of *ulama* (scholars); the *alfa or charno* (religious leaders), *qadis* (judges), and *huffaz* (memorizers of the Qur'an).

2. Salih Bilali's book was reconstructed from memory and cited excerpts from Abu Zayd al-Qayrawani's *risalah*, or Muslim creed of worship, according to the Maliki *madhhab* descendant, Bilali's descendants and Shad Hall of Sapelo (1930 WPA works progress administration interviews); Bilali may have been Frederick Douglass's ancestor (Diouf 1998, 199). Yarrow Mamout is featured in an oil painting by Charles Wilson Peale dated 1819.

3. The etymology of the word *"marabout"* is derived from the term *"al-Murabitun,"* or the people of the *ribat*, a place of spiritual devotion and chivalry similar to a monastery; the *murabit* became *marabout* through French usage.

4. John Owen was the twenty-forth governor of North Carolina (1828–30) and the second owner of Omar ibn Said; ibn Said's third owner was the governor's brother, James Owen.

5. In *The Christian Advocate,* for example, Omar's earlier story of being imprisoned ran as follows: "As no one claimed him, and he appeared of no value, the jail was thrown open, that he might run away; but he had no disposition to make his escape. The cause of the jail being thrown open was, he was found to be 'a bright mason'" (306–07). From what we can tell, ibn Said was certainly not a bright mason. He was educated, and he had mastered Qur'anic teachings adequately before his captivity; he was fully aware that the Qur'an lays stress upon the manumission of slaves. And it would appear that Omar is adapting the discourse of his captors but was ultimately not confined by the rules of that discourse.

6. Osman and Forbes further note, "Fourteen of Omar's manuscripts are extant, thirteen others are quoted by interested parties. His writings include three Lord's Prayers, two twenty-third Psalms, two lists of his masters' family's names, a commentary on Christian prayer, and several parts of the Qur'an. His last known manuscript is a copy of the Qur'anic sura 110, *al-Nasr* [Victory]" (331–43).

7. See Yusuf Ali's translation of *The Holy Qur'an.*

8. For a detailed account of Omar's "Afrika" petition, see John Hunwick, "I wish to be seen in our land called Afrika: Umar B. Sayyid's Appeal to be Released from Slavery (1819)," *Journal of Arabic and Islamic Studies* 5 (2003–2004): 62–77.

Works Cited

Alford. Terry. 1977. *Prince Among Slaves.* New York: Oxford University Press.

Ali, Abdullah Yusuf. 1990. *The Holy Qur-ān: English Translation of the Meanings and Commentary.* AL-Madinah AL-Munawarah: King Fahd Holy Qur-ān Print. Complex.

Alryyes, Ala. 2011. *A Muslim American Slave: The Life of Omar Ibn Said.* Wisconsin: University of Wisconsin Press.

Asad, Muhammad. 1993. *The Message of the Qur'an.* Melksham, Wiltshire, Great Britain: Redwood Press Limited.

Austin, Allan. 1997. *African Muslims in Antebellum America: Transatlantic Stories and Spiritual Struggles.* New York: Routledge.

Curtin, Philip D. 1967. *Africa Remembered; Narratives by West Africans from the Era of the Slave Trade.* Madison: University of Wisconsin Press.

Diouf, Sylviane. 1998. *Servants of Allah: African Muslims Enslaved in the Americas.* New York: New York University Press.

Horn, Patrick. 2012. "Coercions, Conversions, Subversions: The Nineteenth-Century Slave Narratives of Omar ibn Said, Mahommah Gardo Baquaqua, and Nicholas Said." *Auto/Biography Studies* 27(1): 45–66.

Hunwick, John. 2003. *The Arabic Literature of Africa, Vols. 1–4.* Leiden: Brill.

Judy, Ronald. 1993. *(Dis)Forming the American Canon: African-Arabic Slave Narratives and the Vernacular.* Minneapolis: University of Minnesota Press.

Osman, Ghada and Camille Forbes. 2004. "Representing the West in the Arabic Language: The Slave Narrative of Omar Ibn Said." *Oxford Journal of Islamic Studies* 15(3): 331–43.

Willis. John Ralph. 1967. "Jihad fi Sabil Allah: Its Doctrinal Basis in Islam and Some Aspects of Its Evolution in Nineteenth-Century West Africa." *The Journal of African History* 8(3): 395–415.

"The sense of that crush I feel at certain times even now": Jacob Stroyer and the Defense of Fort Sumter[1]

by Susanna Ashton

JACOB STROYER.

In the summer of 1864, fourteen-year-old Jacob Stroyer was sent to work in Fort Sumter. He did not go willingly. Stroyer was a slave owned by the wealthy Mrs. Matthew R. Singleton and was sent from the large Kensington plantation outside Columbia, SC to labor for the Confederate cause. The Confederate Corps of Engineers called upon slave owners to contribute their enslaved people's labor to the problem of construction and fortification of roads, bridges, and key defensive sites. Stroyer explained that fifteen slaves from his plantation "were sent to work on fortifications each year during the war."[2]

Today Fort Sumter looms large in the memory of our nation—whether it be as a symbol for the valiant defense, pained surrender, and eventual reclamation by Federal forces, or as a reminder of the triumphant and strategic hold on it by Confederates for much of the War. For Stroyer, however, the memory was fraught with a conflicted sense of what his role had been. Indeed, in 1879, when he initially wrote the story of his life he glossed over the entire experience with just a few sentences. Only six years later, when he rewrote his life story as *My Life in the South* (1885), did he try to explain at length what he could not forget about that place. And perhaps it is a troubled record such as Stroyer's that can tell us more than any military historian about what was truly at stake in those battles over the Charleston Harbor.

Being tithed out in 1864 for war service was actually the second time Stroyer had been so used. He must have thought he knew what to expect. In the previous summer of 1863 he had been impressed into a two-month service and had been, as he explained, "freighted" to Sullivan's Island outside Charleston. From the island the slaves could wistfully observe Union gun boats, knowing full well that the fleet was "part of the means by which the liberty of four and one-half millions of slaves was to be effected."

The work of the slaves on Sullivan's Island was generally to repair forts, build batteries, and mount the guns, while young boys such as Stroyer, then only thirteen, waited on officers and acted as messengers and water carriers. There was no significant fighting on Sullivan's Island during his weeks there and although Confederate forces skirmished with Union troops camping nearby, young Stroyer saw little actual combat. However, more poignantly, some of the conflict that did arise came from acts of self-emancipation: Stroyer reported that there were slaves who managed to swim across the inlet to Union lines on an adjacent island and that Confederate scouts who set out in pursuit were fiercely repulsed.

Despite the acute proximity of the freedom promised by the Union troops (much less the proximity of the black Massachusetts 54th Regiment, which made its heroic charge on the Fort at Battery Wagner across the harbor in that July of 1863) and Stroyer's painful awareness of what his service to the Confederates represented, the youngster reported some glee at the adventure and comparative freedom of serving the army instead of doing field work back at the Singleton plantation. He even reported an "exalted pride" in having gained some knowledge of a world beyond their own plantation: "I thanked God that it afforded me a better chance for an education that I had at home and so was glad to be on the Island," he wrote.

Stroyer's brief experience encamped on Sullivan's Island did not, however, prepare him for what was to come. For, by 1864, the walls of Fort Sumter still held by the Confederates were in desperate need of repair. Stroyer was assigned to Fort Sumter as part of a team of slave laborers charged with repairing the fort as quickly as it had collapsed under Union assault. This second assignment promised to be far worse than his earlier one, although he recalled with the calm voice of the future minister and educator he was to become that: "I carried my spelling book with me, and although the Northerners were firing upon us I tried to keep up my study." That memory of comparative quiet belied an experience of unrelenting terror and chaos in 1864, however.

The teenager had been sent into the heart of one of the most intense military sieges in modern warfare. Union Major General John. G. Forster launched a bombardment of the Fort on July 7th of 1864 and for the rest of the month an average of three hundred and fifty rounds daily was shot at the besieged site. Many were shot from Forster's batteries on Morris Island, but attempts to destroy the fort with floating rafts of gunpowder were also made. Thanks to the enslaved men's endless work of repairing the walls, the fort held fast. While the most intensive assaults ended by September when Union supplies of ammunition began to run low, historians with the National Parks Service at Fort Sumter estimate that an estimated seven million pounds of artillery projectiles, about forty-four thousand in all, were fired at Fort Sumter before the fort was evacuated on February 22nd of 1865.

As Stroyer reported it, the black men leaving Fort Sumter warned the new ones being ferried over in the dark of night that they might well die before even reaching the fort, as crossing itself was so perilous. Daniel Castlebury, an elderly slave who was being returned for a second tour of duty at Fort Sumter was so terrified that he tried unsuccessfully to hide under boards on the transport sloop, rather than be forced back to the fort.

Even if they could successfully avoid the mines in the Charleston Harbor, Union sharpshooters from Morris Island would shoot at the boats as "oars dipping into the salt water at night made sparks like fire." Another boy from the Singleton plantation was struck by a shell while climbing from a boat before he ever made it into the fort.

Once inside the Fort, Stroyer entered a nocturnal existence of terror and toil. The slaves were locked in during the day and only allowed out at night to work on the fortifications. Parrot shells and mortar came at all times, but the Union sharpshooters who shot at anyone who "showed their heads on the rampart," worked best in the daylight. The slaves were to use cotton bales, loose rubble, timbers, sandbags, and basically whatever they could lay their hands on to build and rebuild the walls. Thousands of bags of sand were brought in from the city at night.

Not surprisingly, it was the slaves who were exposed to the greatest dangers. Stroyer wrote that "the only time the few Confederate soldiers were exposed to danger was while they were putting the Chevaldefrise [wooden spikes pointed with iron] on the parapet at night."

When not passing heavy sandbags up and down the walls, slave laborers were still not safe. Whereas Confederate soldiers took shelter in the relative safety of the bomb-proof section of the fort, slaves were locked into a section known as the "rat-hole" on the eastern side of the fort, facing Morris Island. It was so airless and suffocating that despite the increased danger when they were outside of it, Stroyer wrote that they were nonetheless "glad to get into the fresh air."

Unprotected slaves also died from the constant rain of shells simply when they lined up to receive their daily rations of hard-tack biscuits and raw salt pork. And death from mortar explosions, collapsing rubble, and exploding parrot shells was common, but conditions were exacerbated by gratuitous cruelty of the overseeing officers. Stroyer speculated, for example, that an officer, who at one point ordered Stroyer and his fellow slaves outside of the fort to a small stone projection where they were fully exposed to Union missiles could have done it for "no other reasons…than that we might be killed off faster."

Similarly, when bombs burst above the fort the slaves were directed to huddle in the open middle, while Confederate soldiers hunkered down in protected spaces. The shells would supposedly burst in the air and scatter widely, sparing the center, but Stroyer reported that when shells exploded, though, slaves would scatter in confusion, trying to find cover. Afterward the air would clear to a scene of severed black bodies.

One time, warned by a sentinel that a mortar shell was aloft, Stroyer ran to hide among some timbers but was followed by other slaves who frantically piled atop of him. He nearly died from the weight: "The sense of that crush I feel at certain times even now."

In another assault a mortar shell landed upon the lime house where Stroyer and others had fled for safety and, as he recalled it, the explosion that ensued killed twelve or thirteen of the men hiding within. Stroyer survived but sustained a severe facial injury from the incident and was, perhaps luckily, then removed to a hospital on shore. Having survived that, he was sent back to the Singleton plantation for the duration of the war.

Out of the three hundred and forty men who Stroyer reports served in slavery on Fort Sumter, he claims only forty-one including himself survived. These numbers were the recollection of a man writing twenty years after the event and do not jibe well with the military dispatches from the Confederate commanders at the time, who seem to indicate a dozen or so deaths of black workers and perhaps forty-five to fifty injured during the summer of 1864. Yet new sources and voices offer us new ways to understand not only history but the scars of memory and while we might never be able to reconcile these accounts, perhaps reconciliation is really beyond the point.

After the War, Stroyer went to schools in Columbia and Charleston and eventually made his way to Worcester, Massachusetts, where he continued to study and became an African Methodist Episcopal minister and pastor of the Salem Colored Mission for twenty-five years.

Stroyer never saw himself as a veteran for any cause, but the wounds he incurred at Fort Sumter and the horror he witnessed there, defined his life. He died in Salem in 1908 and was buried in Salem's Greenlawn Cemetery with a carefully phrased tombstone. It reads, in part:

> BORN A CHATTEL OF COL. MR. SIN-
> GLETON NEAR COLUMBIA S.C. 1848
> WOUNDED BY THE BURSTING OF A SHELL
> WHILE AT WORK WITH OTHER SLAVES
> REPAIRING THE DAMAGE DONE BY THE
> UNION GUNS DURING THE THIRD
> BOMBARDMENT OF FORT SUMTER
> IN THE CIVIL WAR.
> EMANCIPATED BY THE PROCLAMATION
> OF PRESIDENT LINCOLN.
> EDUCATED BY HIS OWN LABOR…

Stroyer's emancipation may have technically turned upon a legal proclamation, but those who knew him, knew that it was endurance and hard labor that earned him his freedom. His life was not marked by irony or shame for his service at the hand of his oppressors. Instead, Stroyer chose to commemorate the misery of that summer of 1864 with an account that would surely destroy any sense of romanticism over the symbolic or actual battles over Fort Sumter from the North or the South. He survived to embrace his freedom, but he forever was troubled by the sense of that crush.

Notes

1. Special thanks to Russell Horres, volunteer, and to Rick Hatcher, historian, both with the Fort Sumter National Monument, for help with research for this piece.
2. This and all subsequent quotations are from Jacob Stroyer (1885), "My Life in the South," in "*I Belong to South Carolina" South Carolina Slave Narratives,* ed. Susanna Ashton, Columbia, SC: The University of South Carolina Press, 2010, 155.

Bibliography

Adger, John B. 1899. *My Life and Times 1810–1899.* Richmond, VA: The Presbyterian Committee of Publication.

Stroyer, Jacob. 1885. *My Life in the South.* Salem, MA: Salem Observer and Job Print.

LOCATING AFFRILACHIA: A CONVERSATION WITH KELLY NORMAN ELLIS

by Meredith McCarroll

In 1991, poet Nikki Finney was invited to fill in as a reader on a panel titled "The Best of Appalachian Poets." Upon arrival, though, she discovered that the title had been changed to "The Best of Southern Writers." Friend and fellow poet Frank X Walker was puzzled by the change in title, and consulted a dictionary for clarity—only to have his frustrations confirmed. His dictionary defined Appalachian as a *white* dweller of a narrowly defined mountainous region. To give voice to that which this definition had silenced and to make visible that which it had erased, he coined the term "Affrilachian," and built a movement with a group of young poets at University of Kentucky, including Kelly Norman Ellis. In 2011, the group celebrated its twentieth anniversary. That same year, I began a project on black Appalachia, and had the privilege to conduct a series of interviews with twelve of the Affrilachian Poets. In these conversations, I delved into questions of identity-building at this intersection of race and region. With a New Black Aesthetic sensibility of the limitation of definitions, and a postmodern conception of the emptiness of terms, I was particularly curious to see a group of doubly invisible poets creating a new definition that denotes both race *and* place. In the following conversation with Ellis, which took place in Lexington, Kentucky, at the Affrilachian Symposium, we work to locate Affrilachian Poetry, both spatially and conceptually—understanding who counts as Affrilachian.

ᘉ

Meredith McCarroll: How did you come to think of yourself as a poet?

Kelly Norman Ellis: That happened here at University of Kentucky. I'd always wanted to be a writer. That was because my grandmother was a writer—and was a very talented writer. Actually, a short story that I found after she died is the first chapter of my dissertation. While I was looking for all these literary foremothers, my grandmother was doing what Zora Neale Hurston was doing. She was writing in her kitchen on lined paper. So I am very much influenced by my grandmother and my mother, who is a storyteller. All of my aunts are storytellers. They just do it. They do voices and jump around.

So that defined how I saw myself in terms of loving words. I still thought that writers were other people. Who do you study in school? They are mostly white, male. But my parents had great bookshelves, so I'd pull down Alice Walker, or James Baldwin, or Richard Wright, but still it didn't seem as if I could do that because I didn't have the community around me.

When I came here for my Ph.D., Nikki [Finney] was here. Hearing her read was something different than having those words on a page. It's important, powerful stuff, but when you see the physical presence of a black body—a female body— reading with such authority and such investment, you do say, "I want to do that."

So I started leaving poems in her box. She'd write on them, mark them up, and put them in my box.

When Frank [X Walker] started having readings, he asked me to read. I said, "Sure, whatever," but as the time got closer and closer, I thought, *I can't do that.* I was teaching at Kentucky State at the time, and was teaching composition. I was asking them [the students] to write about family, and I wrote this poem, "Raised by Women" and read it at the open mic then. And everything changed. I was twenty-seven years old. My friends started saying, "You're a poet." It was still hard to grasp. So in the mid-nineties here at UK is when I started to see myself as a poet. A young poet who didn't quite know what I was doing, but I was doing it nonetheless.

MM: When you first heard the term "Affrilachian," was Appalachian already something that was on your radar?

KNE: No. I'll tell you why. It wasn't on my radar because in my mode of thinking, those were white people. Even though I grew up part of the time in Knoxville, Tennessee, it was like, "Oh, that's white folks." The logic of it didn't get across to me. I knew that there was a difference when I moved from Mississippi and moved to the mountains. You know, people ate the same stuff, but it was different. They ate white beans; we ate red beans. When we finally moved away, I longed for the mountains and I found myself back.

So when Frank said Affrilachian and we talked about why…what the dictionary said…before that I never saw myself there. I saw myself as a black southerner, and that still had a lot to do with Kentucky. My consciousness as a black person and a woman was precedent. So it took this experience of going into eastern Kentucky—my body physically being in Whitesburg or being in these communities. Meeting black people in Hazard, teaching at University of Kentucky, teaching at Kentucky State. Going into North Carolina, in Boone and places like that. That is when I started gaining an identity myself as an Affrilachian. And it took me researching to find out who are the other black writers here. It opened up another way of looking.

MM: I think that everybody has various identities, but I don't think many people wake up in the morning and think about these identities—especially if you are in a position of privilege. But you are saying that for you race trumps place.

KNE: Race and gender.

MM: So to throw in place, did that shift your thinking about who you are or did it shift your thinking about what Appalachia is?

KNE: It shifted my thinking about what Appalachia is. University of Kentucky really shaped me in so many ways. You know, I came here to get a PhD in English. I don't think I really knew what that meant other than, "I'm gonna study words. I'm gonna study books." I took this course in southern literature, and there were two other black people in that big seminar and I remember us inserting blackness into the class. And that was the first time, too, that I started seeing this discussion of the black South. There was also this discussion about Appalachia. So I didn't just see the South anymore. There was Louisiana South and there was Appalachia and there was Oklahoma. All these nuances in the South. So it became more complex. Just the vastness of it amazed me. So to be a southern writer also means you can be black or Latino or Native American. You can be all of these things. I don't know if it made it harder; it made it a lot more interesting. I felt a lot more invested in studying it and doing it. It wasn't just an academic exercise.

MM: When I teach African American literature, I do this exercise where I put them in partners and give students excerpts from poems and ask them to determine the race of the poet.

KNE: [Laughter]

MM: You know what happens. If it is Sterling Brown...

KNE: Oh, he's black.

MM: If it is Phillis Wheatley...

KNE: White.

MM: Right. But if it is Dunbar...certain of Dunbar's poems...

KNE: Oh, he's black if it's dialect.

MM: Yep. So I found that even politically engaged and aware students tend to fall into this trap in terms of their expectations. Then there is a totally different set of expectations associated with Appalachian writing that I talked about earlier.

KNE: Churning butter!

MM: So how do you navigate these different expectations? Do you feel like you're writing to other people's expectations or are you just writing your stories?

KNE: On one hand I am paying attention to craft as I edit. I want it to be a sound poem aesthetically that satisfies me. And the other is that I just want to write the poem. If it's a Katrina poem or if it's Mountaintop Removal or some issue of race I've noticed in class with my students, I just want to do that work. I just see a charge to do the work and write the stories. And I think doing that allows us to, I hope, portray the humanity of people who live urban lives or rural lives in our region. I would still do it if I was transplanted to California. I'd still be writing about the people I met here and how they informed who I am.

MM: As I have talked with several of the Affrilachian poets, one thing that struck me is that no one has said to me, "When I'm an Affrilachian poet, I do these things. I meet this criteria."

KNE: I think that the word "Affrilachian" is more inclusive. It's not about a particular cultural moment. It's about a lot of cultural moments. It's not about necessarily the banjo. With the banjo we go, "oh, Appalachia!" But it is more than that. It's about everything from the crack pipe to prison life to raising your children, rape, incest, love. It's the same thing everybody else is writing about. But I do think that Nikki made people realize, "Oh, I can do that? I should be writing about 7th Street. These people right here." That model located me. Think about Gwendolyn Brooks in Chicago. She locates herself. She says, "I'm here, in Bronzeville; I'm on the South Side of Chicago." But it doesn't mean that she's not other things.

MM: Yes; I always tell students that the more specific you are, the more you can say. If you want to write about blackness, forget it. But if you write about riding the bus into East Knoxville in a steamy August, then you are talking about being a woman and being black, as well as other things.

KNE: That's absolutely right. It is like the Lorraine Hansberry quote, "In the specifics of your life is the universal." So when I name it—when I say 7th street, Lexington, or Spalding Bakery right over here, it locates the humanity of those people. We might tend to go, "Oh *those* people?" Yeah, that is us. We're like you and unlike you.

MM: So if the point is that we are similar and we are dissimilar, what is the point of a new term? Isn't that just the human experience? Why call it "Affrilachia"?

KNE: I understand that. At this conference at Berea years ago, this woman was irate and said, "How dare you call yourselves 'Affrilachians.' You can't just make up a word!" To me, the term "Affrilachian" said we're not invisible. Simply the act of writing a poem—for a black person in West Virginia, or Kentucky, or North Carolina—it is a political act that says, "I'm not invisible. I'm here. I'm not what you think you know." The word "Affrilachian" shocks you into a whole new way of seeing and that is the value of the word.

Affrilachian Poets—the group—that's us, the group of people who travel around and read poetry. But the term "Affrilachian" is not a copyrighted term. An Affrilachian doesn't need permission from us to be Affrilachian. I think that is the freedom of the word.

It is a way of claiming space. I don't have to be country, I can be urban. I can be all this crazy mix of things and still be from this place.

MM: It seems to me that Affrilachian Poets are at an interesting place. In 1991, "Affrilachian" was primarily Kentucky and black. What about now? How did you begin and where do you find yourselves?

KNE: One of the things we did at the beginning was take out the map and look at the counties. I remember the moment I realized that John Edgar Wideman was Appalachian. And that is what he's writing about. He's writing about that boundary. And then to think about where our people migrate to. Birmingham is one of those points.

MM: It's like the Appalachian diaspora.

KNE: Yes! Atlanta. Ohio. I talked to Rita Dove at a conference and she claimed it. Henry Louis Gates claimed it. There's always this recognition: "I knew it all along, I just needed that word to help me." Appalachian felt exclusive to black people. It's a model of not being named by someone else.

MM: Du Bois's concept of double consciousness comes to mind here. For him, double consciousness—that twoness—is a burden because he is perpetually in the object position. He doesn't get to say, "I feel black and American," but rather, "I feel that I am always seen as black and American."

KNE: Learning what this word—"Affrilachian"—means has taught me a lot about claiming who I am as a writer and as an artist. This process has taught me to claim your space. You think about groups of writers like the Fugitive Poets. "I'll Take My Stand," I'll do it. During the Harlem Renaissance, Dr. Locke said, "We're the New Negro." They didn't wait to be defined or recognized by scholars. Teaching at Chicago State, Haki Madhubuti has taught me to define yourself. Don't be defined.

As I am editing an anthology on Black Appalachia, and as I think about the Affrilachian Poets, I have to remain true to the region because part of the beginnings of this had to do with being invisible. "White dwellers of the mountainous regions of Kentucky and West Virginia…" We're not invisible. I've had to struggle at different points with the editor of the press because it is important to me to have a section devoted to Booker T. Washington and excerpts from *The Souls of Black Folks* when Dr. Du Bois was in Tennessee, and some of the WPA Slave Narratives, and Paul Laurence Dunbar. It's important to me because that says we were always here. We were *always* here. We were in coal mines. We were slaves. We were at Cynthiana. We were all of these places that we walk every day. When I am talking about being Appalachian, I'm saying that person needs to have some foot in this place. So even if you're born in California, but if you spent fifty years in Kentucky, you're an Affrilachian. And if you have roots here that you return to again and again, if your body comes back here and spends time in

Tuscaloosa, spends time in North Carolina, then to me, you are Affrilachian. That's my only prerequisite.

It's not to be exclusive, but to say that there is a point to this.

MM: But by definition, it has to be a little exclusive for it to be valid. And it doesn't mean that it can't be evolving.

KNE: That's right. It does.

MM: So where do you see the Affrilachian Poets evolving?

KNE: That's a great question. I've thought about that and I'll be honest: I don't know. This has shocked me because at different times when we've tried to make it be something, it says, "no I don't want to be this movement." It is such an organic thing that with each new step we take we go, "Oh, ok. Let's do that." So I have not a clue. Twenty years ago, Nikki was the only published writer. Twenty years later, we're all teaching, we're writing books. And it all began because we just wanted to read some poems to each other and to feel like we had a place. I think that for us, for me, by documenting who we used to be and who we are—it carves out a place for other writers. At some point they will take for granted that they are Affrilachian. It just will be. And they'll be able to create knowing that they have a tradition. And I think that for young black writers, particularly, wherever they exist in the United States—when you find that you're a part of a tradition, it is huge. It changes things for you. You have models. My models have been Lucille Clifton and Anne Sexton. I love them both. But when you see a black woman doing what you're doing, it changes everything. So I want us to be that tradition that black writers, and black southern writers, and black Appalachian writers can go to. They can say, "Oh, Frank X Walker did this. Keith Wilson did this. Nikki Finney did this. So I can do this."

MM: Makalani Bandele explained to me that he always thought of himself as environmentally conscious, but it wasn't until he took on this identity as Affrilachian that he started thinking about mountaintop removal. It became more local than global. His focus has shifted. It seems to me that the idea of Affrilachia is going to survive because it can shift, because it can evolve. It makes it harder to write about. If there were four tenets that defined the Affrilachian Poets, it would be much easier, but I think you wouldn't still be here twenty years later.

KNE: When I find out that somebody is from the region, I want them to know that they have a tradition. But…I think you're right that it will survive because there are no rigid boundaries. It isn't as if all Affrilachian Poets have to write about family, or write a black poem. If you look at Nikki's new work, there are certain poems that could have been written by a white person. But there are some that are black poems, or lesbian poems. I think what is important is that we feel free to do all of that. To be…just be. I do think it gives people a sense of pride. And I think it makes us different from some of the different groups that came along at the same time. I think it is a big enough family that you can always step out and step back in.

MM: Yes, this is what I heard again and again as I talked with Affrilachian Poets. The idea of family as binding this group together. But it is not a romanticized sense of family. But the idea is that you love them enough to be able to step away when you need to. And to step to them and say, "You can't do this anymore."

KNE: That's right, you step away. And you can say, "I don't like that." But you continue on because you love them. I have not been able in the same way to find a literary family. We hold people accountable to what they bring to the table. Nobody is mean-spirited, but we might say, "Hey, that's the same image you've been pulling on for six months." But also, I trust them. When your poem feels tight, that makes me feel good. With us, there is some kind of organic attraction that we have for each other. Respect for one another. It's the family model of respect and the sense that I know people have my back.

How Many Midnights?

by Tom Williams

I

Adam thought he heard a church bell tolling twelve, but when he looked at his watch it read eleven fifty. He still had ten minutes to find the sign. His laptopp bounced in its black case against his thigh. The road he walked, Coahoma County Road Six, was hard, packed dirt and cut through cotton field after cotton field, the plants eerie in the light of a fat, full moon. He shared the road with no pedestrian. No car had passed since he'd left Clarksdale.

Big Son, the guitar player who'd told him where and when to go this evening, had warned Adam that loneliness might turn him around. Now Adam wondered if he'd been sent here as a joke. Was Big Son, the seemingly guileless and toothless player of the raggediest guitar Adam had ever seen, somewhere in the shadows, enjoying the image of a thirty-five-year-old black man from Indiana, stumbling toward a meeting place that might not exist? Adam thought his eyes had adjusted to the near-dark but couldn't discount the idea that Big Son was hidden nearby, passing around the bottle of Crown Adam had given him. Then, as his heart chilled and his sensible self told him to turn back, he saw what Big Son had promised would be there: a red arrow pointing east, with the words Patterson Farm hand-painted in black on it. Adam breathed, a long clearing of his lungs and mind, and looked down the road ahead. He clutched his laptop to his chest.

II

Two weeks earlier, he'd been sitting in a club chair in his agent's office. Doug, his former classmate, and for the last five years the sole champion of Adam's fiction, had no good news to share, not for the novel or the story collection that had been visiting certain addresses in Manhattan, Boston, St. Paul, as well as in the smaller cities of the publishing world.

"I've kind of suspected this, Adam." Doug strolled behind his desk. Adam sat straight as a stick. "But I didn't have the words, you know."

In his peripheral vision, Adam saw Doug rounding his desk, smiling and running a hand through his thinning blond hair. Adam closed his eyes. In workshop, Doug handed in more excuses than completed manuscripts. Since he'd become an agent, he'd threatened to write a roman à clef about the corruption in his industry, but Adam believed Doug hadn't written a word of fiction in years. Still, for most of his clients, Doug had an undeniable record of success. Multiple book contracts. Film rights. One mystery writer even had an iPhone app. Yet with Adam—the writer Doug claimed was his best—he couldn't even sell a book to a second cousin who was an acquisitions editor at a two-title-a-year house in Nashville.

Adam now opened his eyes, saw Doug sitting in the front of his desk, leaning closer. "Garrison, he put it to me this way," he said, his hands clasped before him as if in prayer. "And he liked your stuff. Wrote that really pleasant rejection I showed you. He just, just, just,…"

Adam's shoulders rose. Doug's stammering often accompanied his trying to say something uncomfortable, usually a comment that might be taken as racist. Adam, his only client of color, looked at his watch. "I don't have a lot of time," he said. "Go ahead."

"Remember," Doug said, flattening his hands on his desktop. "This is how editors think, you know. But it's like, Garrison said, you might as well—the way you write, that is—you might as well be white."

Adam closed his eyes and nodded. Smiling, he stood, shook Doug's damp hand, and listened to a few more rambling professions of loyalty and friendship, then departed Doug's offices, not knowing what he'd do next. Kill himself? Get married? Go to work at an advertising firm? Wait for Garrison in a dark alley and scream, "Black enough for you now, motherfucker?" Nothing seemed appropriate, nothing might provide him what he needed. He certainly didn't imagine himself back in his apartment, listening to his father's cassettes of his grandfather's records, then find himself captivated by Tommy and Robert Johnson, a pair of names you'd find dozens of in any phone book yet evocative of whispered rumor and secret deals. He didn't envision himself driving down to Clarksdale, where he'd find some curious relic like Big Son. At no time at all did he think he might consider asking this unknown but amazing player of electric blues how one might travel to a certain Mississippi crossroads and what might happen on a particular night of the year.

III

Now it was midnight. His watch, an inheritance from his grandfather, confirmed the time. Adam looked both ways, as if crossing a busy street. A shudder brought his shoulder blades closer together, though he felt no wind and sweat slipped down his sides. He wanted to cry out, just to hear a human voice or bring Big Son and his cronies out of their hiding places. No telling how many skinny white boys the old man dragged out here to laugh at the lengths they'd go for otherworldly guitar technique. But what if it was true? He'd thought this back in Indy. What if such an opportunity existed, where for one's soul some uncommon talent would be received? And what if instead of a guitar, one brought the tool used in one's trade? What would be the harm to find out?

The minute hand of his grandfather's watch clicked past midnight. He'd stay no longer than twelve ten. Even in his New Balances, the most comfortable shoes he'd brought to Mississippi, his feet throbbed. All along, he'd wondered what else might explain the phenomenon of standing at a crossroads, waiting for the devil to arrive. Perhaps one simply gained confidence from the venture. Perhaps one strove to improve his craft so none would laugh uproariously once they heard of such a nocturnal visit. If for nothing else, his trip to Clarksdale had given him access to Big Son and his hour upon hour of stories. He'd not himself ever been to the crossroads at the appointed time, which explained for the bluesman his lack of fame and relatively long life, a life that Adam had thought might make for a fantastic book—fiction or nonfiction—that no New York editor would deem "not black enough."

Five more minutes, he promised himself, then looked ahead. He'd never been anywhere south of Louisville before, yet his own grandfather had left Eastern Arkansas in the thirties for Indy, where he'd raised Adam's father to believe that they'd found a better place for themselves and their families. In the Indianapolis suburbs, where Adam was born and raised, his grandfather and father preached that he could be anything he wanted to be. And if that was a writer, then it was all right by both of them. Now Adam wondered if his grandfather had erred in leaving the South. He didn't know. He could see, though, that it had been nearly five minutes since his last resolve. He looked around and sighed, considered the long, sore-footed trek back to the Best Western on Highway 61. Then a few hours of sleep, a drive back north, where he didn't know what awaited him besides an unmade bed, a sink of dirty dishes, bills that needed paying, and the promise of summer work teaching composition at a community college. He looked left once, then right, then turned left once more in time to hear, unmistakably, a voice saying, "You're not local."

He wasn't a big man, but he was definitely black, a nimble, behatted fellow whose manner, light complexion, and wardrobe put Adam in mind of Gregory Hines. Adam required at least five blinks and two dry swallows before he could respond. "You're not…"

"Him?" the other man said, pointing to a space on the ground between the pointed toes of his gleaming shoes. "No, sir. A representative, yes. A regent or emissary. An agent, if you please."

Adam envisioned the words before him, as if he'd right-clicked on a word for potential synonyms.

"But back to my first line of thought," the man said. "What brings a sophisticated gent like you to Mississippi, of all places? You here for a reason? Not just a chance meeting in this lonely place?"

Adam nodded, then rasped, "Yes." His mouth hung open and he breathed out of it, then swallowed again. He touched his damp face with a trembling hand. Had the already sweltering temperature increased? The man tipped back the brim of his hat. He looked as cool as the driver of an air-conditioned Lexus. "Don't you know this is just a myth?" he said. "A concoction of African wisdom and bad folklore scholarship?"

Adam didn't move. He didn't even blink. His vision had adjusted by now to the moonlight, though, and the man before him was smiling. "Just playing with you, boy," he said. "So let's see it."

"See?"

"You're not toting a guitar, but you don't strike me as the musical type. But whatever it is, the instrument with which you hope to create, you know." He pointed to Adam's side. "What's in the case, cuz?"

Adam's eyes followed to where the man's slim fingers pointed. He kneeled, set the case on the ground, and tasted dust when he inhaled. Still watching the man—unsure if he might at any instant vanish or sprout horns—he unzipped the cloth case and produced his MacBook.

"Good to see folks getting with the times," the man said. "Makes everybody's job easier. Plus, a laptop's a lot easier to goose than all those Remingtons and Olivettis I used to see." He took the laptop out of the case and spun it on his finger, like a Globetrotter with a basketball. Adam reached for the computer, recalling its cost and expired warranty. Then the man stopped spinning the laptop and opened it up.

"Battery's a little low," Adam said.

The man shook his head. "Not a problem." With one hand, he held the laptop before him, while the fingers of his other hand manipulated the keyboard. "PC's are more my speed," he said. "But don't fret. I got you faded."

On the screen, faster than Adam had ever witnessed, the icons lined up in all their regular spots. As soon as he considered the hard yet fruitless work they represented, one by one, they vanished. Not directed to the recycling bin, they were just gone, until all that was left was the Internet icon. "What are you doing?" he said.

"You had all that stuff backed up, didn't you?" the man said. Then he laughed, his gold-filled mouth open wide and roaring. Surely somebody nearby could hear such mirth, Adam thought, but after a long second or two, no one else joined the pair. Then, on the screen, a new icon appeared, resembling the Microsoft Word icon save for the red outline and the unmistakable horns and coiled tail. "A little corny," the man said. "Subtlety's never been his speed." Once more, he pointed toward the ground between his handsome calfskin shoes.

Adam blinked, enthused that everything had gone so fast and seemed so simple. Yet he worried as well that he'd gone too far without thinking, without weighing any consequences. This was, he knew, no joke.

The man snapped shut the laptop and said, "That's it, bro. Now it's your turn."

"Who are you?" Adam said, the question formed and spoken at the same instant. He looked down at his laptop, expecting smoke or some mephitic scent but finding it looked none the worse for wear.

"Does it matter what you call me?" The man shrugged, turned to walk away.

"How will I write?" Adam said. "Should I just keep doing what I was doing?"

The man paused, turned around. He doffed his hat. Adam expected horns but saw hair as close-cropped as his own. "You know, that's what troubles me," the man said, dragging a hand over his scalp. "All y'all come here because you've been doing what you thought would work and nobody's listening. Or reading. Or buying. Then you see a little smoke and magic and voilà, say, 'Should I just keep doing what I was doing?'" This last phrase he spoke in a perfect impression of Adam, who always wondered if he sounded more Midwestern than needed.

"All y'all?"

"Tommy and Robert, of course. But Bill. Eudora, too."

"William Faulkner?"

"The one and the same."

"Eudora Welty?"

"You know any others?"

"Oh my god," Adam said.

"No, no. That's Flannery O'Connor's man. Don't tell me you haven't been doing your reading, bro. That's unconscionable."

Adam laughed for the first time since he'd left Big Son behind. Had the bluesman been wearing the same kind of porkpie as this emissary of hell? He said, "I've just been writing in a particular way for over fifteen years now. Do you know what I mean?"

"Listen, cuz." The man stepped closer. "Trust me. Time's right, you'll know what to do."

And with that, he was gone. The sun loomed ahead suddenly, red and enormous. Adam stood at the crossroads. He looked east and west.

When he woke in his soft Best Western bed, the sheets up past his shoulders and the air conditioner humming, Adam yawned and pressed his left hand—his writing hand—to his chest. What day was it? What time? Had he, like Young Goodman Brown, fallen asleep and only dreamed it all? After he leapt to the floor and fumbled for his laptop, the interminable wait for his computer screen to appear kept him wondering: If he dreamed it what would happen with his writing? If he'd been at the crossroads, what would happen when he....He wouldn't fill in the blank.

Everything else looked the same on the screen. No horns or tail decorated his Microsoft Word icon. He was no more fallen a creature than when he'd driven south from Indianapolis. He fell back in bed. He'd check out, drive out of Clarksdale, then forget he'd ever been so close, so close to…. Another sentence he couldn't finish. But what was that on the soles of his New Balances? Dirt? Of course, the streets of Clarksdale weren't any cleaner than those of any small town. What was true was this: He needed to go back home. Should he say anything to Big Son? No, he needed to get the—he paused, couldn't say the word. He looked at the alarm clock, then picked up his grandfather's watch. He needed to vacate Clarksdale, where he no more belonged than a choir director in a juke joint.

IV

Always an early riser and adherent to the principle of writing in the morning, Adam found, back home, a fairly productive June. Like Thomas Mann, he aimed at three pages a day, from six to ten, then a two-mile walk, followed by a shower and two summer sections of composition at the community college where he had a tenuous promise of full-time work in the fall. He was trying to assemble a story—or a novella or perhaps the beginning of a novel—about Big Son Jenkins. Thirty pages in, he believed he was only writing the pages that would take him to the story he needed to tell. After all, as he'd told himself again and again since his return from Mississippi, he was only thirty-five. He had time.

He'd told no one of his visit to Mississippi, especially not his father and Doug. On a visit to his grandfather's grave, he thought of what it might have been like to travel the South with him. He wished he'd paid more attention to the older man's stories, recalling only the manner in which they were told—full of animated gesture and voices Adam didn't recognize. Was that what he'd been seeking, more than some supernatural shortcut? A connection with a kind of black man who'd lived—what else to call it—a more authentically black life?

He tried not to think about it much.

Instead, all summer, Adam maintained his routine, then modified it when the school year started and he had five classes. By winter break he had nearly three hundred pages, and after spring break he'd produced enough material to contemplate whether to contact Doug. Send the manuscript and a synopsis to Garrison, he wanted to say, but no, not yet. Patience seemed his new watchword. When the appropriate time came, both he and the manuscript he toiled over would be ready.

V

It was midnight. Had Adam checked the calendar, he would have seen a year had elapsed since the night of his vivid dream of a visit to the crossroads in Mississippi. He might have recalled, had he tried, that Big Son Jenkins claimed this was the same crossroads Robert and Tommy Johnson had visited. He might have recalled how suspicious he felt but how that did not stop him from believing he had to discover for himself, for his career, just what might happen, if he'd run into someone there, someone who'd have a specific deal for him.

But none of this entered his thoughts as he strode toward his writing desk and pushed aside the notes and numerous process-analysis essays from his composition classes. The cigarette he lit—from a pack of Kools he didn't recall buying—caused him no discomfort as he switched on his laptop and there found his place not in the novel based on Son Jenkins's life but something else, a fiction that instantly felt recognizable and offered no obstacles in composing. It was, quite frankly, the kind of writing he'd been trained to mistrust: too quick, too careless, too easy. When he stopped writing—not midscene or midsentence as Hemingway and Dubus had counseled—he had little sense of what he'd written and where it might go.

In the morning, he printed the document. He shook his head as he read something that bore little resemblance to anything he'd ever written, yet he didn't toss any of the twelve pages, nor did he sit down to revise them. And later that night, as well as for the next nineteen midnights, he returned to his desk, effortlessly picking up where he'd left off while smoking cigarette after cigarette without messing his desk or coughing up any phlegm. At times his fingers would slow and his shoulders stiffen, yet he kept on, and when he finished, he didn't even run a spell-check on the document. The printer whirred into action. The pages spat out with a speed he couldn't measure. He didn't search for an envelope. One sat ready on the table by his front door, along with his car keys, wallet, and the ink pen with which he copied an address. He left his grandfather's watch behind. The night air felt thick in his lungs as he drove to the post office. No one stood in line for the automated postage machine. He dropped the manuscript in the bin.

VI

"Why didn't you tell me you were working on this?" Doug said over the phone.

"It sort of came out of nowhere," Adam said.

"Jesus."

Adam winced. He almost said, "No, the other team."

"It'll sell," Doug said. "The question really is for how much. Who do you want me to try first?"

"Garrison," Adam said.

"Sure?"

"He's the one." Adam looked at the nearly empty pack of cigarettes on his desk. He didn't want either of the Kools remaining. He crumpled up the pack and shot it toward a wastebasket. He missed.

"If I didn't know you like I do," Doug said, "I'd say you wanted to prove something to Garrison."

"Maybe," Adam said. "I've got to go." He heard Doug say something else, but that didn't keep him from hanging up. He needed to contact the chair at the community college, tell her he would not be coming back in the fall.

VII

The success of his novel didn't surprise Adam. Nor did the next nor did the one after that. In four consecutive years, he wrote a novel that sold more copies than the previous novel, as well as all other works of fiction published in that particular year. Garrison called him his workhorse, while Doug even said it might be wise to take some time off, though both his agent and editor had appeared to discover there was no reason to monkey with

Adam's process. Critics expressed astonishment at his performance, claiming always the quality remained or in fact improved from book to book. A Jamaican novelist said Adam's work was a little facile in the *Times* and in *Entertainment Weekly* a biracial female poet claimed he told the same story over and over, which kept, for a while, the praise from being total. That is, until both reviewers, on the same day in June, died in separate accidents, the Jamaican fellow at land, the biracial woman at sea.

Though Doug and Garrison and many others encouraged him to move to Manhattan—and in truth he'd once dreamed of living there—Adam told all who asked, he had everything he needed in Indianapolis. Each novel was optioned for film, but he refused to travel to LA to write the screenplays, (though each film found itself with excellent adaptations and positive reviews). Perhaps because of his staying in Indianapolis, a rumor emerged that he couldn't have possibly written all the books. Only a team of writers could maintain such productivity and quality, people said. Never mind that those who whispered such remarks often found themselves with bowel troubles, cracked foundations, ingrown toenails, or flat tires afterward. To combat the whispers, at Garrison's urging, Adam agreed to grant interviews. No matter the interviewer—male, female, foreign, or domestic—Adam spoke of his old writing process, claiming he rose early every day, wrote a small amount, fussed over and focused on his work one word at a time. "Like most writers," he claimed. When the questions pushed hard, wanting him to divulge too many secrets, he remembered Big Son had told him Robert Johnson played often with his back to the audience, lest anyone take note of the magic he wielded so easily. Adam did tell the truth about how he still used his MacBook, despite the many new versions on the market that did so many wonderful things, though he refused every request to photograph its screen.

When he finally agreed to take a break, instead of another novel, he produced a dozen stories, each composed in a single evening. All were published in the slicks, then a collection, which his publisher released at the time his next novel was arriving in manuscript to Garrison (to whom he now sent everything directly, and who never complained about the chronic paper cuts he suffered). About this time, it was overheard often that, if this one man could write all these books, then he must never sleep. Throughout eleven months of the year, Adam slept well. He ate well, too, and slept with comely women who didn't bother him about moving in or dating exclusively. He left his doctor's office with a pat on the back and the assurance he had the body and health of a much younger man. Every now and then, right before he went to bed, his eyelids would fly open and he'd feel the sensation of a hand on his shoulder that neither harmed nor healed. But soon his heart would quiet, his eyes would soften, and he'd find his way toward another good night's rest.

VIII

Then his father grew ill. It happened all of a sudden—he learned about it from his mother after a reading of his latest novel in Bloomington—and Adam cursed himself for being so self-involved. When was the last time he'd seen his father? Weeks before? Had he not appeared thinner then? Had there been a new shuffle in his gait? What in the world had Adam been thinking? That his father would live forever?

It was cancer, the same disease that had ended Adam's grandfather's life. It was late in discovery and devouring his stomach. The worst kind of cancer, the doctor said, a white man not much older than Adam who later whispered how much he loved all Adam's novels. Adam thanked him, knowing nothing could be done. Was this the price for that evening outside Clarksdale? Or the first installment on the plan?

He entered his father's hospital room, found him asleep, and considered telling him what had happened so many midnights ago, knowing at the same time his father wouldn't believe him—just another story from his imaginative and talented son, of whom he couldn't be more proud. Adam had brought with him a copy of his latest novel, which had been nominated for and was expected in some quarters to sweep all the annual prizes. He laid it on the nightstand, watched a spasm of pain twist his sleeping father's face. Adam said, "It's my fault." His father stirred, his coppery forehead glazed with sweat. "Adam?" he said weakly, wincing as he rose and rested his weight on his elbows. He turned, then slumped back down on the mattress. "Don't strain yourself," Adam said.

"Least of my worries," Mr. Carmichael said. He tried to smile, but looked at the ceiling and groaned.

Adam said, "I wish there was something I could do."

"Might just be my time," his father said. His shoulders rose beneath the white hospital blanket.

Adam reached out a hand, then clamped it against the other. It occurred to him that he needed to remember this pain, that he'd one day revisit it in his writing, but that thought didn't stay with him long. His eyes tracked toward his new novel, which had been called "a searing journey into the lives of Black Americans," but bore no trace of similarity to his own experience. In truth, unless he read any of his fiction, he'd often forget exactly what it was about. He let go his hands, tapped the hardcover. "When you have some time," he said. "I thought you might like to take a look at this."

Mr. Carmichael turned his head. He sighed. "I'm sorry, son," he said. "I don't want to spend any of these days telling anything but the truth. Your books, proud as I am of you that you wrote them, they're just not my cup of tea."

Adam's hand rose from the book. He watched his father's eyes close.

IX

But it wasn't just his father. He recalled the two prominent critics of his work, now silenced, were black. At a reading in Fort Wayne and the next night in South Bend, he saw black students in the audience, but they yawned and looked at their watches, then bolted the auditoriums after they'd checked in with their teachers to secure their extra credit. Back home, he disguised himself in sunglasses and a Colts cap and lingered in several bookstores. In the big chains, he found his books in sections ranging from fiction to best-sellers to African American studies, and occasionally a black man or woman would pick up one of his novels or the collection of stories, but rarely did any purchase one. Though he was cheered one evening to see a pair of high school students depart with his books in their shopping bags, two nights later he saw them arrive at different hours, each with their receipt sticking out of the paperback and on their way to the returns counter. Meanwhile, in the small black-owned bookstores, he didn't know which was worse: that Afrocentrica had no copies at all or that two sun-faded mass-market paperbacks of his sat in a lonely corner of Amistad Books.

What to do? He couldn't talk to Doug or Garrison. He didn't want to trouble his mother, now a widow. A spontaneous return to Clarksdale began with much promise yet on arrival yielded the solemn news that Big Son Jenkins had died the same day Adam's first novel was released. While in the city, he drove in what he recalled to be the direction of Coahoma County Road Six but got turned around on Highway 61 and was headed back to Memphis with the sun sinking low.

Never much of a drinker, he tried several nights in motels between Memphis and Indianapolis to get drunk, but a case of beer or a bottle of gin only made him a little sleepy. When he woke, he was as alert and vital as if he hadn't touched a drop, and painfully aware of every thought in his head. In his car, he turned up the music, always blues, especially by Charlie Patton, Son House, Bukka White, Tommy and Robert Johnson. When "Cross Road Blues" came on, he turned it up even louder. The song didn't mention a scenario like the one Adam experienced. It merely evoked the sense of a man driven to a point where he must make a decision. To Adam, the most compelling line was when Robert sang, "Save poor Bob, if you please." What those lines meant to poor Bob, though, Adam could only guess.

What he did know about both Robert and Tommy Johnson was that neither, in his lifetime, had experienced as much fame as Adam. Was that the price for them? That each would record, really, only a handful of songs, none of which were known too well outside of Mississippi? Only after they'd died—Tommy in his fifties, Robert in his thirties—did their fame finally grow. And, not too ironically, Adam felt, the bluesmen's principal audience now was as white as his own. Yet Tommy and Robert had played before Southern black men and women until the days they died. Adam's own grandfather claimed to have seen Tommy play some out-of-the-way juke near West Memphis when he, Mr. Carmichael, was a teen. Would Adam's work experience the opposite when he died? Would it be, at long last, read by African Americans? What about the Johnsons, though? Were they compelled to play? Long after they knew they had only mastery and not celebrity? Did Tommy feel his heart misery before he played his first note at that final party? Did Robert know that he might face some jealous husband on the night he died but still arrive with his guitar? One thing Adam knew for certain: another midnight awaited him. He'd return to his Mac, with many more midnights to go.

He was thinking about all this, the Johnsons, and his father and grandfather, too, along with his own fate, when he arrived home. But when his hand touched the doorknob, he felt slowed by another thought, as sudden as inspiration. The MacBook? What if he didn't have it anymore? That very machine drew him to his writing room, didn't it? Hadn't the devil's agent programmed it? Just as he'd tuned Tommy and Robert Johnson's guitars?

Soon he was inside his house, then back outside, his MacBook clutched against his side. He was moving quickly to the car and driving before he knew his destination. In his mind he tried to fashion what would be the way to disable or destroy the machine. Unfortunately, Indiana offered few mountaintops from which to hurl it, and he didn't think he could find his way inside a demolition yard. What he had was water, creeks and lakes and reservoirs. The Wabash was the state river of Indiana, subject of the state song, too, "On the Banks of the Wabash, Far Away." He had his choice of Lafayette or Terre Haute—each a little over an hour away—then headed south, to Terre Haute, a city he'd never visited, to which he wasn't sure the directions. Yet once he'd made the decision, he didn't slow down, as if to pause for a moment of reflection might take him back where he'd begun.

X

Adam stopped at a red light. The air conditioner cooled his face but only briefly, as the front seat of his Lexus suddenly felt hotter than any thermometer could measure. "Don't go thinking you're slick," a voice said.

Adam turned. No one sat next to him, though he smelled a faint and familiar cologne and heard the dry notes of laughter. The traffic signal turned green, but Adam didn't press down on his accelerator. He found no one in his backseat and heard only the beating of his heart. The rest of the uneventful drive brought him home, where the security system secured the fact that no one had entered since he left. Once inside, he felt fairly certain that his hallucinations were just that: vivid hallucinations, both auditory and olfactory, and they followed him into the kitchen where he never cooked, the guest room that had never seen a visitor. Like the Lexus outside, all the items inside had been purchased through his writing: the plush furniture, sparkling appliances, art works by Bearden and Basquiat (about whose successes he often wondered). Yet he felt no real ownership of them, had shared them with no other person. He passed a bookshelf that contained every title he'd published. When he picked up a copy of his first novel it felt as foreign to him as if it had been written in a forgotten language. The stiff pages seemed sharp enough to slice. He wanted to compare it with some of his earlier efforts, which he kept locked in the bottom drawer of the file cabinet in his writing room. Had he really gotten better? Would he be able to tell? As he strode in that direction, though, a familiar voice said, "Over here."

Adam paused. "Where?" he said, still clutching the book as if he might use it to defend himself.

"Where else?" the voice said.

Adam walked toward his writing room. He looked at his grandfather's watch, though he knew it was midnight, just as he knew whom he would see inside when he opened the door.

He shouldn't have acted surprised to see his old friend—who'd never said his name—seated in Adam's folding chair, the very same chair he'd first sat down in to write those fevered words that made up the book he still held. Now the devil's own agent was dressed in a track suit and slippers, as if he'd been roused from sleep and threw on the first thing he could find. "Not expecting company this time of night?" he said

Adam shook his head. He dropped the copy of his novel to the carpet. "It's natural," the man said, leaning back in the chair so that three legs hovered above the floor. "Why do you think Faulkner hid out in Hollywood? To write dialogue for Joan Crawford? Shoot."

Adam leaned against the door frame. His forehead felt slicker and slicker, but he didn't raise his sweaty palms, knowing how futile it would be to wipe his brow.

"Gotta tell you, though. That was pretty clever," his companion said, still perched in the chair on one leg. "Get rid of the tool and lose the trade? That's a fresh idea."

A fat bead of sweat slipped into Adam's eye. He blinked. He could envision the Mac-Book bumping along the Wabash's silty bottom, surrounded by ancient catfish and nuzzled by snapping turtles. As sudden as temptation, a thought of suicide occurred to him, but would that only double his damnation? "I didn't really think everything through," Adam said, his voice hollow and distant, as if supplied by a ventriloquist.

"Boy, we depend on that," the devil's agent said, and with that the chair's legs came slamming to the floor. Adam jumped back. But his guest was on his feet and approaching.

"Everybody thinks he's going to find the one trick, the one loophole," he said. "But I'm here to tell you that there isn't one. You could have all the time left in the world and you wouldn't find it. And a deal, my friend, is a deal." Then, in less than instant, he was gone.

XI

Adam woke. He looked around his bedroom with no memory of how or when he got into bed. Yet he felt refreshed, awake and alert, not troubled at all. His appetite was normal, his weight half a pound lighter than the day before. Perhaps his hair needed trimming. His elbows and knees were refreshed by handfuls of lotion. While standing there, he felt certain he'd reached some high point, endured some crisis, and now had before him a new life to live.

This thought carried him through the day, as he set about occupying himself with the simplest of tasks, all of which possessed, for the first time in years, a luster and spark. Shining shoes, filling the gas tank, and mowing the lawn felt consequential again. He wondered why his shoulders seemed so loose, why in the shower before heading out for a meal, he felt each stream of water. What promise each day held! A glass of ice water refreshed like nothing else. He begrudged no one an autograph as he sat for dinner one evening at a restaurant, a chain that had recently earned a bad reputation for how it treated minority customers. But not on this night, not for Adam Carmichael. As he savored the last bite of apple pie, he wondered why he didn't treat himself more often.

In the months that followed, he would not allow himself to say he'd beaten the devil, wouldn't even let the words rattle in his head like dice in a cup. The happiness within him had not been present for years prior to his sojourn in Mississippi. All along he'd believed writing had made him happy and the proper recognition of his work would distinguish him. Now the only writing he did was on a check or grocery list. When Doug or Garrison called, Adam would describe a ball game he'd watched or a woman he'd met at the movies. Never would he provide them with the details they wanted—what the next book would be about, when it would arrive—because he didn't think of books, the next one, the former one, all the earlier manuscripts no one wanted to read. All that time he'd spent. Now he felt as though he'd found the way to live life best, in the details of living in the world as you knew it, not in what you might make of it. Most nights he made it into bed by nine, where he'd lie as peacefully as he had been as a boy in his pajamas, and fall asleep without remembering a moment of being awake.

XII

The church bells were tolling again. By the time he knew he wasn't dreaming about Mississippi, he was already near his writing room. The door opened easily. When he sat, the folding chair conformed to his shape. The Kool fit between his lips, a lighter lay in his hand. His grandfather's watch showed midnight, but the second hand stopped moving. His MacBook sat on his desk, smelling faintly of the river. It hummed as the screen glowed. The tears that slicked his face would dry soon. The work would begin again tonight. He'd be hard at it a long time.

Do You Remember?

by Laura Good

I met him when I was young, only a child with hair that curled tightly against my head. My mother would spend hours braiding it, pulling and pulling so that between each braid you could see my scalp. On the ends of the braids she would tie the painted beads that she had gotten from my grandmother. My favorite bead was the white one with tiny blue waves painted on it. I had never been to the beach, but I imagined that the ocean was a place where someone could float and never be harmed.

He lived across the street from me. Sandy hair, a gap in between his teeth, and red lips that looked like he was always wearing lipstick. I used to tease him, calling him a girl with those red lips. I remember how he would wipe his lips on his forearm, grinning as he pulled away and showed me his arm, white without any trace of red. We spent hours in the backyard catching frogs and putting them in glass jars. We never kept them for long, though. I couldn't imagine being trapped inside a tiny glass frame against my will, dreaming of the open grass I used to live in, and neither could he. We decided it was best just to look at them, name them, and then set them free.

When I was young, my mother never said anything to me about him, nothing about how we shouldn't be friends. But thinking about it now, every time he came inside my house my mother would look at us with those eyes. They were eyes that weren't looking at us but past us. It was like she was looking at something else. Something serious. She would be sitting at the table painting beads, like my grandmother used to do before she passed away. Her brush would be poised in the air, red dripping from the bristles, and then she would give us the look that looked serious and far away. I never thought about it until now, what that look meant. Maybe she knew what would happen one day when we were older.

Our first kiss happened during the rain. We had been in his house watching one of our favorite TV shows, our legs touching at the ankles. We always sat close like that. I liked feeling the warmth of his skin against mine. It started to rain. Lightly at first. But then the pounding sound of drops got louder and louder. He looked at me and grinned his gap-toothed smile.

"Let's go," he said.

He took my hand and we ran into the backyard. The rain was cold against my skin, but heat came up from the ground in a light fog. He took off his shoes and waded into the creek.

"Wait up," I yelled. I untied my laces and pulled off my socks one at a time. I followed him into the creek, stepping on rocks so my toes wouldn't be so cold. He got further ahead of me so I tried to walk faster. My head was down as I concentrated on staying on the rocks and not falling in the water. When I finally looked up he had stopped. He was smiling as he grabbed my arms and pulled me toward him with too much force. I stumbled into the water as our lips hit each other. We laughed and it felt strange, but also wonderful. We kissed again, softly this time.

Sometimes at night I have this dream. I'm in the creek with you, but you're too far ahead of me.

"Wait up," I say, but it's like you can't hear me. Or you don't want to.

It's raining harder and harder and I can't see the rocks beneath my feet. You keep walking farther ahead and I can still see you, but you're only a speck, like a smudge in a photograph. I wonder, if you turned around, would you be able to see me?

I was only a baby when my grandmother died. She was sick for a few weeks and then, the doctors said, all that could be done for her was to make her comfortable until the time came. I only knew this because my uncle told me when I was older. My mother never talked about her death, only her life. I knew my mother missed her, the way she was always painting beads. She never seemed to smile very big and always wore long, flowy skirts that cut off at her ankles. The skirts, I had learned, were my grandmother's. I never thought to ask about my grandmother because I hadn't known her. All I knew was the stories my mother would tell when she braided my hair. Getting older meant that the pulling and braiding didn't hurt anymore. I would listen to the sounds of her fingers combing through my hair as she talked about my grandmother. She was beautiful, my mother told me, and loved to paint. Beads weren't the only things my grandmother enjoyed. She liked making pictures using a special paint made from seashells. My mother had tried to make this paint, but she couldn't remember the recipe. I came in one day to find a hundred tiny shell pieces on the kitchen floor, and my mother huddled on the floor with her head in her hands. She could remember how to make the beads, though, and so that's what she did.

My grandmother had been in love with a white man. It was the reason for our carmel-colored skin. My grandmother had been black as night, my mother had said, but she fell in love with a man who often came into the grocery store where she worked. I never learned what happened to him, my grandfather. Apparently he disappeared a few months after my mother and her twin brother were born. I imagined that he was perhaps alive, and I often wondered if I would ever run into him. Maybe we would both be eating at the same restaurant or taking the same taxi, and I would be sitting with an elderly white man with no idea that he was my grandfather. It was cruel, I thought, that he was allowed to exist without knowing about me or my mother. But, then again, I guess I wouldn't need to know a man who had decided to abandon his family.

When we were in high school, things started to change. Years of running in backyards with fireflies and frogs seemed to matter less, and skin seemed to matter more. I'll never forget the first time I realized that we wouldn't be friends anymore. I passed you in the hall and you were standing with your friends. I asked if we still had plans after school. We had talked about getting milk shakes and burgers down at Birdie's Bar because we'd both been craving the taste of Birdie's burgers.

I'll never forget the look on his face. His friends stood behind him, confused as to why I had walked up and asked him a question, why I had decided to talk to him in the first place. He tried to look like he didn't know what I was talking about, but I could tell that behind the look in his eyes was something else. Was he ashamed of me? Of himself? Had he forgotten the first time we kissed? The first time we made love? He pretended like it meant nothing, but behind it all I could tell he was feeling something else.

That was only the beginning, the first time I saw that you had realized I was black and you were white. It hadn't mattered before. It didn't matter when we were alone. But now, as I stood asking for burgers, you stood looking like you didn't even know who I was. As time passed it was only worse for me, worse for us. All of it eventually faded until we stopped speaking. You told me it was because we grew apart. I knew it was because you had grown up.

My mother told me that it wouldn't work out between us. Not as friends, not as lovers, not as anything. She told me one day when we were sitting at the kitchen table. She was painting beads and I was reading a magazine. She explained that the world wasn't ready to accept friendships like ours. We were too different, she said, not only because of color but because of our lives. He would grow up to be a white man, a man who was handed everything in life. He would carry a suitcase and go to work and then go home to a blond wife and three blond children. That was the way it would be, she said. I remember crying in bed that night, wanting to prove her wrong. We were different, I had hoped. Just because my grandfather had been the man to run away didn't mean my man would be. Looking back I think I was just sad because by then I decided that I loved him. I loved him like a child loves the feeling of summertime grass between her toes and the feeling of the ocean on her face.

The first and only time we made love was outside. It was on a warm night beneath the stars. He had driven his truck all the way to the outskirts of a town in an open field. I could hear cicadas chirping and the sound of our hearts beating as we undressed. It was slow and soft and sort of strange, the way our bodies looked together in the moonlight. We were yin and yang, two parts of a whole. I remember, once it was over, telling him about the ocean.

"I want to see it someday," I said. "And I want you to be there."

He smiled and promised he would. Two weeks later, I asked him to eat a burger with me and he had forgotten all about the ocean.

Now that I'm older, I don't wear my hair in braids anymore. I go to a salon once a month and use a relaxer that smells like burning plastic. It makes my hair soft and smooth and long. Sometimes I think that if I saw him he wouldn't recognize me. I wore braids up until the last moment we saw each other. It was the last day of the summer, before he went back to college and before me and my mom moved to a different town. It wasn't good to be here, she had decided. I guess she heard me crying all those nights. Or maybe she thought moving would help her forget my grandmother. Maybe she was hoping she could find shells.

On the last day we saw each other, I saw him standing in his driveway. He had taken out the trash and stopped on his way back in the house. He was staring into our window and he had a confused look on his face. I looked back at him, wondering if he could see me. I thought about holding my hand up and waving. I even felt myself do it, felt my arm move up. But I didn't. I wondered what he was thinking. Was he troubled by how he'd treated me? Was he thinking about the night we made love, how our bodies had moved perfectly in sync? Or was he just staring off into space, thinking about something only white boys think about?

Sometimes I dream that I'm in the ocean with you. We're swimming in the water. It's too deep for us to stand, so we're just floating. We feel safe and warm, like nothing can touch us. We hold hands and drift far off into the sunset. I fall asleep a little too long, and when I wake up I realize that my hand is empty and you're not there anymore.

I got married to a man named Jared. He was talk, dark, and handsome. Or at least that's what my mother said the first time she met him. She held on to his hand and smiled into his eyes. She promised she'd fix us some biscuits.

As she got older my mother had stopped painting the beads. One day she handed me a small box with a thousand painted balls inside and told me to keep them. She didn't want them anymore, she said. She didn't want any of it. So she turned to cooking, which she wasn't very good at. Her biscuits were hard and her fried chicken was always a little too burned. But Jared smiled when he ate the biscuit, buttering it and eating the entire thing.

The night after we first made love, he told me that he loved me and that he knew we'd get married one day. I smiled, imagining us living together with three children. Two boys and a girl, I hoped. We would live somewhere far from here, maybe near the ocean. It was funny that the first thing that popped into my head when Jared proposed, a few months later, was the gap-toothed boy with red lips who lived across the street from me. I didn't know why, and I wished immediately that I hadn't been reminded of him, yet there he was in my memory—holding my arms and pulling me so close that our lips hit.

We went to the beach for our honeymoon. It was my only requirement, somewhere with a beach. And so we traveled to Jamaica where the water was clear and people drank out of coconut shells. I loved Jared. I loved him the way a woman loves the feeling of a bed and her feet on the ground. I liked the way we looked sleeping together, the way our arms were tangled so that you couldn't tell where my arms stopped and his arms took over. With Jared, I'd always be safe. With Jared, there would be no beads or broken shells. I wouldn't have to take up cooking in fear of my husband leaving me for a white woman and whiter dreams. I didn't need to go swimming in the ocean. I could just stand on the beach looking out at the waves, watching them come to the shore only to retreat again out into the endless abyss of blue.

Lenard D. Moore

Plain Truth

I was born into a segregated world
that did not want my kind,
but I did not know
what not to do in the 1950s.
I rose whenever I wanted to
or whenever there was a need.
I was the sun and still am:
rising, setting, rising, radiant, too.
It was a water hose of a time.
It was a dog-biting of a time.
It was a tear gas of a time.
It was a slap-feet-cadence of a time
in a cruel colored chanting country.
Now I walk straight up, straight ahead
through any door because I was born
into a long lineage of strong kin
who hacked down obstacles all day
who climbed cruelest peaks here and there.
I know which knob to turn.

WILLIAM L. RAMSEY

THE PHOENIX RIOT, 1898
—Benjamin Mays's first memory in Greenwood County, SC,
recounted in *Born to Rebel*

From such a fire,
       with the elective franchise,
       his father submissively bowing,
       his father at gunpoint saluting white men,
       all swirling upward in its smoke,

what species of bird could
       reasonably be expected to arise?

But the pine shadows, shaken
       over maimed confluences
       of muscle and tired memory, unspooled
       fresh senses from his soul.

Wounded voices became so quiet
       that winter, burnt cedar so cold,
       the bleak rattle of flames one evening
       broke upon more basic flame, brittle sheets
       of rebellion broke on a bedrock
       of rebellion.

Who can say exactly how it happened?

By spring, at any rate, the crack
       in the window pane, in the wren's
       egg, in the spine of his favorite book,
       in his heart, ran like wax from a single wick
       wherever he dared look.

Kaneesha Brownlee, *Peace and Quiet*,
Chattahoochie River, Georgia.

R E V I E W   E S S A Y

"THREE SONGS ABOUT LYNCHING"

by Julius B. Fleming, Jr.

In 1936, African American poet and civil rights activist Langston Hughes published a trilogy of poems in *Opportunity* magazine entitled *Three Songs About Lynching*. The three poems, "Lynching Song," "Silhouette," and "Flight," use various poetic strategies but portray similar ideologies, imagery, and discursive constructions that were at the core of one of the most heinous forms of violence in the history of humankind. Addressing the routine pathologization of black male sexuality, white patriarchy's creation of white female angst, and lynching's effect on white subjectivity, the three lynching poems chart similar waters in overlapping but divergent ways. One finds a comparable dynamic in examining three excellent texts that analyze lynching's historical and cultural significance in the U.S. nation-state: Kimberly Harper's *White Man's Heaven: The Lynching and Expulsion of Blacks in the Southern Ozarks, 1894-1909* (2010), Koritha Mitchell's *Living With Lynching: African American Lynching Plays, Performance, and Citizenship, 1890-1930* (2011), and Jennie Lightweis-Goff's *Blood at the Root: Lynching as American Cultural Nucleus* (2011). Each author sings a song that is simultaneously tragic and beautiful. Their narratives of lynching and resistance sometimes collide in productive dissonance. But all three texts leave lynching studies in a richer, more exciting, more complex location. We are fortunate to have such a heavy topic in such able hands.

Kimberly Harper's *White Man's Heaven: The Lynching and Expulsion of Blacks in the Southern Ozarks, 1894-1909* offers an intriguing history of lynching that moves outside of North/South dichotomies to situate the Midwest at the center of lynching discourses. Harper is a masterful storyteller, and if readers' familiarity with lynching in the U.S. South anticipates a particular narrative, the stories that Harper tells surprise at every turn. *White Man's Heaven* examines the lynching and expulsion of African Americans in Monett, Pierce City, Joplin, and Springfield, Missouri, and Harrison, Arkansas, between 1894 and 1909. A large part of Harper's intervention, she claims, is to analyze these geographical sites collectively and to foreground African American expulsion—which lags behind lynching in scholarly interest—as a crucial node in the history of violence against blacks. Expulsion, the author writes, "was one of the most extreme forms of social control, as African Americans were forced to leave behind everything…and it sent a message to nearby black communities to remain complacent or else face the same fate" (xxiv).

In the wake of Emancipation, scores of African Americans set out for the territory, heading westward in hopes of building a new life as free people. Many of them, *White Man's Heaven* shows, settled in Mid-western towns and enjoyed relative access to the freedoms of U.S. citizenship. African Americans formed schools, held political office, voted, and were civil servants, to offer a partial list. But the short-lived optimism of Reconstruction soon ran dry, and anxieties around whiteness and white power, and the linked discourse of black criminality, produced a region in which Mid-western towns trekked into modernity just as they were embracing heinous acts of racial violence. Under these conditions, African American life and livelihood were precarious, and amiable relations between races in a town could, with little warning, give way to chaos and racial animus. Unlike the U.S. South, Harper argues, the regional economy of the Southern Ozarks did not rely heavily on African American labor. Thus, the lynching and expulsion of black residents affected only minimally local economies, which in turn meant the economy offered little incentive in the way of deterring violence against black bodies.

Harper organizes *White Man's Heaven* around discrete geographical locations: chapters one, two, and three examine Pierce City, Missouri; chapters four and five turn to Joplin; chapters six through ten focus on Springfield, Missouri in the book's lengthiest engagement with a particular city; and chapter eleven, the shortest, turns to Harrison, Arkansas. The variance in the time and space that each city gets, Harper admits, is a result of what the archive makes available. Using newspaper accounts, legal records, journals, and other historical sources, each chapter tells a similar narrative of declension in which shifting white racial attitudes towards blacks produces all-white towns through acts of violence and racial purging. But in these stories, one is surprised to see widespread attempts among whites to promote the legal infrastructure of the State over vigilantism and extra-legal violence. Whether all-white juries found blacks innocent of alleged crimes, or whether whites rushed into lynch mobs to protest a lynching, refused to hand over prisoners, or called in the National Guard, Harper demonstrates how the flowering of racial discord became increasingly more common as the criminalization of blackness became more firmly rooted in popular discourses.

In *Living With Lynching*, Koritha Mitchell pushes lynching discourses into uncharted territories. This well-researched and convincingly argued book calls into question the customary and circumscribed ways in which we have come to know lynching and its cultural logics. In particular, Mitchell critiques the ways in which lynching photographs have been assigned a privileged epistemic value that supplies and legitimates their archival dominance and evidentiary authority. Not only are these photographs frequently products of those very communities that perpetuated lynching, but they "rarely represent the perspective of African Americans" (Mitchell 4). For Mitchell, such a narrowing of lynching's archive has obscured the innovative ways in which black communities creatively utilized drama and performance to confront and grapple with lynching between 1890 and 1930.

In this vein, *Living With Lynching* critically analyzes what Mitchell terms "African American lynching plays"—a key genre of African American drama that "tells stories strikingly different from those suggested by lynching photography" (1). Grounded in extensive archival research, *Living With Lynching* shifts African American lynching plays from the margin to the center of lynching discourses. Such an expansion of the archive provides students of lynching alternate ways of knowing this familiar and violent practice and, ultimately, offers a different set of optics through which to analyze the United States during the Progressive Era.

Bringing together literature, performance studies, history, and a range of other disciplines and critical traditions, Mitchell assembles a theoretical framework that pinpoints the social, cultural, and intellectual logics that have authorized photography's ascendency and provided little incentive to take seriously the epistemological and aesthetic value of African American lynching drama. The care with which Mitchell details the generic conventions of these plays proves to be a useful foundation for the chapters that follow. Lynching plays, she tells us, are generally "one-acts published in periodicals" (14). They "served as mechanisms through which African Americans survived the height of mob violence." And, unlike most photographs, they "refused to feature physical violence," opting instead to "spotlight the black home and the impact that the mob's outdoor activities have on the family" (Mitchell 2). With these features in mind, Mitchell concludes that African American lynching plays were produced for black communities who potentially used performance to survive the horrors of lynching, while figuring out how to practice the rights, privileges, and protections that U.S. citizenship ostensibly afforded.

This attention to generic conventions and social historical milieu serves as a springboard to another significant claim that the book makes: too often, African American art gets pigeonholed within the realm of "resistance." Why, Mitchell asks, "do scholarly analyses so frequently end with explanations of the extent to which such art responds to white supremacy? Is it possible that black art about lynching is a continuation of African Americans' self-affirmation" (4). To be sure, resistance and self-affirmation can coexist in artistic production. But in exposing the often reductionist social logics that give rise to black art/resistance correlations, and in disrupting the impulse towards this critical stance, *Living With Lynching* is a welcomed expansion of lynching's archive. In fact, this accounts for much of Mitchell's motivation to dispense with the "anti-lynching drama" label, a label that suggests blacks react to lynching discourse rather than initiate discussions on lynching. Mitchell divides her book into two sections. In the much shorter part one, "Making Lynching Drama and Its Contributions Legible," chapter one of two shows how the sidelining of African American lynching plays is rooted in modernity's privileging of those representational modes that, in their estimation, come closest to "the real" and "truth." Within this paradigm, performance has often fared poorly. Building on the work of performance theorist Diana Taylor, Mitchell suggests that scholars have erected partitions between what Taylor terms the "archive and repertoire." In other words, documents get privileged "because they seem simply to record facts and remain immune to the corruption and ephemerality of performance" (Mitchell 6). Yet, Mitchell works against the grain of this separation and lifts African American lynching plays to the status of evidence, while avoiding the trap of reducing creative production to realist testimony.

Despite gaps in the archive, Mitchell quite brilliantly finds a way to think about how these plays possibly circulated within their material environments, particularly among African American social and domestic spaces. Their one-act format and publication in periodicals, she finds, encouraged "amateur performance in private venues," particularly black homes. These embodied performances in black homes could have "provide[d] a training manual for black communities, encouraging African Americans to rehearse an understanding of lynching that allowed them to mourn because it helped them to maintain a sense of themselves as upstanding citizens unjustly under siege" (Mitchell 39). The speculation upon which the book's conclusions about how African American lynching plays circulated may seem suspect. Yet, the author's speculation is, I think, a promising methodological tactic that allows her to confront the harsh realities of archives that index the marginalization of subjects through archival absences.

Chapter two uses Angelina Weld Grimké's full-length play *Rachel* to track how black artists expand beyond stage performance, particularly minstrelsy and musical comedy, to develop what Mitchell terms a "writer-centered conception of black theater" around 1910 (44). *Rachel* epitomizes how black families literally lived with lynching, as its violence continued to affect the families and homes of its victims. While Grimké's aesthetic choices made her work conducive to formal theatrical production, there is a marked shift in the kind of aesthetic choices that later authors of African American lynching drama make. Not only do these writers shift primarily to one-act formats, but Mitchell concludes that they are less invested in "formal staging" and the integrated audiences that *Rachel* had attracted and more concerned with how their plays could affect black audiences and encourage "practices of communal literacy" (57).

"Part Two: Developing a Genre, Asserting Black Citizenship," consists of four chapters that identify and critically analyze distinct characters that recur throughout African American lynching drama. Chapter three examines representations of the black soldier in Alice Dunbar Nelson's *Mine Eyes have Seen* (1918) and Mary Burrill's *Aftermath* (1919), the first two published lynching plays by black authors. In these plays, the black soldier, fighting in the name of U.S. democracy, represents black manhood and an ideal form of black citizenship. But such devotion to one's country becomes precarious in the face of lynching and other forms of anti-black violence that go unpunished. This paradox of fighting for equality on behalf of a nation that spurns your desires for precisely that is at the core of Dunbar Nelson's and Burrill's plays and, as Mitchell sees it, likely became a part of conversations in those communities that came into contact with these plays.

Chapter four examines the transition from the black soldier to the black lawyer, who became the "centerpiece of conversations about identity and citizenship" (Mitchell 115). Examining Georgia Douglas Johnson's *A Sunday Morning in the South* (1925) and Myrtle Smith Livingston's *For Unborn Children* (1926), Mitchell shows how, like military service, the court became key space in which blacks waged their battle for full citizenship. Like the solider, black lawyers exhibited a keen faith in the U.S. legal system, only to "have it fail them and their families in the most painful ways" (Mitchell 122). The ironic criminalization and ultimate lynching of black custodians of the law, and those who sought to enter the profession, reveals the glaring contradictions in U.S. rhetorics of equality and freedom and the harsh realities for blacks who were fighting in various theaters of war to secure and perform full citizenship.

In chapter five, Mitchell continues her commitment to exploring how black women, particularly mothers and wives, lived with lynching perhaps more than anyone else. Their experiential realities take center stage in three plays by Georgia Douglas Johnson: *Blue-bood* (1926), *Safe* (1929), and *Blue-Eyed Black Boy* (1930). In the wake of the havoc that lynching wreaked on the bodies of fathers and husbands as well as black homes, these women were left to perform the work of repair and survival. But black women's relationships to lynching often preceded the theatrical act of violence. Whether they remained silent about being raped by white men to avoid the possibility of black male retaliation—and black men's likely death as punishment for what might otherwise be read as valor—or whether they resisted bringing black children into a world in which black bodies lived in perpetual states of vulnerability, these women—in body, spirit, and action—lived with lynching and, as Mitchell puts it, managed to "keep on keeping on" (2).

The final chapter offers an analysis of the "pimp" and "coward" in G.D. Lipscomb's *Frances* (1925) and Joseph Mitchell's *Son-Boy* (1928), the only two male-authored plays in Mitchell's archive. "Black men," she writes, "began writing lynching plays in 1925, several years after Angelina Weld Grimké initiated the genre, and Alice Dunbar-Nelson and Mary Burrill began revising it" (175). The figures of the pimp and the coward are certainly not as noble as the soldiers and lawyers that populate the book's earlier chapters. But these figures are crucial to understanding how a range of blacks coped with and responded to lynching. They were less concerned about enacting a kind of citizenship-based manhood as they were surviving, even if this meant making seemingly heartrending compromises to conciliate those who, at any moment, could take their lives in the ritual act of lynching. And while these figures may not move toward self-affirmation in the same ways as other lynching plays, they did, however, "encourage difficult conversations—within the plays and among African Americans reading them" (Mitchell 177).

Neither the lynched body nor photography, *Living with Lynching* argues, is the sum of lynching's archive. They fail to offer the most textured narratives about how various peoples—not just lynching's perpetrators—lived with lynching and its devastating effects on bodies, homes, and the fabric of black life in the U.S. nation-state. Certainly the limitations of the archive leaves one wondering, for example, how did class, region, and a host of other variables, factor into communal uses of African American lynching plays? But these plays, and their performances, Mitchell convincingly argues, offer new ways of knowing that require us to engage lynching on different terms and from different sites. The contribution that Mitchell makes to studies of lynching is significant. And if we, scholars and laypersons alike, take seriously Mitchell's Baldwin-like cautions about the relationship between archives and the production of knowledge, we must necessarily study, conceptualize, and ultimately live with lynching anew.

If *Living With Lynching* investigates lynching's effect on the everyday lives of African American communities, Jennie Lightweis-Goff's *Blood at the Root: Lynching as American Cultural Nucleus* spirals out to account for the broader national practices that fuel and sanction anti-black violence. *Blood at the Root* is a provocative and creatively conceptualized text. It fuses familiar academic methodologies, such as close reading, with the author's bold incorporation of personal narrative, which both opens and closes the book. Lynching, the author posits, too often gets imagined as a distinctly southern brand of anti-black violence. Yet, such a neat correlation between racial violence and geography, the book contends, is not only misleading but indexes a larger tendency to individuate anti-black violence and, thereby, invisibilize the nation's complicity in these practices.

Rather than study "pathological individuals," then, *Blood at the Root* take as its object of study "pathological cultural formations" (Lightweis-Goff 5). A "discursive shift," the author writes, has replaced "pathological *racism* with the pathologist *racist* in accordance with the paradigm that elevates the individual, rather than the collective, as the prized unit of American capitalism" (9; original emphasis). It is this turn from the singular to the collective, from the private to the public that drives Lightweis-Goff's engagement with lynching. For the author, the individuation of violence is a ruse that allows a national amnesia to underplay the nation-state's role in anti-black violence. In other words, this "discursive shift" conceals the ways in which lynching was not a sectional or regional problem; it was, instead, forged in the mold of normative relations of racial power that operated in the broader U.S. nation-state.

The process of promoting individual blame and forgetting how the nation has long been imbricated in lynching practices, the book argues, is not simply a semantic or discursive violence but has material consequences. The author, for example, argues that U.S. law has failed at "imagining group psychology" and prosecuting "collective accountability"

(6). But it is precisely this collective blame that the author teases out and brings to the fore, constantly probing the limitations of capitalism's logics of individuality. Using psychoanalysis, critical race theory, body studies, and theories of citizenship and public and private spheres, as well as an impressive archive that ranges from literature to photography and tourist sites, the author sets out to theorize the how nationalism, citizenship, and publicness are produced in and through the same ethos that motivated lynch mobs to wreak havoc on black bodies through physical and discursive acts of violence.

As much as *Blood at the Root* is concerned with probing publicness and white group psychology to better account for national complicities in lynching, it does not gloss over how African Americans have long used the public sphere to stage revolutionary acts of self-making and political dissent and to lay claim to the guarded category of U.S. citizenship. The author's quite brilliant reading of Ida B. Wells shows how African Americans have not only refused the regionalization of lynching, as Wells does, but have developed various strategies of claiming personhood and including themselves in publics that have historically policed the terms upon which black bodies could belong to and move within this restrictive public space.

Chapter one, "America is Mississippi Now: The Portable South and the Exile of Richard Wright," turns to Wright's autobiographical writing to more closely examine and critique the ways in which the South has become a metaphor for racial violence. Turning to the publication history of *Blackboy*, Wright's 1945 autobiography, the author shows how the publisher's process of selecting which materials to include played into fantasies about southern violence. The publisher exorcises sections that render anti-black violence a national problem, rather than a sectional one. In the portions that make the cut, Wright, the author posits, performs a "burdened subjectivity," which contributes to his participation in what she terms "practice lynchings." Using the psychoanalytic concept of introjection, Wright, she claims, engages in various moments of violence that threaten the lives of others—from a kitten to family. These performances of violence evidence how Wright has incorporated "trauma into his own subjectivity" (Lightweis-Goff 49). While it is unclear how much Lightweis-Goff is promoting "practice lynching" as an analytic for reading character behavior or using it as a critique of publication history, or some combination of both, this chapter convincingly shows how Wright constructs a "portable South" to demonstrate that anti-black violence was not confined to particular geographical spaces, though one has to wonder if the idea of portability folds back into a narrative of origins that hinges upon a logic of southern exceptionalism.

In Chapter two, "Beneath the Skin: George Schuyler and the Fantasy of Race," Lightweis-Goff brings together literature, psychoanalysis, and racial science to explore how the private interiors of black bodies—both physical and psychical—have been central to the survival of racial hierarchies. This chapter pivots around a smart and fascinating linkage between the fantasies of scientific racism and the aesthetic use of fantasy in African American literature. Both iterations expose how black interiority becomes a key site for shoring up the dominance of white supremacy, whether through the biologization of racial difference or the creation of psychic fear to thwart black male/white female relationships, even at the level of the dream. Through a brief reading of Jean Toomer's poem "Portrait in Georgia" and a more extended treatment of George Schuyler's novel *Black No More*, the author convincingly shows that "[j]ust as the body could be penetrated by racial violence, so too could the mind be invaded by white supremacy" (68).

If the spectacle of lynching tended to rely on western modernity's obsession with oc-cularcentrism, the auditory, *Blood at the Root* claims, was also central to performing these acts of violence and should figure more prominently in contemporary analyses of lynching. Chapter three, "Peaceful and Unfathomable and Unbearable Eyes: William Faulkner's Elisions of Witness," explains how Faulkner develops aesthetic strategies to diminish both his and his audiences' relationships to lynching, minimizing its structural prominence and downplaying collective guilt. Yet, Lightweis-Goff shows that the auditory is a key epistemological mode for uncovering lynching's operations. It reveals how those who ab-scond the position of witness by artfully repressing their own knowledge of anti-black violence have more knowledge than what meets the eye. This compelling chapter listens to Faulkner's fiction and interviews on what Ralph Ellison calls the "lower frequencies" to brilliantly uncover different ways of knowing lynching in American cultural production.

Chapter four, "The Lynched Woman: Kara Walker, Laura Nelson, and the Ques-tion of Agency," is, in my opinion, the book's most provocative and risky chapter. One can find here a forceful critique of how Black Studies scholarship often downplays the "circumscription of agency" that subtends racial violence and inequality (Lightweis-Goff 121). The preference for what the author terms "agentic" subjectivity, and overinvest-ments in its representation, has contributed to an almost impulsive rush to condemn white spectators who observe injured black bodies. The suspicion that whites will con-sume these images in less than ethical ways has produced what the author terms "anxiet-ies of audience" (Lightweis-Goff 115). Examining Kara Walker's *Cut* and photographs of Frank Embree and Laura Nelson that appeared in *Without Sanctuary: Lynching Pho-tography in America*, this chapter argues that such tendencies not only understate the material conditions of oppression—by overemphasizing agency—but they also foreclose potentially productive moments of voyeurism. The chapter's quite intriguing attempt to "save voyeurism" is optimistic. But readers are left wanting concrete examples of how such a paradigm succeeds on the ground, and they are offered little in the way of figuring out the stakes of such a polemic. Much of the critique of agency is underdeveloped, and even as the chapter avoids ahistoricism, one wonders what the author sees as the role of history in the book's jettisoning of agency and the model of cross-racial visual encounter that it proposes. But these shortcomings, it seems, are, in part, a result of spatial limita-tions. Instead of a chapter, such weighty and complex arguments would almost require a book to flesh out thoroughly.

Bibliography

Harper, Kimberly. 2010. *White Man's Heaven: The Lynching and Expulsion of Blacks in the Southern Ozarks, 1894-1909*. Fayetteville: University of Arkansas Press.

Lightweis-Goff, Jennie. 2011. *Blood at the Root: Lynching as an American Cultural Nucleus*. Albany: SUNY Press.

Mitchell, Koritha. 2011. *Living With Lynching: African American Lynching Plays, Performance, and Citizenship, 1890-1930*. Urbana: University of Illinois Press.

R E V I E W S

"KNEELING IN THE MIDST OF WONDER": EKPHRASIS AND THE ART OF JONATHAN GREEN

Kwame Dawes and Marjory Wentworth, eds. 2013. *Seeking: Poetry and Prose Inspired by the Art of Jonathan Green*. Columbia, SC: University of South Carolina Press. Pp. 160. $39.95 Hardback. $19.95 Paperback.

Reviewed by Anne Keefe, Emory University

Seeking is a collection of ekphrastic writing, mostly poems, that take the visual art of Jonathan Green as their subject matter. Inspired by the narrative surrounding Jonathan Green's painting by the same title, *Seeking* is a lyrical embrace of the details of the visual that spark and enliven verbal responses. Edited by Kwame Dawes and Marjory Wentworth, the collection features twenty-nine poets and prose writers in a beautifully designed compilation that centers on a gallery of sixteen full-color, vibrantly reproduced images of Green's work. Interludes adapted from spirituals and slave songs by Andrew Calhoun serve as transitions between authors, capturing those haunting voices from the graveyard that first inspired Green himself to reach back to his Gullah roots and his own experience of seeking.

Seeking simultaneously re-historicizes voices and memories in danger of being lost to time while exploring the sacred coming-of-age Gullah tradition of "seeking" as a rite of passage suspended in time. As co-editor Marjory Wentworth describes, the project began in 2003 when Green visited Mepkin Abbey, a former rice plantation supported by slave labor in Moncks Corner, South Carolina. Touring the grounds with the abbott Father Francis Kline, Green was moved by the sacredness of the unmarked slave cemetery on the property and began sketching ideas for the painting that later became *Seeking*. The overgrown grave sites were for Green a connection to his own past experience of "seeking," a traditional practice of the African American Gullah community in the low country area of South Carolina and Georgia in which the seeker—a young person of about twelve years old—is isolated in the woods with little or no food in order to seek, to pray, and to find his or her own way to the presence of God. The ritual-induced dreams that the seeker has on his or her journey are then interpreted by a spiritual guide and elder in the church, in Green's case his grandmother, to determine whether the seeker is worthy to be accepted for baptism. Green remembers his dreams as "leading people out of darkness to see more light" ("From the Artist" xv), and his art in this collection seems to do just that for the poets and authors engaged with these paintings.

As an act of engagement or encounter, ekphrastic writing has often been mischaracterized as a kind of competition between poet and painter.[1] *Seeking*, however, is yet another

---

1.   See, for example, James Heffernan's characterization of ekphrasis as a Medusa model in which the male poet seeks to silence or speak in place of the still, feminized image (3); as well as W.J.T. Mitchell's groundbreaking chapter "Ekphrasis and the Other," in which the difficulty of interchange between word and image is captured as hope, fear, or indifference.

example of the ways in which contemporary authors seek out the visual as a collaborative force. Rather than the verbal translation or domination of the visual through mere description, the ekphrases in *Seeking* exhibit what I have elsewhere called the "ecstatic embrace" of verbal and visual (Keefe 2011, 135), a relationship in which word and image are drawn together in the encounter in ways that enliven and enrich the form, sound, imagery and language of the lyric. In *Seeking*, authors rarely depend on mere description (the hallmark of an unsuccessful ekphrastic poem, in my opinion) and instead seize upon the details of Green's seeking experience—the details that surround the painting's own creation narrative—as imaginative entry points into that lyric space of the seeking quest. The white string tied around the forehead to mark the seeker, the white clothing that will dirty and stain as a week alone in the woods slowly passes, the voices imagined and not—these elements become, as they do in Mary Hutchins Harris' poem "The Seeking Child," ways into a relationship with the painting and its history that will bring seeking to life for the reader:

> ...to find his place in the world
> of upturned leaves, the odor of graves
> dug for a folded body, how ruts
> in the mud taste at dawn.... (33)

As Harris has it, the poem places us in the dank woods at dawn, bringing the tastes, smells, and sounds at the periphery of the visual to the foreground of our experience as readers.

 Harris is not alone in privileging senses other than the visual in the lyric space of the poem, as it seems that seeking takes place in the dark realm of the haunted for so many in this collection, a space of indistinction and possibility where we cannot be sure of what we see, a place that suspends historical time, an "interspace" as Charlene Spearen has it in "No Longer Seeking Allegories." We seek new knowledge, to come of age, as in Bryan Penberthy's "October in Eden," where to seek is to hunt, to crouch alone in the dark forest of the unknown "trying to decipher dusk," and ultimately to have one's eyes opened to "the world's unfairnesss" (9): the adult knowledge that the hunt reveals, sex and death, the trick of attraction and desire. The seeker must suspend oneself and yet, as Ray McManus captures in "Last Stand," we fear that what we might discover that will lead us back to ourselves:

> Sometimes we are what
> we seek. Sometimes
> we dig in too deep
> and there is no way
> to tell shade from shadow. (27)

Curiously, it is the painting that grounds the experience:

> It positions the viewer. You must sit
> yourself in the middle; give your mind away.
>   (Spearan 24)

To tell shade from shadow, to give the mind away, these authors look and look again to the visual. For Nikki Finney, the act of painting becomes the bridge between "the boy, now man," and "between the living / and the dead" (23).

Like the conceptual poet Cole Swensen suggests of contemporary ekphrasis in her essay "To Writewithize," the ekphrastic responses in *Seeking* "don't *look at* art so much as *live with* it…. There's a side-by-side, a walking-along-with, as their basis" (123, emphasis in the original). These poems embrace the visual, as if walking together into the forest at the edge of Mepkin Abbey, scared and excited about what might be discovered. "At the brink of something," as Susan Laughter Meyers puts it in what, for this reader at least, was the most arresting lyric in the collection, "Singing at the Edge of Need":

> I was small, I was hunger, I was thirst—
> wings flitting in a brush pile. O Grandmother,
> I was small, kneeling in the midst of wonder,
> quaking and singing at the edge of need. (12)

Bibliography

Heffernan, James A. W. 1993. *Museum of Words: The Poetics of Ekphrasis from Homer to Ashbery.* Chicago: University of Chicago Press.

Keefe, Anne. 2011. "The Ecstatic Embrace of Verbal and Visual: Twenty-First Century Lyric beyond the Ekphrastic Paragone." *Word & Image* 27.2: 135-47.

Mitchell, W. J. T. 1994. "Ekphrasis and the Other." *Picture Theory.* Chicago: University of Chicago Press. 151-81.

Swensen, Cole. 2011. "To Writewithize." *American Letters & Commentary* 13: 122-27.

VISION AND POWER ON A NEW PLANE

Natasha Trethewey. 2012. *Thrall: Poems*. New York: Houghton Mifflin Harcourt. Pp. 96 $23.00 Cloth.

Reviewed by Joseph Millichap, Western Kentucky University

Winning the Pulitzer Prize in 2007 made Natasha Trethewey a respected poet and a regional figure, but then she emerged as a national personage and a major poet in 2012 by way of her initial appointment as Poet Laureate and the publication of her fourth collection, *Thrall*. She is widely known and much admired today, as demonstrated by her reappointment to an atypical second term as laureate, while *Thrall* continues to enjoy a very positive reception from readers and reviewers. Most recognize that Trethewey's newest volume reiterates and develops the subjects and the forms discovered in her earlier books. In this reviewer's reading of her new collection, *Thrall* engages and enlarges her personal and poetic interests in children and parents by means of a sharpened focus on the conflicts of love and knowledge that reveal the relationships between daughters and fathers in poems that are at once open and formal.

Trethewey's subjects and themes prove both personal and professional; her mother was a black social worker, while her father is a white professor and poet. Whether autobiographical or fictional, filial relations in *Thrall* are rife with racial tensions and artistic anxieties. Trethewey's evocations of her literal and literary father figures shape her poems that concern them, but they help define by contrast her other subjects and themes that include many other aspects of her black mother's cultural heritage and of her own creative legacy as a bi-racial poet. All of these complicated elements are revealed once more and then developed both more fully and deeply in *Thrall*, her most impressive collection of poetry to date, in my view as well as those of most other reviewers and critics.

Trethewey's major sequence in *Thrall* consists of a cluster of ekphrastic poems recreating familial portraits from eighteenth-century Latin America, including the example colorfully reproduced on the book's jacket. As the poet's concluding note to a group of them entitled "Taxonomy" explains: "Casta paintings illustrated the various mixed unions of colonial Mexico and the children of these unions whose names and taxonomies were recorded in The Book of Castas" (81). In some sense, perhaps, *Thrall* exists as Trethewey's own book of castas, for it considers the bi-racial children of all the Americas, herself included. In the fourth section of "Taxonomy," a poem entitled "The Book of Castas" supports this reading. The sequence models Trethewey's overall text by presenting in a smaller scale the most important elements found in *Thrall*. In the poem she variously describes the eighteenth-century collection as "the catalog / of mixed bloods," the "guidebook to the colony," and the "typology of taint" (24). Trethewey's essential focus here is on one bi-racial daughter, as it is throughout her volume; "her name / written down in the Book / of Castas—all her kind / in thrall to a word" (26). The cast, or color, of these bi-racial progeny, as well as the caste, or class, assigned them within their culture therefore are determined by their white fathers to whom the children then are always in thrall.

For her paired epigraphs to *Thrall*, Trethewey could not have chosen two more patriarchal modern poets than Robert Penn Warren and the precursor to his Fugitive years, T. S. Eliot. The epigraph from Warren comes from his own ekphrastic work, the long poem "Audubon: A Vision" (1969). Trethewey quotes Warren's well-known lines, "What is love? / One name for it is knowledge" which conclude a section of "Audubon" entitled 'Love and Knowledge.' The epigraph, then, alerts us to the anxious balance that we find in Trethewey's poems between love and knowledge, especially as it appears in the tensions between the poet and her father figure, her primary themes. Trethewey's organization of individual poems into sections, sequences, and pairings reveals this collection's thematic patterns. These thirty-two poems are gathered into three sections of about the same size in terms of page numbers, introduced by a single poem set apart, "Elegy," which ironically focuses on her father who is still very much alive.

The first section of eight poems consists of her ekphrastic presentation of the casta paintings, including "Taxonomy," though she concludes it with an interrogation of her own father in her significantly titled poem "Knowledge." In the second section, which consists of sixteen shorter poems, Trethewey again proceeds from art to life, though the balance shifts from reimagined works of art to remembered personal events, ones connected more with verbal rather than visual texts such as her own and her father's poems. The book's longest single selection, "Thrall," opens the third section of seven poems all in the realm of the graphic arts, and reiterates the overall themes of love and knowledge. The pivotal selection of this last section, "Enlightenment," links painting and the past to poetry and the present by way of recreated visits by both Tretheweys to the home of a Founding Father, Thomas Jefferson, at Monticello. This section of her book seems more optimistic, as Trethewey turns inward, toward her own writing in the gathering of four short but meaningful poems that conclude *Thrall*.

Trethewey's first three collections—*Domestic Work, Bellocq's Ophelia*, and the Pulitzer Prize-winning *Native Guard*—are each important works in differing ways, yet *Thrall* unifies and extends Trethewey's poetic vision and power onto a new plane. Her personal and poetic relationships with her literal and literary fathers figure in the earlier work, but daughters and fathers become her pervasive subjects and themes in *Thrall* by embodying American anxieties about race and society as well as universal tensions over art and culture. These anxieties also inform her writing about her racial heritage from her mother and her literary legacy from women writers both black and white. It is impossible for any reviewer to predict the course of literature, yet if her work continues to flourish as it has in the last decade, Natasha Trethewey well may become the finest Southern poet of our new century.

THE RISE TO RESPECTABILITY

Calvin White Jr. 2012. *The Rise To Respectability: Race, Religion, and the Church of God in Christ*. Fayetteville, AR: The University of Arkansas Press. Pp. 239. $34.95 Cloth.

Reviewed by Lucy Mensah, Vanderbilt University

In his own words, Calvin White Jr. writes that the purpose of his book, *The Rise to Respectability: Race, Religion, and the Church of God in Christ*, is to "fill the hole in the current historiography," addressing the absence of scholarly work on the Church of God in Christ, or the COGIC (5). White's objective is to write a revisionist history of African American religion and political involvement by including the COGIC as an integral part of racial uplift and the politics of respectability. While the COGIC was critiqued by other black religious denominations as being conservative and regressive because of their "emotional" religious expression, White examines how the contrary can be argued: in his view members of the COGIC were quite progressive in their inclusion of women in religious activities, their cosmopolitanism through mission trips, their political engagement with national institutions, and their role as a safe haven for members of the Civil Rights Movement. White's book is indeed valuable to the broader religious and political conversations about the role of black churches in racial uplift and black religious engagement with "secular" agendas such as civil rights.

White goes to impressive lengths to portray an engaging narrative about the growth and development of the Church of God in Christ. He pulls predominantly from oral interviews and newspaper accounts as a means of building his portrait of the COGIC. His book is an excellent model of how integral oral culture can be in addressing gaps in our historical knowledge. He uses the figure of Charles Mason—who was ultimately responsible for the rise of the COGIC—to tell a story of resistance to the challenges the church faced in gaining respectability as a mainstream black religious denomination. As White recounts, the COGIC faced not only legal disputes with religious members both inside and outside its denomination, but also individual members faced physical harm from the white community who felt threatened by the COGIC. The title of White's book, *The Rise to Respectability*, names the rise he charts through cultural, political, economic, and religious challenges which resulted in the church as it stands today, a respectable and politically engaged religious denomination.

White is skilled in tying the COGIC to the larger social, cultural, and political issues facing the national black community during the early twentieth century, particularly the Great Migration, urbanity, and the effects of modernity following the industrial development of the nation. As White argues, what was most at stake for the black community was the necessity of appearing respectable in the face of increasing tensions among various black religious denominations. They disagreed on black religious expression in a modernizing U.S. that still sought to marginlize black society. In a sense, White's book is about the politics of black worship.

White's book is divided into six chapters, each of which deals with a specific challenge the COGIC faced and how its members met this challenge. His introduction foregrounds the overall challenge that would follow the COGIC from the late 19th century up through the Civil Rights Movement: the COGIC, valuing African heritage, lacked respectability and sophistication compared to their Methodist and Baptist counterparts, who modeled their worship on Victorian, and more broadly, Western, standards of etiquette and behavior.

Chapter 1, "In the Beginning, There Stood Two," traces the lines of influence that informed the worship practices of the COGIC. White offers a microhistory of Charles Harrison Mason, a dominant leader of the COGIC and Black Holiness Movement. Mason's religious upbringing sets the stage for the central characteristics of COGIC's religious expression. Mason's upbringing as a child of former slaves, immersed in slave religious culture, was the basis of COGIC's conservatism when it came to keeping African religious tradition as an integral part of COGIC's religious expression. Traces of slave culture could be found in the grassroots formations of COGIC churches, the decentered organization of the church, and "emotionalist" worship practices, such as shouting. Mason's lack of formal religious training was a prime difference between the COGIC and other denominations. While members of other denominations critiqued this lack of education and formal training, White argues that Mason's model of the "slave preacher" spoke to the segment of the black population which was poor, non-educated, and worked primarily in low paying jobs, such as sharecropping and domestic work. What White reveals through the tension of the COGIC and its counterparts is an intersection of religion and class, a topic that brings insight into how black class dynamics informed different modes of worship.

White also notes the in-fighting that occurred within the COGIC. Another COGIC leader, Charles Price Jones, was more of an intellectual. This difference is treated in chapter 2, "We Will Let the Courts Speak for Us," which covers the legal disputes that emerged from inner tensions within the church. Mason and his congregation supported heteroglossia, or speaking in tongues, while leaders such as Jones argued that Mason misread the Bible in promoting such a practice and, therefore, should be prevented from using church property for worship. What began as a denomination looking inward for sanctification, shifted to one looking outward, as Mason was forced seek legal representation in order to keep his property. White portrays an interesting weaving of religious and legalistic discourse as legal opponents debated whether heteroglossia was a diversion from reading the Bible.

White's third chapter, "Mason Told Us Not to Fight," offers information on another important challenge for Mason and his congregation. The introspection desired by Mason's congregation was challenged, this time by the United States' entry into World War One. Although the U.S. Military Service act was openly contested by many religious and pacifist organizations, the COGIC faced special difficulties in their refusal to go to war. Despite the fact that Mason supported the war financially by encouraging his congregation to purchase war bonds, Mason was still considered in violation of the Sedition Act (1918) by politicians and oppositional black religious denominations. White portrays Mason and his congregation as largely misunderstood and misread, falsely accused of having pro-German sentiments and being influenced by the United States' enemies.

Chapters four and five, respectively titled "Come Over to Macedonia and Help" and "Memphis, the Hope of a Promised Land," are meant to convey Mason's launch into the project of racial uplift. Chapter four tackles the issue of sanctification, and how sanctification held the dual purpose not only of bringing members closer to holiness, but also of instructing them on respectability and self-care. COGIC's mission trips to Liberia, for example, signal the denomination's global reach in promoting racial uplift in other African diasporic communities. However, White also rightly critiques this agenda as racist and paternalistic.

In conjunction with missionary work, COGIC actively involved black women in the dissemination of the church's principles abroad. In part, Chapter four not only addresses COGIC's cosmopolitanism, but also its democratic underpinnings as a space open to black women's leadership and participation. This, in White's opinion, separates COGIC from other black religious denominations in this era. Chapter five also deals with black women's contribution to racial uplift, primarily in the form of auxiliary groups, sexual abstinence, and dress.

While White's text has very noticeable strengths, there are also two important weaknesses that detract from his overall argument. Although the title of White's book is *The Rise to Respectability*, his actual engagement with the politics of black respectability is limited. White does not stray far from simply defining respectability in terms of Victorian and Western conduct and behavior. Given that respectability is at the center of White's text, White's engagement with the subject should have been more extensive. He hardly discusses the meaning of respectability, its historical context in the black community, or the complexities involved in the pursuit of respectability. Blacks have long been scrutinized in their public behavior and comportment, and it would have been beneficial for White to underline the fact that the pursuit of respectability does not automatically grant blacks access to social equality.

Secondly, White's divisions between the religious practices of black congregations and secularism are too rigid. White's argument depends on a division between the middle-class comportment of black Baptists and Methodists and the slave-influenced religious expression of the COGIC. However, it would be hard to believe that black Baptist and Methodist congregations were not influenced by the religion of their slave ancestors, which makes White's division seem simplistic. Furthermore, White gives the impression that COGIC's engagement with secular activities was first initiated by their involvement with protests against the lynching of Emmett Till, which he explores in his sixth chapter, " 'Dar He.'" However, again, White's rigid divisions do not stand considering that the COGIC never really was able to avoid being involved in secular activities; White's entire book supports this very notion. Despite these issues, however, White's book stands as a much-needed platform in directing more scholarly attention to a neglected denomination.

REIMAGING SOUTHERN GEOGRAPHIES

Thadious M. Davis. 2011. *Southscapes: Geographies of Race, Region, & Literature*. Chapel Hill: University of North Carolina Press. Pp. 458. $39.95. Hardcover.

Reviewed by Ondra Krouse Dismukes, University of Georgia

In *Southscapes: Geographies of Race, Region, & Literature*, Thadious Davis examines the south as three-dimensional space, chained to a hurtful history of slavery that provides a canvas – a figurative black, blank space from which southern-born authors extrapolate meaning. This space is also the canvas, or stage, for the production of a re-envisioned southscape. Davis's reference to chains functions as a metaphor for the way southern-born African American authors are linked to their slave past, not merely in terms of geography, but also in terms of the history embedded in their memories and extended through an African American literary tradition.

Davis studies the geographic locations of Mississippi and Louisiana, and the politics surrounding their histories of racial injustice, to note the backdrop against which Mississippi natives Endesha Ida Mae Holland, Sterling Plumpp, Etheridge Knight, and Richard Wright, along with Louisiana native Ernest Gaines generated literature that articulated these locales as raced spaces. Subsequently, Davis asserts, contemporary African American authors from these same locales—namely Natasha Tretheway, Olympia Vernon, and Shay Youngblood from Mississippi; Sybil Kein and Brenda Marie Osbey from Louisiana; and Randall Kenan from North Carolina—re-envision the South, not as the raced space created by their literary forbearers, but as a site of cultural memory. These contemporary authors provide, in Davis's view, the third dimension of the space, and new links in a chain of tradition of southern-born African American writers who share geographies of slavery.

While Davis draws upon theorists such as Jean François Lyotard, Michel de Certeau, and Yi-Fu Tuan, it is French historian, Pierre Nora, who provides the theory of situated memory that founds the image of enchainment, which functions as both a structural analogy and a contextual metaphor for the book. Although Davis cites Pierre Nora's rather startling conclusion that the purpose of history is "to annihilate what has in reality taken place," it is the more subtle observation that Nora makes regarding memory's location in those persons, places, and/or things that crystallize images of the past. Davis finds a similar idea in Toni Morrison's notion of cultural memory. In short, the image of a chain of interlinked memories governs Davis's idea of "southscapes," articulated connections between authors and their environments during the period of segregation.

For example, Chapter Two, "Poverty & Porches: Controversial Mississippi," posits the Mississippi Delta imaged in the work of Endesha Ida Mae Holland and Natasha Tretheway as a "bluescape," presenting "in visual imagery the private and public landscape of pain and pleasure associated with the blues music that originated in Mississippi Delta" (78). This bluescape is defined by the porch and by the lynching of Emmett Till. On one hand, the porch is the protected landscape for cultural production in the form of participatory storytelling that involves house residents and community passersby. A house without a porch served as a reminder of poverty and segregation, of being literally cut-off from such cultural production, which many African American sharecroppers in this area experienced. On the other hand, the history of the lynching of Emmett Till reminded writers, such as Endesha Mae Holland and Anne Moody that their own black bodies were vulnerable "spaces" in the public sphere. Through Sterling Plumpp, Davis links shared social history to a mythic blues persona. In other words, Davis finds embedded in cultural memory contradictory images: on one hand, the horror of the Till lynching and on the other, the recurring comforting image of the porch; the intersection of these competing images represent an exposure to and a shelter from the racism that circumscribed the southern geographical landscape of the Mississippi Delta and, consequently, of the raced identities of the authors.

Later in this chapter, Davis juxtaposes the "bluescape" inspired by the dark history of segregation in Mississippi with Olympia Vernon's postmodern fiction and posits it as "'fugue space,' the unmapped evoking the hyperreal and signifying a heightened state of consciousness in which actions occur at sharp angles from the normal and a polyphonic thematic in which voices narrate contrapuntal stories of bodies struggling, futilely, to recover racial history and social memory" (113). In essence, Vernon's postmodern fiction refuses to submit modernist interpretations of the South as a hopeless, smothering, killing space; instead, as Davis sees it, Vernon offers Mississippi and Louisiana as locales in which African American bodies struggle, but retain a hopeful dream of recovering from the memory of the painful history.

Similarly, Davis' following chapter, "Power and Profession: Richard Wright's Mississippi and Its Expatriate Legacies," re-examines the history of Mississippi as it relates to Wright. Wright wrote *Black Boy* (1945) when "he had no hope of becoming a professional man" (227) in what was a geographical "no-man's land for blacks of Wright's generation" (136). Wright took advantage of the Federal Writers' Project, a program of President Franklin D. Roosevelt's Works Progress Administration designed to provide jobs after the Great Depression. He was able to produce literature that reflected his disdain for the strictures facing African American males in the south, capturing the particularly harsh and haunting memories of racism that emerged after Wright crossed racial lines in marrying Ellen Poplowitz, his second wife. Feeling even more vulnerable to racist attack, he moved to Paris, and later to London. The constant sense of flight that characterizes much of Wright's work owes much to his sense of being dispossessed in America, in general, and in his native Mississippi, in particular. Wright's case provides a particularly strong illustration of the transformation of raced space from two dimensional space lacking hope and horizon to three dimensional space that reshapes the space through distance from oppression of segregation. For Wright, a racially contentious Mississippi intersects with his angst, ordering his life and limiting his opportunities. However, when Wright moves from the South he charts a path taken up by Shay Youngblood. She follows Wright from the South and on to Paris, re-envisioning the south through a multi-layered postmodernism that provided for black, gendered, and queer bodies. Both Youngblood and Vernon elucidate a South that offers them the literal and the figurative space in which to assert control over the same space whose politics robbed their forbearers of any such control.

Davis shifts her focus from Mississippi to Louisiana in the fourth chapter of *Southscapes* where she explores both the potential and the failure of Louisiana as a space for modeling a more expansive construction of race. In "Mutable Geographies," she offers an extensive overview of the history of Louisiana and how the confluence of African, French,

Spanish, and Native American cultures created a space that could potentially have become a model region for the South in terms of race politics; however, the economic import of slavery forced the new Creolité population, Louisiana Creoles of Color, to occupy the lowest rung on the socioeconomic ladder. Davis examines the literary production of Creolité authors, including *Les Cenelles*, an anthology comprising the work of seventeen male Creolité poets, and the work of Alice Ruth Moore (later Dunbar-Nelson), wife of African American poet Paul Laurence Dunbar. To show the embedded nature of race mixing and the consequential racial subjectivity that Creoles of Color experienced, postmodern writers from Louisiana, similar to their counterparts in Mississippi, re-envision raced space in ways that edify, rather than negate the voices of people of color. For example, poet Brenda Marie Osbey creates a sense of homage to her African slave ancestors in her poetry and in her descriptions of the above-ground cemeteries where their bodies lie. Likewise, poet Sybil Kein calls attention to the beauty that emerges from cultural amalgamation; by writing in Creole, French, and English, she preserves the Creole history in the very material that represents the conflation of cultures.

In the penultimate chapter, Davis coins the term "chaining" to intimate Ernest Gaines's reliance on his past to produce literature, not only in terms of the history of Louisiana that he revisits in his fiction, but also in terms of his characters who reflect his personal experiences of the South. Accordingly, the Louisiana landscape emerges in his stories of plantation and prison systems, incorporating Louisiana folk culture; Gaines himself becomes the raced body connecting generations. Randall Kenan, Gaines' postmodern disciple, recreates Gaines's model of chaining in the remapping of his native North Carolina. That is to say, Kenan is two generations and twice as many states removed from Gaines in terms of his literary production; however, like Gaines, Kenan revisits the folk culture of his native North Carolina and presents it anew in his fiction. From a postmodernist perspective, Kenan enters what Davis calls a "chimeric space" (314). Where Kenan not only recalls the history of slavery in North Carolina, but also interrogates the travesty of human abuse toward other humans, and the ability of individuals to defy such dehumanizing forces.

An interesting dynamic emerges between the first and sixth chapters of *Southscapes*. While the first chapter provides the theoretical concept for Davis's discourse and moves directly from her theoretical framework to a discussion of the work of contemporary poet Natasha Tretheway, there seems to be a gap between the first dimension, the regional politics of the South, and the third dimension, in which Tretheway pays homage to the Louisiana Native Guard and restores their abandoned place to historical record, as well as restoring her physical tie to her native Mississippi. In *Southscapes's* sixth and final chapter, however, Davis fills the void of the second dimension of the chaining metaphor. In this last chapter, Davis argues that, through her poetry and fiction, Alice Walker contemplates a new geography of the South, one in which the site, or space of the wound also becomes space for healing. By giving Walker the last word, Davis not only reconfigures the South in terms of its shared history of racism and segregation, but also shows how the collective cultural memory of the raced South can yield fertile ground for reclaiming African American cultural production and healing from a hurtful past.

CAPITAL PUNISHMENT AND RACIAL INFECTION:
TRANSFORMING AMERICAN JURISPRUDENCE IN THE CIVIL RIGHTS ERA

Barrett J. Foerster. 2012. *Race, Rape, and Injustice: Documenting and Challenging Death Penalty Cases in the Civil Rights Era*. Ed. Michael Meltsner. Knoxville: University of Tennessee Press. Pp. xiii + 208. $39.95. Hardcover.

Reviewed by Shadi Ghazimoradi, Queen's University at Kingston

At the height of the civil rights movement in the summer of 1965, twenty-eight law students volunteered for a summer internship, which would send them south to collect data on the sentencing practices of juries in rape cases. Supervised by the NAACP Legal Defense Fund, the students set out to determine whether the citizen jurors involved in southern rape cases were racially motivated, thus sending men to their deaths on grounds of skin color. Staggering statistics showed that black men convicted of raping white women were usually executed, whereas men convicted of rape in circumstances involving other racial combinations commonly received prison sentences. While the racial bias at work in southern courtrooms was common knowledge among both the court and the general public, scientific proof was needed if any changes were to be implemented in the legal system. This scientific data is what the Fund and the students set out to collect.

Approximately 45 years after that fateful summer of 1965, one of the twenty-eight law students, Barrett J. Foerster, who had gone on to become a Superior Court judge in Imperial County, California, decided to write the story of the events of that summer and the impact that the student researchers' efforts had on death penalty laws throughout the country. As he mentions toward the end of the book, Foerster believes that "the events leading to the now widespread use of 'guided discretion' statutes in capital and non-capital cases all had their origins in that boiling, violent summer of 1965" (141). This book is a detailed and captivating account of the journey that forever changed capital punishment laws in the country's jurisprudence.

The book begins by describing the nature of the mission and the students' initial introduction to both the project and its directors. The research project was organized by Anthony Amsterdam who brought in Marvin Wolfgang, a University of Pennsylvania professor considered to be the father of modern criminology. Wolfgang designed the research approach and the data collection method, and would later present the findings of the research to the courts. At a meeting at the University of Pennsylvania campus, the students were informed of the details of the research project and given the "Capital Punishment Survey" booklets that would be their data collection tools that summer. Foerster and his peers were then sent to the southern states to begin the arduous task of poring through court cases and death penalty briefs in an effort to statistically prove whether the question of who lived and died in southern rape cases depended on the races of the defendant and his victim.

Foerster explains what he believes to have been the main driving forces behind the rape-capital punishment survey. Firstly, the Reconstruction of the 1870's had left behind an almost entirely all-white judicial system primarily concerned with maintaining white domination in the South. Defendants in interracial rape cases concerning a black man and a white woman were severely punished "to serve as a deterrent to miscegenation" and, as Foerster puts it, in the "Martinsville Seven" case, "the punishment meted out under-scored the relative value of human life as seen by the southern judicial system: One white female, wrongfully assaulted, deserved to be compensated by extinguishing seven black lives" (11-12). Secondly, death by execution—particularly by electrocution—was increasingly being viewed as "barbaric and unnecessary punishment," a view fueled by eyewitness accounts of the horrendous sufferings which the condemned experienced in the electric chair (12). The third factor was the growing concern that death was an inappropriate and excessive form of punishment for rape, and thus in violation of the Eighth Amendment. This last notion, and capital punishment's disproportionate application to a racial minority—which violated the Fourteenth Amendment's guarantee of equal protection for all—were the grounds upon which the Fund's lawyers ultimately challenged the death penalty in courts, "eventually toppl[ing] the house of cards on which capital punishment in the South had been built" (13-14).

Chapters 2 to 4 describe the law students' backgrounds and their departure to the South. On May 22, 1965, the law students were put into groups and sent to examine court briefs and documents in over 230 counties. Foerster's team was assigned to cover Louisiana and Mississippi, and he recalls the many obstacles the students faced along the way: unaccommodating clerks who denied access to court files (even though they were public property), resistant judges and lawyers who withheld information, and hostile members of the local community who did not appreciate the strangers' intrusion. One of the biggest threats to the project, and to the students' safety, was the infamous Ku Klux Klan, a white supremacist organization which was responsible for lynching numerous African Americans in the nineteenth and twentieth centuries. After the state government enforced rules banning lynching and violence against blacks, Klansmen began looking to the courts to instill terror in the African American community by condemning more and more blacks to death by execution. Not surprisingly, these Klansmen were particularly hostile to civil rights activists who, they felt, were invading the South and threatening its longstanding caste system. In one of the book's most haunting episodes, Foerster recounts what happened when one of the students, Tim Brayton, heard about a Klan rally happening outside Columbia, South Carolina, and decided to attend. Foerster describes the spectacle of the robe-clad Klansmen setting fire to the cross as a "man-made inferno" (35). In the face of such harrowing circumstances, the law students were only able to overcome "the massive resistance of southern officialdom" with the help of "the loose network of civil right attorneys who cooperated with the Fund" (48).

As the summer of 1965 drew to a close, the survey booklets containing data from 250 counties were delivered to Wolfgang who, with the help of his graduate students at Penn, began the arduous task of assembling and analyzing the data. The Fund's lawyers did their best to secure delays for court hearings until the data had been analyzed. What Wolfgang was doing – determining the role of racial discrimination in sentencing practices through statistical analysis – was, as Foerster notes, the first intervention of its kind. The statistics spoke for themselves; black defendants convicted of raping white women were eighteen times more likely to be put to death than other racial combinations. Yet if Wolfgang was to make a persuadable case to the court, he would also have to examine the role that nonracial variables played in the frequency of the death penalty. Such an examination, however, revealed that nonracial variables had, in Wolfgang's own words, "no bearing on the imposition of the death penalty in disproportionate numbers on blacks. The only variable of statistical significance that remains is race" (qtd. 72).

Chapters 5 to 7 record the very first cases in which the Fund's statistical data was presented before the court as evidence of racially infected sentencing in the South. Among these cases were those of Isaac Sims, Jr., Robert Swain, and Billy Maxwell. With Wolfgang's completion of the statistical analysis in 1966 and the unsettled fate of Billy Maxwell's case, stays were granted to several death row inmates until resolution could be reached. Following this, other lawyers from around the country began requesting stays, and all eyes were focused on Wolfgang to see what he would do with the statistical analysis of the students' data. Maxwell's court brief explained the students' research in the summer of 1965 and presented Wolfgang's conclusion that "Negro defendants who rape white victims have been disproportionately sentenced to death" (qtd. 94). When the justices announced their decision after the hearing, it became clear that the court was doing its best to sidestep the issue of racial bias and, and to the Fund's dismay, that the court had rejected the Fund's appeal for jury-sentencing standards. However, the notion of sentencing standards was later embraced in a dissent (penned by three of the nine justices) which supported its claims with the Fund's arguments on the racial infection of current sentencing practices. Other cases began to emerge at around this time which called upon the Fund's study and its results, constantly reminding the court of the discriminatory practices which governed sentences of life and death in the South. The law students' work and Wolfgang's findings were constantly discussed in courtrooms, slowly but surely causing justices, judges, and the nation's citizens to question the fairness of the death penalty.

In Chapter 8, Foerster chronicles the events that eventually led to the monumental reversal of death penalty laws across the country. Four Death Row petition cases (*Furman v. Georgia*, *Jackson v. Georgia*, *Branch v. Texas*, and *Aikens v. California*), all of which involved black male defendants and white female victims, were selected to be reviewed by the Supreme Court in order to determine whether capital punishment was indeed, as the Fund claimed, "cruel and unusual punishment." In January 1972, the justices convened to vote. Five of the nine justices found, as Foerster states, "that capital punishment violated the Constitution's ban on cruel and unusual punishment.… The court appeared to be on the verge of changing two hundred years of accepted jurisprudence" (117). Tentative at first, the decision was finalized and announced to the public on June 29, 1972, shocking the entire nation and arousing various reactions from the public.

After the court's decision to abandon the death penalty, outraged legislators convened to create statutes by which the death penalty could be reintroduced into the legal system. These statutes provided standards to be considered by judges and juries in imposing capital punishment, and mandatory death sentencing practices were put to an end. The new legislations eliminated—or at least largely minimized—the influence of judges' and juries' racial biases in sentencing a convict to death. But these reforms didn't stop there; eventually, jury-sentencing standards were also introduced into cases not involving the death penalty, thus ensuring racial equality in cases not involving capital offense.

Foerster's intent in writing *Race, Rape, and Injustice* is, as he states, to record the efforts of the law students during that eventful summer of 1965 and to show the ways in which the students' achievements managed to trigger a domino effect which transformed the country's legislative system. He traces the Supreme Court's decision to abandon the death penalty back to that summer when the foundations for eventual grassroots changes were laid: "There was no one moment of inspiration when a majority of the bench suddenly resolved to abandon the death penalty in this country. The justices had been struggling with the issue since at least 1966, a year before the moratorium on executions began. And from the struggle had emerged a slow evolution of thought" (130-131).

Foerster's book is a fascinating read and one I would highly recommend to anyone interested in contemporary American history. It provides deep insight into the social, legal, and cultural climate of the civil rights era, and gives a comprehensive account of the lesser-known names whose hard work made tremendous changes in the legal system possible. Though the book does become somewhat tedious and excessively detailed in some sections, it is for the most part an enjoyable and engrossing read, and Foerster's elegant use of language is highly commendable. Sadly, Foerster's death in November 2010 meant that he never saw the publication of the book (which he'd submitted to the publisher shortly before his death). Yet this great work speaks for itself.

In the final chapter, Foerster discusses Harper Lee's *To Kill a Mockingbird* and its portrayal of Tom Robinson who, because of the racism of the Alabama town he lives in, is wrongfully accused of raping a white woman, sentenced to death by an all-white jury, and later killed while trying to escape from jail. Foerster takes comfort in the fact that "no such trial would take place today" (152), and pays tribute to the people whose devotion made this possible, including Marvin Wolfgang, Anthony Amsterdam, Michael Meltsner (who edited Foerster's book and wrote the introduction), Marvin Frankel, and Norman Amaker. Yet above all he gives credit to his fellow law students whose bravery initiated what Foerster terms the "'Seven Years' War' through the state and federal courts." It was through their efforts that, he states emotionally, "Mockingbirds have been saved" (155). The epilogue provides a glimpse at the later lives and careers of the project's directors and advocates, as well as those of some of the student researchers. The book ends, appropriately, with a paragraph on the influential life and career of Marvin Wolfgang, whose vision and determination forever changed American jurisprudence.

C O N T R I B U T O R S

Susanna Ashton is a Professor of English at Clemson University. Her edited collection, *"I Belong to South Carolina": South Carolina Slave Narratives*, which includes Jacob Stroyer's autobiography, was published by the University of South Carolina Press in 2010 and received an Outstanding Academic Title award by *Choice*. Currently, she is working on book entitled *A Plausible Man: the Life of John Andrew Jackson*.

Jenifer L. Barclay is a Visiting Assistant Professor at Washington State University. She received her Ph.D. in history from Michigan State University in 2011 after completing a Pre-doctoral Fellowship at the University of Virginia's Carter G. Woodson Institute for African American and African Studies from 2009 to 2011. Her current book project is *The Mark of Slavery: The Stigma of Disability, Race, and Gender in Antebellum America*.

David Borman is a Ph.D. candidate and Graduate Fellow in the Department of English at the University of Miami in Coral Gables, Florida. His work focuses on contemporary literary accounts of return to Africa and the forms of international belonging suggested by such narratives.

Ashley Bourgeois is completing her doctoral degree under the direction of Professor Susan Bordo at the University of Kentucky. Her dissertation project, *Remnants of the New Left: Scenes of Liberation in Contemporary Fiction and Film,* explores erotic pleasure potentials that extend beyond sexual intercourse to active forms of human labor and communal life.

Kaneesha Brownlee received her B.S. degree in Graphic Communication from Clemson University in 2002 and an A.A. degree in photographic imaging from the Art Institute of Atlanta in 2006. She currently works as a retoucher/color specialist for PureRed.

Kelly Clasen received her Ph.D. in English from the University of North Texas in 2011. She directs the Academic Resource Center at Newman University in Wichita, Kansas.

Ondra Krouse Dismukes ia a doctoral student, Ford Foundation Fellow, and teaches multicultural American literature at the University of Georgia.

Julius B. Fleming, Jr., is a PhD candidate at the University of Pennsylvania, where he teaches a course on African American migration narratives and works on his dissertation.

Shadi Ghazimoradi is a doctoral candidate at Queens University, Kingston, Canada, with interests in Iranian studies, critical theory, race and ethnicity, and comparative literature.

Laura Good graduated from Clemson University in 2012 with a B.A. degree in English and a minor in Fiction Writing. While at Clemson, she served as a student organizer for the Fifth Annual Clemson Literary Festival, and received the Undergraduate Award for Excellence in Fiction Writing.

Michael Ra-Shon Hall is a Ph.D. candidate in Interdisciplinary Humanities at the Graduate Institute of Liberal Arts, Emory University. His areas of research and teaching include contemporary American and African American literature; visual culture; travel, tourism and imagination; and cultural histories of travel as refracted through material artifacts.

Akel Ismail Kahera is Associate Dean for Research and Graduate Studies in the College of Architecture, Arts and Humanities at Clemson University. He is the author of *Deconstructing the American Mosque: Space, Gender and Aesthetics*, published by the University of Texas Press in 2002, and *Reading the Islamic City: Discursive Practices and Legal Judgment,* published by Lexington Books in 2011.

Anne Keefe is the NEH postdoctoral fellow in poetics at the Fox Center for Humanistic Inquiry at Emory University. Her poetry collection *Lithopedia* (2012) won the Bull City Press first book award.

Meredith McCarroll is Director of the Writing Center and a Lecturer in the Department of English, and the Writing Fellows Coordinator for the Pearce Center for Professional Communications at Clemson University. She is working on a book about Affrilachia poets.

Shaila Mehra is a Visiting Assistant Professor of English at Oklahoma State University. Her current book project focuses on the politics of gender difference and the legacies of black cultural nationalism and the Black Aesthetic in postmodern African American literature.

Lucy Kwabah Mensah is a doctoral student at Vanderbilt University; her research has focused on motherland, autobiography, and migration in the work of Gloria Naylor.

Joseph Millichap is Professor Emeritus of English at Western Kentucky University and has contributed to *SCR* occasionally, notably on Southern writers such as Robert Penn Warren, Thomas Wolfe, and especially Eudora Welty.

Maja Milatovic is a final year Ph.D. candidate at the University of Edinburgh, researching the ancestor figure in African American women writers' neo-slave narratives. In addition to African American literature and the Black Atlantic, her research interests include Indigenous studies, digital humanities and education, and more broadly, critical race and whiteness studies, postcolonial, feminist, and trauma theory.

Lenard D. Moore is an Associate Professor of English at the University of Mount Olive, where he directs the Literary Festival and advises *The Trojan Voices*. He is the author of *A Temple Looming* published by WordTech Editions in 2008 and other books. His poetry also has been published in many anthologies, including *Villanelles* issued by Knopf in 2012.

Angela Naimou is an Assistant Professor of English at Clemson University. Her first book, *Salvage Work: Literature Amid the Ruins of Legal Personhood,* is forthcoming from Fordham University Press. Her essays have appeared in *Callaloo* and a special issue of *College Literature* on human rights.

Kenton Rambsy is a Ph.D. candidate in African American Literature at the University of Kansas and serves as the digital initiative coordinator for the Project on the History of Black Writing. He writes about African American artistic culture and digital humanities.

William L. Ramsey is Associate Professor and Chair of the Department of History and Philosophy at Lander University. His poetry has appeared in *Poetry, Poetry Northwest, Southern Poetry Review*, and elsewhere.

Rhondda Robinson Thomas is Assistant Professor of English at Clemson University. Her *Claiming Exodus: A Cultural History of Afro-Atlantic Identity, 1774-1903* was published by Baylor University Press in 2013. She also edited the scholarly edition of Jane Edna Hunter's 1941 autobiography *A Nickel and a Prayer*, published by West Virginia University Press in its Regenerations series in 2011. She is working on a book to be titled *"Slaves of the State": Colored Convicts and Ivory Towers in Post-bellum South Carolina, 1889-1900.*

Tom Williams is the author of two books of fiction, *The Mimic's Own Voice*, a novella, and the forthcoming novel, *Don't Start Me Talkin'*. His short fiction has appeared recently in such journals as *The Collagist, Florida Review,* and *Triquarterly*. Currently, he chairs the English Department at Morehead State University.

❧

Students in photograph on the back cover: "Student League for Black Identity" organization posing in front of the Fort Hill historic home at Clemson University. *Taps* 1975 (Clemson University yearbook). Volume 65.

www.ingramcontent.com/pod-product-compliance
Lightning Source LLC
Chambersburg PA
CBHW030830090426
42737CB00009B/950